WHO ARE
THE JEWS

University of Nebraska Press
Lincoln

WHO ARE THE JEWS— AND WHO CAN WE BECOME?

Donniel Hartman

The Jewish Publication Society
Philadelphia

Library of Congress Cataloging-in-Publication Data
Names: Hartman, Donniel, author.
Title: Who are the Jews-and who can we become? / Donniel Hartman, the Jewish Publication Society, Philadelphia.
Description: Lincoln, Nebraska: University of Nebraska Press, [2023] | Includes bibliographical references and index.
Identifiers: LCCN 2023007294
ISBN 9780827615618 (paperback)
ISBN 9780827619142 (epub)
ISBN 9780827619159 (pdf)
Subjects: LCSH: Jews—Identity. | Judaism—21st century. | Zionism—History—21st century. | Judaism and politics. | BISAC: RELIGION / Biblical Studies / History & Culture | RELIGION / Judaism / General
Classification: LCC DS143 .H278 2023 | DDC 320.5409569409/05—dc23/eng/20230716
LC record available at https://lccn.loc.gov/2023007294

Set in Lyon Text by A. Shahan.

To Adina
For the story we have told
To Mia, Sophia, Elori, Libi, and Lavie
Who make telling the story the
most important thing in my life

There are three kinds of patriots, two bad, one good.

The bad are the uncritical lovers and the loveless critics.

Good patriots carry on a lover's quarrel with their country . . .

—WILLIAM SLOANE COFFIN

Contents

Acknowledgments

This book is dedicated to my wife, Adina, who has shared my life for over forty years. Together we developed and told our family's Jewish story. Without you it would not have been possible. And to my grandchildren, Mia, Sophia, Elori, Libi, and Lavie. Shaping the story the Jewish people can tell ourselves about ourselves is my attempt to pass on a Judaism to which you will be proud to belong. I can only pray that this story will inspire you to add your own chapters.

I owe an infinite gratitude to my children, Michal, Roie, Yitzchak, Avital, and Talya, for the joy and meaning you give to my life. The greatest honor of my life is to be your father. I am also deeply grateful to my mother, Bobbie Hartman. You are my constant and unconditional source of encouragement, and my best and most loyal reader and supporter.

I have been thinking, teaching, and writing this book for over a decade. In the midst of this process I have been blessed to work within the community of friends, colleagues, and students of the Shalom Hartman Institute. They have been the significant others with whom I have talked and from whom I have learned. Whether it is to learn together, share an idea, decipher a difficult text, or read a chapter of someone's manuscript, they always give of themselves and their time. In an ideal world, everyone will be able to live, write, and grow in such a community. I have been blessed to live in it.

From its beginnings, I shared this work with a number of people who played a critical role in shaping its outcome. First and foremost, my editor Charlie Buckholtz has been my partner and Hevruta throughout this process. Your invaluable contribution to this book, our third together, goes far beyond form, to the heart and clarity of the arguments.

You have added depth and beauty to my words and refined my ideas. I could not have written this book without you. My deep thanks as well to Shalhevet Schwartz, the book's research assistant, who invested a tremendous amount of work in developing and perfecting the notes and bibliography. Your work has given the book much added depth and enhanced the learning experience of the reader.

My colleagues in the Hartman iEngage research team, Yehuda Kurtzer, Tal Becker, Mijal Biton, Lauren Berkun, Elana Stein Hain, Yossi Klein Halevi, and Masua Sagiv, have been my key thought partners throughout this process, helping me to shape the content of every page of this volume. Who I am today, what I understand, and the essence of what I believe needs to be said is a direct byproduct of the gift of learning from and with you. Thanks as well go to Israel Knohl and Ishay Rosen Zvi, whose invaluable comments and criticisms dramatically improved the quality and coherency of the book.

I want to thank the students of the institute, in particular the rabbis, lay leaders, and educators who heard multiple versions of this work over the years. You and your students were my first and foremost audience, in dialogue with whom my ideas were tested, refined, and corrected. Your intellectual and spiritual search for a Judaism and Israel that matters, and the interest you showed in the ideas of this book, were a critical source of strength and inspiration.

I would like to thank my most recent partners, the Jewish Publication Society (JPS) and the University of Nebraska Press, for accepting my book for publication. Your professionalism and dedication to details is a gift. JPS Director Rabbi Barry Schwartz: thank you for embracing both the book and me as an author, for simultaneously creating a challenging and loving environment, and for your comments which significantly improved the quality of the arguments. And finally, I thank the JPS managing editor, Joy Weinberg, the master of Occam's Razor, who painstakingly and lovingly went over every word and argument, improving the language and the content and ensuring that what was written could also be heard. I am deeply in your debt.

Finally, there would be no Shalom Hartman Institute were it not for our dedicated friends, supporters, and board of directors. They not only sustain the institute but provided me with the financial support to write this book and the framework within which to pursue my life's work and dreams.

In particular I would like to thank Bob Kogod, the now chairman emeritus of the institute, my lifelong friend and partner. Bob, you not only supported me throughout my life; you were also the first person to open my eyes to the idea of Jews with complex identities and the need for a Jewish story which took this into account. Some forty years ago you introduced yourself to me as being a Jew, an American, and a Washingtonian. At the time, being a provincial Jerusalem yeshiva student, I thought it was odd—I now know otherwise. You were giving voice to a new reality in modern Jewish life and identity. This book, and indeed much of my life's work, is inspired by this understanding.

Introduction

In 1971, three months after my bar mitzvah, my family moved from Canada to Israel. I immediately picked up the overt message communicated to young Israeli boys at the time: we would soon be soldiers, guardians, and protectors of the nation and state. As a little boy (literally; I was only four feet eleven inches, under sixty pounds), the idea of being the guardian of anything, let alone responsible for an entire country, made me dizzy with excitement. My people were counting on me.

That's why I was so confused and upset a year later (grade nine, studying in an Orthodox-Zionist yeshiva high school whose faculty consisted exclusively of ultra-Orthodox non-Zionist rabbis), when my teacher told us that we were *forbidden by Jewish law* from going into the army. As students of Torah, he explained, we were soldiers in *God's* army, which took precedence over serving in the military forces of a secular political state.

That night I shared my bewilderment with my father. He sat me down and said he had something he wanted to study with me.

He opened the Talmud Tractate called *Berakhot* ("Blessings") to page 32a, and we began to learn:

> And God said to Moses: "Go down from the mountain." (Exodus 32:7) [The Rabbis ask]: "What is the specific interpretive significance of this way of phrasing this command?'" "Go down from the mountain": [God says to Moses, for] I have given you greatness only for the sake of this people. And now that they have sinned, what need do I have of you?[1]

A little background. In what was supposed to be the pinnacle of the biblical story of the covenant between God and the Jewish people—the "happy ending" to a vexed Exodus following centuries of Egyptian bondage—Moses ascends Mount Sinai to receive God's Torah and deliver it to God's people, but in a plot twist that becomes the Bible's central motif, God plans, and the Jewish people laugh. In this archetypal instance, their laughter takes the form of a Golden Calf.

It's a disturbing moment in the Jewish story. The entire narrative has been building up to Moses's transcendent encounter with God, and his delivery of God's word to the people. It was for this that they were taken out of Egypt: "I will take you to be My people, and I will be your God" (Exod. 6:7). As biblical readers, we are on the edge of our seats—but the revelation is interrupted; the triumphant culmination never comes. Instead, God, in the verse quoted above, commands Moses to depart from the Divine Presence, descend the holy mountain, and confront his sinning people.

According to the Bible, the explicit meaning of this command is: *Get away from Me, because I'm giving up. I've had it with these people, their rebelliousness, their ingratitude. I'm finished. I'm going to wipe them out and start a new people with you and your descendants.* Or, in the Bible's words, "The Lord further said to Moses, 'I see that this is a stiff-necked people. Now let Me be, that My anger may blaze forth against them, and that I may destroy them, and make of you a great nation'" (Exod. 32: 9–10).

The Rabbis of the Talmud, however, reversed the original sense of the story—reinterpreting God's command not as a rejection of the Jewish people and an elevation of Moses but the exact opposite. *Go down from the mountain*, the Rabbis admonish, using this moment to voice a core tenet of their own emergent Jewish theology: Judaism is, at its bedrock, about a collective. The Jewish story has no place for select individuals to climb the mountain and commune with God in private spiritual ecstasy, while the rest of the people wander and stray. Without a Jewish people, there is no Torah; indeed, there is no Judaism.

At school, my teacher had argued that we serve our people best in isolation from the vast majority of them—far removed from others through our commitment to Torah. My father responded with the counterteaching that a commitment to Torah is misguided, meaningless, and irresponsible if undertaken in separation from the needs of the Jewish people. "Go down from the mountain"—*to be with the people. Fulfill your responsibility to ensure their safety, and then build a Judaism in their midst. For only there, in their midst, will Torah take root, and only then can you be with Me.*

Not Just Some of Our Stories, the Sum of Our Stories: Defining the "We"

Since Judaism is so strongly identified with engagement in collective life, it seems reasonable to ask, *who are the Jews*? This people to whom I am bonded and bound . . . who are they? What makes us, us?

The anthropologist Clifford Geertz posits that the answer to the question of who a community or culture is lies in its stories—or, more precisely, in the "ensemble of stories we tell ourselves about ourselves."[2] As distinct from the medieval Jewish philosopher Rabbi Saadia Gaon's model that our people are a people strictly by virtue of its doctrines and laws, the story metaphor avoids prescriptive definitions of Jewishness that attempt to tightly control it. By its very nature, a story is messy, contradictory, subjective, open-ended. A story spins off unruly subplots, often unintentionally, and ours can certainly count many such spinoffs over the three millennia of its evolution; indeed, it continues to generate new ones to this day. Further complicating things, the very question of which plot is the main plot, and which are the subplots, is open to divergent interpretations.

It shouldn't surprise us, then, that the story Jews have told ourselves about ourselves is neither simple nor monolithic. While it can certainly lay claim to a humble, redemptive beginning with our liberation from slavery, the subsequent journey has been famously meandering, geographically and otherwise: at times tragic beyond human imagination and at times suffused with wonder, transcendence, and joy . . . at times a story of failure and at times success . . . at times replete with righteous-ness, at times riddled with sin . . . at times awash with mutual love and care, at times drowning in animosity and mutual delegitimization . . . at times walking with God, at times alienated and wandering . . . at times at home in our land, at times dispersed throughout the world.

Delving into our story through this lens, I found that the more I learned, the less possible it seemed to discern any shared features around which our collective identity can be said to have coalesced.

To be clear, there have been no shortage of answers *proposed* to the question of *Who are the Jews?* and what the Jewish people fundamen-tally share. Various Jews and Jewish movements have been eager to self-anoint their ideologies as the content that all Jews must hold in common. Invariably, though, these answers are more prescriptive than descriptive: there is no *we*, their underlying logic goes, unless *you* become like *me*.

But if we are the sum of the stories we tell ourselves about our-selves, we must first and foremost be willing to hear the complexity and diversity roiling within the "sum" of our stories. An answer to the question *Who are the Jews?* must be broad enough to accommodate three thousand years of multiple understandings and divergent accounts.

This is one of the essential differences between our titular question—"Who are the Jews?"—and the more familiar, stubbornly persistent, ever-contentious discourse around "Who is a Jew?" The latter is prin-cipally a matter of membership policy pertaining to questions like: "What is a legitimate conversion?," "Who is a legitimate rabbi (to conduct conversions)?," "Is Jewishness matrilineal or patrilineal, or both?" in which one's position on these questions is often a function of one's denominational affiliations or one's reading of halakhic sources.

"Who are the Jews?" takes on a much broader question: Given the fact that Jews disagree on so many issues, that the way we understand our stories divides us more than it unites us, and that we cannot even agree on the question "Who is a Jew?"—*in what sense can we think of ourselves in collective terms at all?*

Desert-Island Jokes and Jews:
Are Shared Arguments Enough?

If there is any shared trait that consistently typifies the Jewish people over the course of our long history, it is our seeming second nature to argue, question, disagree—with each other, the tradition, communal authorities, and God. Indeed, in discussing the current state of Jewish communal disunion, which too frequently seems to bleed into pathological dysfunction, we often find ourselves telling jokes about the divisive Jewish temperament. Consciously or not, we do this to reassure ourselves that it has, in effect, always been thus—that arguing and disagreeing about all things Jewish doesn't mean we are fundamentally alienated or estranged from one another, but that, rather, our fighting is a sign of our closeness. We argue because we are connected; it is the way we connect. Arguing with each other is the one permanent characteristic of who we are.

Hence the classic joke about the argument that broke out in a shtetl over the proper way to conduct a particular ritual. As the debate grows hot, the two factions turn to the elder rabbi of the town for clarification of the correct tradition. His ruling: the local custom, every year, for as long as anyone can remember, is to argue about it.

Another version has the rabbi hearing one side and declaring this speaker to be right; and then, when hearing the other, declaring that speaker to be right as well. When challenged on the incongruity of his rulings, he (of course) declares the questioner to be right, too!

Or perhaps the most famous Jewish joke of all: the Jew who ends up stranded on a deserted island and builds two synagogues: the one s/he goes to, and the one s/he *doesn't* go to. The punchline: Jews disagree so vehemently as to how things were and ought to be, they define themselves not merely by where they pray but by where they are not willing to pray.

But a shared argument does not forge a shared identity. The comfort offered by an old joke is functionally a mirage, masking a far darker and more fractured communal reality. For over two hundred years, with the advent and spread of denominationalism into Jewish life, we have become increasingly separated, alien, and often hostile to each other. This emergent reality creates a powerful centrifugal force, which in turn undermines the possibility of a collective Jewish identity that includes the vast majority of actual Jewish people.

"You Go Your Way and We Ours": When Judaism Becomes What Divides Us

As early as the 1860s, the Reform and Orthodox Jewish communities in Germany and Hungary appealed to their respective governments to be recognized as two distinct "Jewish peoples." The founder of ultra-Orthodoxy in the nineteenth century, Rabbi Moshe Schreiber (known as the Hatam Sofer), was strident in his desire to engineer the greatest separation possible from Reform Jews: "I would be of the opinion to separate them from our midst, to desist from giving our daughters to their sons, and our sons to their daughters. . . . Let their community . . . go their way, and we ours."[3]

Today the Jews are even far more divided than our nineteenth-century predecessors. We are divided denominationally among Ultra-Orthodox, Orthodox, Conservative, Reform, Reconstructionist, Renewal, Traditional, Humanistic, and Secular communities, each with multiple subdenominations. We are divided between those who affiliate with a denomination, and the largest group of Jews in North America, who classify themselves as "Nones."[4] We are divided geographically if not nationally and culturally between Israelis and World Jewry. We are divided between those whose mothers are Jewish, those whose fathers are Jewish, those who converted in ways that some reject, and those who self-identify as Jews by virtue of marriage, family ties, or living in the midst of a Jewish community in Israel.

Furthermore, nowadays we are more divided than unified by broad principles of the shared story that once held wide sway among us: respect for Torah, synagogue attendance, Shabbat observance, supporting Israel, heightened loyalty, mutual care, and communal protection against antisemitism. Today, disagreement is so pervasive that it is virtually impossible to identify any shared feature of Judaism that all Jews hold in common.

In this context, the religious divisions portrayed in the classic Jewish jokes have become anachronistic, even quaint.

Diversity and denominations are not unto themselves a problem. Quite to the contrary—they are essential for creating communities of meaning, for when we Jews disagree on most issues pertaining to Jewish law, faith, and ethics, it becomes imperative that each of us finds an authentic Jewish communal home that speaks to us. Jewish unity unto itself is not a value if it demands the papering over of difference. However, when denominationalism leads to a Hatam Sofer–like division between "theirs" and "ours," we are no longer connected through a shared argument or story. Instead, the argument has led to distinct collective identities, each with its own story, in which the other has no part.

In this context, it is not only hard to answer the question, "Who are the Jews? "—it is not even clear that the question makes sense.

Let's take the first joke: the rabbi settling a debate over a communal ritual with the punchline, "We always argued about it." The "moral" of this joke is that everyone—even those on opposite sides of a question of shared communal practice—can be part of a Jewish tradition designed to hold such opposites within a greater whole. But a moment's consideration reveals that the joke assumes a reality in which people on separate sides of a contentious issue could approach the *same* rabbi, both recognizing his standing as a respected authority and intending to accept his decision as final. Whether this was factually accurate in a premodern era, or merely a wishful, wistful backward projection, the notion of a common authority and shared tradition that unites Jews has clearly come to an end.

In our new denominational tribalism, Judaism not only has ceased to unite us—it has become the primary *threat* to our unity, the thing that divides us more than anything else. We no longer share a common tradition—much less, as in the "we always argued about it" joke, a common rabbi whose authority we can accept to interpret it. Our fractured communal landscape seems on the surface to be far more reflective of the canonical "desert island" joke, which mirrors the deeper denominational factionalism of the modern period. We no longer go to the same synagogue or debate fundamental issues of tradition. We each have our own denominational space, built exclusively with those who share our beliefs and practices, and nurtured equally by the deep sense of commonality found among members and the demonstrative rejection of those who are not "us." My identity is defined equally by the synagogue I go to and the synagogue I avoid.

But even the "desert island" joke is, on closer consideration, nostalgic for an era long past. In today's Jewish landscape in Israel and North America, with its blossoming of those who self-define Jewishly as "Secular" and "None," the odds of a Jew who has had the misfortune of getting stranded on a desert island thinking to build a synagogue is slim to none.

The Jew within and the Dissolving Collective

The challenge of answering "Who are the Jews?" cuts even deeper than the formidable task of formulating a common story in the midst of such divisive times. In both North America and Israel, where over 85 percent of the Jewish people reside, the basic assumption that Jewishness is essentially a collective identity *at all* is being questioned.

In North America, the premise of Jewish collectivity is challenged on two fronts: individual (rather than collective), and complex identities.

Individual Identities

Whereas in the predominantly antisemitic societies in which Jews historically found themselves Jewish identity had been largely communal in nature—the primary, if not exclusive, identity of a Jew, the dominant contemporary trend favors individual, rather than collective, identities; Jews increasingly express their Judaism as a personal, familial experience, as distinct from principally a communal one.[5] The current largest "denomination," 40 percent of Jews, are those who do not classify themselves within Jewish communal frameworks and prefer the category of "Nones," a powerful expression of their individuation and move away from group identity labels. Diminishing Jewish membership in communal organizations and institutions is somewhat reflective of this broader historical shift in consciousness. Collective identity, uncoupled from Jewishness, is expressed via other means.

Complex Identities

In the postmodern diasporic phenomenon of "complex identities," individual Jews are likely to claim multiple identities simultaneously. A Jew can feel and be considered Jewish while also feeling and being American or Canadian, gay, transgender, feminist, conservative, liberal, progressive, or any other number of contemporary identities. Jewishness is no longer exclusive and often not predominant in an individual's identity[6]—and hence Jewish peoplehood risks becoming diminished in significance, perhaps even devolving into a purely private, individual expression.

In Israel, on the other hand, while collective Jewish identity is alive and vibrant (at least among non-Haredi Jews), there is a phenomenon of *within-ness* specifically within the boundaries of the State of Israel. The national framework of sovereignty, coupled with Israel's sustained isolation from its neighbors, has created such a strong sense of community that many Israeli Jews have come to see *Israeliness itself* as the primary content of, and qualifier for, Jewishness and vice versa. Indeed, in much of the Zionist narrative, Israel is not a subclass of Jewish peoplehood but its only viable and authentic expression. Israelis with this view see Jews outside of Israel as part of their community, but with some important parameters—that is, only to the extent that the Diaspora Jews want to make aliyah and move to Israel or are in existential danger and in need of Israel's assistance. Within the Jewish state, Zionism has yet to embrace a positive global Jewish collective identity encompassing Jews who are at home outside of Israel and not in need of rescue.

About This Book

The premise of this book is that the story the Jewish people tell ourselves about ourselves is in need of a revision focused on identifying resonant through-lines that inspire wide swathes of Jews to listen, discuss, and retell it. We Jews need a story we can see ourselves in, one that offers meaning and moral guidance to help us navigate our lives, and one we want to pass on. We need a metastory that can deepen our understanding of who we are and, more importantly, who we want to become.

The volume is divided into three parts. The first, "What's Our Story?," presents a thesis regarding the metastory Jews have told ourselves about ourselves—the root stories of Jewishness. This story is divided between two concepts and their respective covenants. The first, Genesis, defines Jewishness as a modality of being, an identity Jews affirm independent of what we do or believe. The second, Exodus, understands Jewishness principally as a modality of becoming, a system of beliefs, values, and practices that challenge and demand that a Jew become more. I show how these two covenants have shaped rabbinic understandings of Jewishness (the process of becoming a Jew and the boundaries of Jewish identity) and then demonstrate how the categories of Genesis and Exodus can serve as a lens through which to understand key developments in the Jewish story over the past two millennia.

In parts 2 and 3, the book shifts from a story of who Jews were and are to how the metastory of Genesis and Exodus can reshape the possibilities of what Jewishness might become. Part 2, "A Zionism for the Twenty-First Century," elaborates on some of the central challenges facing Israel today: overcoming the "original sin" of religion and state, convincing secular Israelis to embrace their Exodus Judaism, rising above Israel's deeply entrenched rejection of the value of Jewish life outside its borders and "othering" of Israeli Palestinians, reembracing the pursuit of peace in political discourse, and challenging Israeli society to return to its core liberal Jewish and democratic values.

Part 3, "A Diaspora Future," begins by analyzing the unique shift from the Jewish experience of otherness to one of "at-homeness" in North America and its profound consequences: intermarriage as a new normal and Diaspora Jewry's eroding relationship with Israel (in part because of the rise of ultranationalist and ultra-Orthodox political forces and Israel's continued occupation of the Palestinian people in the West Bank and Gaza). The penultimate chapter builds a framework for a new, encompassing understanding of Zionism for the vast majority of liberal North American Jews, and the final chapter offers a narrative of Jewish collective identity for twenty-first-century Jews by Choice—which, in the twenty-first century, is all of us.

In essence, the book you are reading is an invitation to a conversation I have been having—with colleagues, students, friends, and anyone else who would listen—over the last ten years. It is a story of interplaying ideas that have shaped Jewish life, thought, and identity over the millennia, and equally a story of the future: a way to link who we have been with who we might become.

"Genesis" and "Exodus" Caveats: Some Notes on What They Don't Mean

In using the language of Genesis and Exodus to denote the two primary modalities of Jewishness, I am not making the literal claim that they exist exclusively in the books of Genesis and Exodus respectively, or that there is a singular distinct Jewishness characterized throughout the book of Genesis, matched by its perfectly complementary book of Exodus counterpart. Quite the contrary: there are multiple manifestations of Exodus Judaism in the book of Genesis, and extensive expressions of Genesis Judaism in the book of Exodus. Both reappear throughout the various books in the Bible. In fact, my essential argument is that the two are inextricably intertwined throughout the biblical narrative.

I use "Genesis" and "Exodus" because the covenants with God embodying these two dominant modes of Jewishness first appear in these biblical books, respectively, in explicit and developed terms. They are both heuristic categories—shorthand for alternate notions of Jewishness—and actual distinct biblical covenants between God and the Jewish people.

It is also important to clarify that the dichotomy between the Covenants of Genesis and Exodus does *not* parallel the common distinction between Jews as a people/nationality and Judaism as a religion.[7] That distinction essentially evokes two parallel stories of Jewishness: one about who the *Jews* are, and another about what *Judaism* is. One is a secular sociopolitical story that positions Jews in parallel with French, Germans, and Greeks; the other religious and faith-based, viewing Judaism as analogous to Christianity, Islam, and Buddhism. By contrast, the Covenants of Genesis and Exodus, as we will explore, are both integral to Judaism as a *religion*. In our story, both define a covenantal relationship between God and the Jewish people and reflect a way to live a full Jewish life.

WHO ARE
THE JEWS

PART ONE   What's Our Story?

1

The Genesis Covenant and the First Jews

Can we find a way to talk about Jewish collective identity that infuses it with an enhanced sense of clarity, meaning, and purpose? Can we tell a story that considers both who the Jews are and what we can become?

In part 1, I argue that the metastory Jews have told about who we are since our earliest origins is born out of the active, living synthesis of two competing claims about the essential nature of Jewishness: the Genesis Covenant/Genesis Judaism and the Exodus Covenant/Exodus Judaism. In the Genesis Covenant, Jewish collective identity is grounded in who one *is* and the group to which one belongs, independent of what one believes and/or does. The Exodus Covenant, conversely, is grounded in one's relationship to an aspirational system of values, ideals, beliefs, commandments, and behaviors.[1] The friction generated by the encounter between these opposing concepts is a central creative tension that has defined Jewish collective identity.

Here, I aim to illustrate how the Covenants of Genesis and Exodus constitute a core lens through which to understand Jewishness, the warp and woof of the Jewish identity metanarrative, such that when one disappears or becomes too dominant, Jewish collective identity becomes threadbare and begins to unravel. Conversely, when they are held in constructive conversation, Jewishness becomes a nurturing, unifying resource. In the generative Genesis-Exodus interplay the sparks of a rich and compelling identity for our time may be found.

Tales of a Traveling Kippah

As an Orthodox Jew, I generally travel around the world wearing my kippah. A remarkable fact I do not take for granted is in how much of

North America I feel comfortable and welcomed as a Jew. I am aware of how unique—and recent—this feeling is against the broader canvas of Jewish history.

My kippah has been a catalyst for many unexpected connections, the most common being what I refer to as the "Jewish Nod." Amid the daily rhythms of North America's relatively tolerant multicultural landscape, very often some fellow traveler begins to stretch their neck in unnatural ways as they try to remain discreet while making "secret" eye contact. The bizarreness of the move attracts my attention, and the moment of eye contact is accompanied by a subtle, almost indiscernible nod of the head. And so, while the neck bends, the gaze remains firmly in place—silently communicating that I have been seen, and that they too are a Jew. We are an *us*.

Protocol requires that I respond immediately, in kind, with a reciprocal nod, thereby confirming that I have seen that they have seen me, and see them in turn. At times the formal ritual ends here. At other times a third nod is delivered, a declaration of acknowledgement that they have seen, that I have seen, that they have seen me.

The Jewish nod is brief and fleeting, for in reality, we are strangers to each other and have different short-term agendas—especially if we are on a plane and need to sleep. The alternate reality, however, remains true, and leaves its imprint: among the community of travelers, we are strangers but not *total* strangers; we share a perhaps distant, but still meaningful, connection. Our subtle communiqué is founded on an unexplained yet self-evident bond of a shared identity that transcends mundane reality.

Once, on the first day of a long-awaited ski trip in Colorado, I found myself at the top of a slope outside my skill set as a rabbi. While wiping out over a nasty mogul, I cut my knee on the edge of my ski and was quickly whisked off the mountain to the hospital for stitches. As I lay in the hospital bed, angry at myself and upset over my ruined vacation, a stranger approached me and asked, "Excuse me. Are you Jewish?"

I should mention here that, kippah notwithstanding, one of the main reasons for going skiing in Colorado is to be anonymous. Throughout the year, I am entrenched in the Jewish community. This was my chance to commune with snow. I was not interested in being a Jew at that moment; frankly, I wanted to be left alone. But duty called, and I reluctantly answered in the affirmative.

"Great," he responded. "I am also Jewish and live in Mexico. Do you possibly know someone who I can set up with my daughter?"

At that moment, the last thing I was interested in was someone else's problems, let alone a stranger who wanted to find a spouse for a daughter I did not know.

Yet almost against my will I found my mind wandering . . . *Who do we know in Mexico? Does Adina (my wife) know anyone?*

This stranger had claimed me. He had laid claim to my interest, loyalty, concern, and care simply by virtue of some notion that we were both Jews.

These interactions are the products of a particular motif or thread or subplot within the story Jews tell ourselves about ourselves.

Jewishness without Judaism: The Golden Calf Motif

One of the threads weaving together the story of the Jewish people can be extrapolated from the biblical tale of the Golden Calf, in which even God is unable to complete the handing over of the Torah to Israel.

Fearing Moses has died after disappearing up a mountain forty days earlier, the people panic. Instead of maintaining their faith in the One who has just redeemed them from Egypt with "a mighty hand, an outstretched arm, and awesome power" (Deut. 4:34), they hastily fabricate a Golden Calf and proclaim, "*This* is your God, O Israel, who brought you out of the Land of Egypt" (Exod. 32:4).

The Golden Calf isn't just a moment in the Bible: it *is* the Bible, in a proverbial nutshell. Throughout the Bible, the Jews (in biblical terms, Israelites or Children of Israel) vacillate between monotheism (the belief in the existence of only one God) or monolatry (the belief in the existence of many gods, but with the consistent worship of only one) and idolatry and remain largely indifferent to, and at times in open rebellion of, God's word.[2]

In other words, at such moments when we Jews wished to worship a Golden Calf, we were not necessarily who we were supposed to be, but who we were: Jews on a lengthy dialectical journey toward monotheism who did very little of what we have come to know as Judaism.

Claiming that the first understanding of being Jewish is distinct from most of what we think of as Judaism might sound strange, even heretical. In my defense, I might call as a witness the last chronological book of the Hebrew Bible, Nehemiah, which looks back at the Jewish people's seven-hundred-year journey and says: *Let me tell you what I just heard.*

Here is the prophet Nehemiah's summary of the biblical story:

Forty years, *you* God, sustained them in the wilderness so that they lacked nothing. Their clothes did not wear out; their feet did not swell. *You* gave them kingdoms and peoples and allotted them territory. They took possession of the land of Sihon, the land of King of Heshbon, the land of Og, King of Bashan. *You* made their children as numerous as the stars of heaven and brought them to the land that *You* told their fathers to go and possess. The sons came and took possession of the land. *You* subdued the Canaanite inhabitants of the land. . . . *You* delivered them, both their kings and their people. *You* captured fortified cities, rich lands, and took possession of houses filled with everything good. (Neh. 9:21–25, emphasis added)

God, in short, delivered on *Your* (our) side of the covenant, fulfilling all of our wants and needs. Everything God promised, God did. This, of course, made it all the more galling for God and the prophet when:

Defying You, *they* rebelled. *They* cast your teaching behind their back. *They* killed your prophets who admonished them to turn them back to you. *They* committed great impieties. You delivered them into the power of their adversaries who oppressed them. In their time of trouble, *they* cried out to You; You in heaven heard them, and in Your abundant compassion gave them saviors who saved them. But when *they* had relief, *they* again did what was evil in Your sight, so You abandoned them again to the power of their enemies, who subjugated them. Again, *they* cried to You, and You in heaven heard and rescued them in Your compassion, time after time. You admonished them in order to turn them back to Your teaching, but *they* acted presumptuously and disobeyed Your commandments, and sinned against Your rules, which a person who practices will live by. *They* turned a defiant shoulder, stiffened their neck, and would not obey. You, God, bore with them for many years, admonished them. Your prophets did the same, but *they* would not give ear, so finally You delivered them into the power of the peoples of the land. (Neh:26–30; emphasis added)[3]

This is Nehemiah's summary of the Bible—a close to thousand-year snapshot of a people who remained Jewish, generation after generation, without doing much of anything that could be considered "Judaism." The Judaism of the Bible existed primarily in the eyes and mind of God, who fantasized about a Jewish people who would be faithful to God and God's commandments. But for the Jews themselves, Jewish identity had little to do with . . . *doing*. They were raised on a different narrative, Genesis Judaism, in which being Jewish was just who you were. They were *Genesis Jews*—a form of Jewishness that first occurs in the book of Genesis and becomes the dominant Jewish identity of the biblical period.

Chosen People: An Inherited Identity

In the Genesis Covenant between God and Abraham, Abraham is chosen on condition that he leave his native land and embark on a journey to an unknown land that God promises to show him (Gen. 12:1). His descendants are promised to be a great nation, God's chosen people, only by virtue of being Abraham's offspring:

And the Lord said to Abraham . . . "Raise your eyes and look out from where you are, to the North and South, to the East and West, for I give all the land that you see to you and *your seed* forever. I will make *your seed* as the dust of the earth, so that if one can count the dust of the earth, then *your seed* too can be counted." (Gen. 13:14-16; emphasis added)

Throughout Genesis, generation after generation inherits God's promise merely as a function of being Abraham's seed.[4] The promise begins with Isaac:

And the Lord appeared to [Isaac] and said, "Do not go down to Egypt; stay in the land which I point out to you. Reside in this land, and I will be with you and bless you. I will assign all these lands to you and to your seed, *fulfilling the oath that I swore to your father Abraham.* I will make your seed as numerous as the stars of heaven and assign to your seed all of these lands. And all the nations of the earth shall be blessed through your seed." (Gen. 26:2-6; emphasis added)

Then God passes down the promise to Jacob:

And the Lord was standing beside [Jacob], and He said, "I am the Lord, the God of your father Abraham, and the God of Isaac. The ground on which you are lying I will give to you and to your seed. Your seed shall be as the dust of the earth, and you shall spread out to the West and to the East, to the North and to the South; all the nations of the earth shall bless themselves through you and your seed. Remember I am with you: I will protect you wherever you go, and I will bring you back to this land. I will not leave you until I have done what I have promised you." (Gen. 28:13-15)

Abraham clearly earns his status as God's elect. He undergoes travail after travail—exile, famine, war, childlessness—culminating in the horrific test of loyalty known as the Binding of Isaac: "Sometime afterward, God put Abraham to the test. He said to him, 'Abraham,' and he answered, 'Here I am.' And he said, 'Take your son, your favored one, Isaac, whom you love, and go to the land of Moriah, and offer him there as a burnt-offering on one of the heights that I will point out to you'" (Gen. 22: 1–2).

Early the next morning, Abraham rises, takes Isaac, and embarks on a journey to fulfill God's command. At the last moment, right before Abraham is about to slay his son on the altar of his loyalty to God, God stays the decree. Abraham's willingness to obey God is deemed sufficient to guarantee the chosen status of all his progeny:

> By Myself I swear, the Lord declares: *Because* you have done this, and have not withheld your son, your favored one, I will bestow My blessing upon you, and make your seed as numerous as the stars of heaven, and the sands of the seashore. And your seed shall inherit the gates of their enemies. It is through your seed that all the nations of the earth shall be blessed, *because* you have obeyed My command. (Gen. 22: 16–18; emphasis added)

This is the essence of the Genesis Covenant into which the Jewish people are welcomed simply by virtue of the piety of Abraham and their association with him.

Circumcision and the Sign of the Covenant

The one major exception to this rule is the commandment placed within the Genesis Covenant whereby Abraham and his descendants must circumcise their sons:[5]

> God further said to Abraham, "As for you, you and your offspring to come throughout the ages shall keep My covenant. Such shall

be the covenant between Me and you and your offspring to follow which you shall keep; every male among you shall be circumcised. You shall circumcise the flesh of your foreskin, and that shall be a sign of the covenant between Me and you . . . Thus shall my covenant be marked in your flesh as an everlasting pact. And if any male who is uncircumcised fails to circumcise the flesh of his foreskin, that person shall be cut off from his kin (people); he has broken My covenant." (Gen. 17:9-14)

The inherited and unconditional Genesis Covenant has one condition—circumcision—which, if not followed, constitutes a breaking of the covenant and requires banishment from the community. However, note the language: circumcision is designated as "the *sign* of the Covenant between Me and you." While clearly a condition, it is not the covenant itself but merely an external sign, marked on the flesh, attesting to one's status and acceptance of belonging to the community of Genesis Jews.[6] The core Genesis Covenant remains a mode of being and not doing.[7]

That said, the notion of a sign of the covenant as a requirement within Genesis is nevertheless critical. It means that while one inherits one's status as a Genesis Jew, Genesis still demands that one actively embrace this status. It defines one's Jewishness only to the extent that one actively chooses to be a Jew. While failing to do so, as we will see, does not engender a loss of Jewishness, it is nevertheless a requirement which generates sanctions for those who fail to comply.[8]

A Story of Flawed Ancestors

In keeping with the notion of Genesis as an inherited covenant, and quite distinct from its treatment of Abraham, the Bible makes no effort to associate noble qualities with Abraham's seed. None of Abraham's descendants distinguish themselves through heroic acts of faith or particular greatness of character. While Isaac and Jacob do maintain a faith in God and worship the God of Abraham, the Bible depicts the two as mediocre at best.[9] When one descendant is chosen over another, as is the case between Isaac and Ishmael, and Jacob and Esau, no grounds such as claims of moral or spiritual superiority are given to justify the particular selection (Gen. 21:9–13; 25:23). In the case of Esau and Jacob, the Bible actually portrays Esau in far more positive and sympathetic terms than Jacob, certainly in terms of Esau's caring for his father (Gen. 26:28; 27:4).

As for the next generation, the children of Jacob who inherit Abraham's blessing—and become the backbone out of which the nation of Israel is formed—the Bible renders them as somewhat morally challenged. They disobey their father, plot to kill their brother Joseph, relent and merely sell him as a slave, and torture their father emotionally with a story of his death at the hands of wild beasts (Gen. 37:18–35). Shimon and Levi appear as devious, murderous thugs (Gen. 34). Reuven sleeps with one of his father's half-wives (Gen. 35:22), while Judah sleeps with prostitutes and mistakenly impregnates his own daughter-in-law (Gen. 34). Joseph, the supposed "good apple," comes across as spoiled, arrogant, and self-aggrandizing as he assembles his father and brothers to share his dreams in which they will all one day bow down to him (Gen. 37:5–10).

These Genesis Jews of inherited status become the collective "Children of Israel" (the family of Jacob, whose name is converted to Israel)— and with this identity they go down to Egypt. There they proliferate and grow into a people (Heb. *am*), eventually filling the land of Egypt. The Children of Israel are no longer simply a nuclear family but a nation, and as a result the Bible struggles with their name: "A new king arose over Egypt who did not know Joseph. And he said to his people, 'Look, the *People* of the Children of Israel (Heb. *Am B'nei Yisrael*) are much too numerous for us. Let us deal shrewdly with them, so that they may not increase'.... But the more they were oppressed, the more they increased and spread out, so that the Egyptians came to dread the Children of Israel" (Exod. 1:8–12; emphasis added).

Here they are no longer merely the literal children of Jacob, but a people distinct from the Egyptians in whose midst they live. And for a moment, through the mediating words of Pharaoh, the Bible recognizes this transition by calling them, "the *People* of the Children of Israel"—the only instance in the Bible in which this term is used. Henceforth, the nomenclature "people" is dropped, and they revert back to simply being the "Children of Israel": a nation now, but one still identified and defined through its ethnic roots.

In essence, after Abraham, Jewishness comes to be defined by the totally passive act of being born into Abraham's family.

"I Have Remembered": Salvation and the Guaranteed Covenant

The laconic, unblinking assessments of our ancestors' flaws and dysfunctions do not end with the original patriarchs of Genesis. The book of Exodus never distinguishes the character of the Children of Israel from that of their Egyptian taskmasters—some superior attribute by virtue of which they might warrant salvation and the gift of liberation from Egypt. All that is mentioned is their—and God's—connection to their forefathers:

> And God said further to Moses, "Thus shall you speak to the Israelites: 'The Lord, the God of your fathers, the God of Abraham, the God of Isaac, and the God of Jacob, has sent me to you: This shall be My name forever, this My appellation for all eternity.' Go and assemble the elders of Israel and say to them: 'The Lord, the God of your Fathers, the God of Abraham, Isaac, and Jacob, has appeared to me and said, "I have taken note of you, and what is being done to you in Egypt, and I have declared, I will take you out of the misery of Egypt to the land of the Canaanites, the Hittites, the Amorites, the Perizzites, the Hivites, the Jebusites, to a land flowing with milk and honey""'" (Exod. 3:15-17).

All the Jewish people need to do to warrant God's salvation is to be the descendants of their ancestors. As God's chosen people, their suffering alone is sufficient to activate divine intervention on their behalf: "I have now heard the moaning of the Israelites, because the Egyptians are holding them in bondage, *and I have remembered My covenant*. Say therefore to the Israelite people: 'I am the Lord. I will free you from the labors of the Egyptians and deliver you from their bondage. I will redeem you with an outstretched arm, and through extraordinary chastisement'" (Exod. 6:5–6; emphasis added).

Here, too, as with Abraham's circumcision, redemption of the Genesis Jews is conditioned on the people's willingness to publicly distinguish themselves from their surrounding culture, to choose to belong and identify with their Genesis-based Jewishness. Only those who mark their doorposts—a symbol for the home—with the blood of the Passover sacrifice (see Exod. 12) are in turn distinguished by God from the Egyptians and their fate. As in the case with circumcision, here the blood is similarly designated with the word "sign" (Heb. *ot*) (see Exod. 12:7, 13).[10]

Following the model of the Exodus from Egypt, in the future, when God's patience and compassion run out and God pours God's wrath upon us—even to the extent of banishing us from the Promised Land—one dominant Genesis-influenced biblical motif posits that ultimately, redemption, a return to the land and God's blessing, is guaranteed. Like the Children of Israel in Egypt, we too are guaranteed redemption by mere virtue of our pedigree and the suffering we experience:

> Even then, when they are in the land of their enemies, I will not reject them or spurn them so as to destroy them, annulling my covenant with them: for I the Lord am their God. I will remember in their favor the covenant of the ancestors, whom I freed from the land of Egypt in the sight of the nations to be their God: I, the Lord. (Lev. 26:44–45)[11]

Similarly, the prophet Isaiah declares: "Comfort, O comfort my people, says your God. Speak tenderly to Jerusalem and declare to her *that her term of service is over, that her iniquity is expiated*; for she has received at the hands of the Lord double for all her sins" (Isa. 40:1–2; emphasis added).[12]

Comfort and redemption are guaranteed and will come when the allotted time arrives, as a result of God's grace and as the consequence of the original covenant. As was the case in Egypt, future salvation is in no way contingent on our behavior, on our earning or deserving it.

"A Stiff-Necked People": The Genesis Jews of Exodus (and Beyond)

Both during the Exodus from Egypt and afterwards, in classic "Genesis mode," the Bible continues to depict the Jewish people as uninspired by the divine word. In what essentially encapsulates the story of Moses's prophecy, when God tells him to tell Pharaoh to let God's people go, Moses replies, "The Israelites will not listen to me" (Exod. 6:12)—and as the continuation of the story reveals, he is right.

At every step of their Exodus journey to their Promised Land, the Children of Israel seem a reluctant party at best. Despite witnessing God's miraculous power, at any crossroads of danger or uncertainty, they complain, rebel, sin, and even plead to be allowed to return to a life of slavery in Egypt:

> As Pharaoh drew near, the Israelites caught sight of the Egyptians advancing upon them. Greatly frightened, the Israelites cried out to the Lord. And they said to Moses, "Was it for want of graves in Egypt that you brought us to die in the wilderness? What have you done to us, taking us out of Egypt? Is this not the very thing we told you in Egypt, saying: 'Let us be, and we will serve the Egyptians, for it is better for us to serve the Egyptians than to die in the wilderness?'" (Exod. 14:10–12)[13]

Summarizing their life together over forty years in the desert, as Israel is about to be brought into the Promised Land, predating but echoing Nehemiah's reading, Moses avows:

Hear O Israel! . . . *It is not because of your virtues and your rectitude that you will be able to possess this country*; but it is because of their wickedness that the Lord your God is dispossessing those nations before you, and in order to fulfill the oath that the Lord made to your fathers, Abraham, Isaac, and Jacob. *Know, then, that it is not for any virtue of yours that the Lord your God is giving you this good land to possess; for you are a stiff-necked people.* Remember, never forget, how you provoked the Lord your God to anger in the wilderness: from the day that you left the land of Egypt until you reached this place, you have continued defiant toward the Lord. (Deut. 9:1-7; emphasis added)

The Bible takes great care to consistently depict the Jewish people as nothing more than a people with a story of shared ethnic roots. They inherit the status of God's "Chosen People" not because they embody unique values or noble attributes, but as a family heirloom, and this inherited status seems to exhaust the content of their Jewish identity.

"Saving" the Book of Genesis

For many years, I returned again and again to the book of Genesis, and each time was left deeply troubled by its content and message—or rather, its seeming emptiness. While rich in human drama and insight, with the possible exceptions of Abraham and Rebecca, no figures seem worthy of emulation; no outstanding individuals emerge who seem suited to be role models of any kind. Since the Bible is clearly not a book of history—but a book aimed at shaping the values and thoughts that ought to embody our lives—what purpose do we find in the fifty chapters of overtly mediocre-to-worse ancestors? What lessons about Judaism does it mean to teach us?

I wondered, along with the Rabbis, why it was necessary to include this book in our canon. Isn't the Bible essentially a book of commandments and laws—and if so, why not begin with the first commandment given to the Jewish people (Exod. 12:2), skipping over a patriarchal narrative that does not seem to offer any insight or direction on how to live our lives?[14]

The rabbinic tradition was so deeply troubled by the negative depiction of Abraham's descendants that there emerged a systematic project to rewrite the Genesis narrative through midrashic exegesis. While not overidealizing our forefathers and their descendants, the Rabbis did whitewash many of their shortcomings. Rabbinic stories rehabilitate Isaac and Jacob (who carry on the Israelite line) as faithful pietists, lovers of God and scholars of Torah, and render their brothers Ishmael and Esau as whoring, idolatrous, murderous lowlifes.[15] In these tales, even the Jewish people in Egypt receive a minor upgrade: they were steadfast in maintaining their traditions and values, which ensured they would not assimilate into the idolatrous Egyptian culture.[16]

But perhaps "saving" the book of Genesis lies not in rose-colored revisionism, but in reframing its purpose—not to provide role models but to establish a founding precept of Jewish identity. Perhaps these stories are intended not merely to recount early Jewish life and behavior but to advance a particular definition of Jewishness: an articulation shaped by what I have called the Genesis Covenant. From this perspective, the rabbinic "rehabilitation project" misapprehends the book of Genesis' central point: that Jewish identity, once acquired, *requires no further validation*—not even in abiding by the word of God. God certainly *wants* the Jews to obey God's commands, but the conceptual foundation set forth first in the book of Genesis is that this is not *necessary* for Jewish identity or the fulfillment of the covenant.

A Covenant of Grace

By granting an eternal inviolable covenant to Abraham's descendants, God—and not merely the de facto reality of millennia-long sinning Jews—lays the foundation for what constitutes a Jewish covenantal relationship with God: simply *to be*, to be a member of this people.

The Genesis Covenant is about extending God's grace to embrace the Jewish people unconditionally. Because Abraham chose to walk with God, God commits to walking with his descendants. You don't have to earn God's love and commitment; nor can you forfeit it. To be a Jew is to live under Gods' love, validation, and care; it is an invitation to walk with a God who will always be at your side. The God of the book of Genesis, who stayed with Abraham's descendants despite their persistent mediocrity, moral failure, and at times outright depravity—the God who stays with the Jewish people throughout the Bible, despite their rebelliousness, faithlessness, and bad behavior—is the God who will stay with the Jewish people wherever they go, and whatever they do.

Through this lens, Nehemiah's depiction of the Israelite story should be read not as a failed covenantal history but rather as a history of the origin of Genesis Judaism. The core message of Genesis is simply this: regardless of who you are as a person, regardless of what you do, the covenant with God is sustained.

"A Jew Is a Jew Is a Jew": The Immutability of Jewish Being

Later Jewish tradition embraced and canonized this idea that Genesis Jews were not failures as Jews but to the contrary, figures meant to exemplify one of Judaism's conceptual bedrocks: the permanent and unconditional nature of both our relationship with God and our collective identity. Just as there is nothing an individual can do to void the covenant established by Abraham, so too membership status remains an established fact outside the reach of individual choice. Early rabbinic law ruled that the immutability of membership applies to all "deviants and sinners"—whether born Jewish or having converted. Under Jewish law, even a recent convert to Judaism who retracts that conversion and returns to his or her prior religious beliefs and practices is classified as an Israelite "deviant" and maintains full legal status as a Jew:

> [Once] he has immersed and emerges [from the water] *he is a Jew in every sense.* What are the halakhic ramifications [of his being a Jew in every sense]? If he returns and renounces [his conversion] and then marries a Jewish woman, he is considered a deviant Jew

[but still a Jew nonetheless], and his marriages are therefore still valid marriages [due to the fact that he is still a Jew].[17]

Once a Jew—even if only for a fleeting moment—always a Jew.

The classical rabbinic formulation of the "immutability principle" of Jewish membership calls out from the powerful talmudic pronouncement, "Even though they have sinned they are still called Israel."[18]

In other words, sin, while perhaps generating sanctions, never severs the basic communal membership status of the sinner. By the Middle Ages it had become a widespread internalized axiom of our collective identity that one's Jewishness could never be revoked for any reason, even by actions or beliefs that the tradition deemed deviant in the extreme.[19]

Indeed, throughout Jewish history this has been one of the few collective principles so universally held as to virtually transcend debate. A powerful example can be found among the modern legal responsa of Rabbi Eliezer Waldenberg, who served as head of the Orthodox Jerusalem Rabbinical court in the 1960s. In the following ruling, he addresses the status of a woman who converted to Christianity—and then subsequently petitioned the court to allow her to "reconvert" to Judaism. Waldenberg rejected the request *as posed* on the following grounds:

> It is obvious and simple that according to Jewish law, a Jew is in no way capable of freeing him or herself from the bonds of the Torah and severing the ties and the roots of his or her connection to his or her people. A Jew's fundamental connection to the Jewish people is founded on the fact that s/he was born to Jewish parents, or more accurately to a Jewish mother. . . .
>
> It is, therefore, a central principal of our religion and our holy Torah that no one of the offspring of Jacob can escape from it, whether voluntarily or non-voluntarily. Against his or her will, a Jew remains a Jew, connected to the religion of Moshe, with no recourse to free him or herself from it. It is, therefore, simple and

clear that the conversion to a different religion of this woman, who wants to return to Judaism, *is something that never happened*. She never left the framework of Judaism, either religiously or nationally, and her return to Judaism is like the return of a daughter to her mother.[20]

The biblical ancestors remained the "Children of Israel" despite their almost total rejection of God and Judaism—and in this, as in so many things, they set an example for future generations. Our Genesis Covenant translates this truth into an essential node in the "operating system" of Jewish self-understanding, staking its central claim in the immutability of membership in the Jewish people.

"Are Your Brothers to Go to War while You Stay Here?": Genesis and Loyalty

A second essential implication of Genesis Judaism is the elevation of mutual loyalty as a constitutive principle of Jewish identity. To be a Jew is not only to be a part of a family embraced unconditionally by God. It demands, fundamentally, an unconditional loyalty to one's fellow Jews. It starts with one's willingness to be a carrier of the sign of covenant—to not merely be but to actively and willingly choose to belong. But it goes further and demands more. If the Genesis Covenant creates an inviolable bond between God and the Jewish people so that God is "stuck" with us irrespective of our virtues or faults, it also consigns all Jews to the same fate of "stuckness" with respect to one another.

The traditional text of the Passover Haggadah expresses this idea most powerfully with the introduction of the figure of the Wicked Child:[21]

Who is the wicked child? S/he who says, "What is this [Passover] ritual to you"-to *you*, and not to *her*. And by removing herself from the collective, s/he is a heretic on the essence [of Judaism].

Here we have a definition of what constitutes the paradigm of wickedness in Jewish tradition: seeing oneself as separate from the community. Even more intriguing is that the tradition does not leave it there—in this classic reading, the moral wickedness of removing oneself from the collective is branded not merely as religiously deviant but as *heresy in its essence*. For what lies at the foundation not only of Jewish peoplehood but of Jewish *faith* is seeing one's destiny as inextricably bound together with that of all other Jews.

In a similar vein, Maimonides includes in his comprehensive catalogue of Judaism's core heresies "a person who excludes themself from the ways of the community":

> A person who excludes themself from the ways of the community, *although they have committed no transgressions*, but remain separated from the congregation of Israel, not observing commandments together with Israel, not including themselves in Israel's troubles, not mourning on Israel's days of mourning, but following their own path *as if they were one of the nations of the world*, and not a part of Israel, such a person has no share in the World to Come.[22]

To be clear, Maimonides explicates that the person in question may not have committed a single one of the transgressions enumerated in the Torah; their only deviance is their spiritual and emotional self-segregation from fellow Jews: "not observing commandments together with Israel, not including themselves in Israel's troubles, not mourning on Israel's days of mourning." As far as Maimonides is concerned, this pointed absence actually amounts to embracing a non-Jewish identity, "walking in their ways as if they were one of the nations of the world."[23]

Such a person could be a tireless devotee of God's word, keeping all the commandments and not sinning at all—the kind of person my father used to say is so stringent in the laws of kashrut, they don't even eat in their *own* home. Yet for Maimonides, the mere fact of not seeing oneself as part of the community makes one an archetypal deviant of

Jewish tradition. To remain bound to the People as a whole, just as God is, is the essential substance of the Genesis Covenant, such that if a fellow Jew is in trouble, we do not ask which commandments they observed and which they transgressed. We just stand up and say, *Here I am. What can I do?*

This expectation is powerfully illustrated in the tense biblical stand-off that threatens—for the second time—the Jewish people's ability to enter the Land of Israel. The first attempt had failed because of the sin of the spies, who by accentuating the perils that lay ahead, disillusioned the people from crossing over into the Promised Land (Num. 13–14). Now, forty years later, the tribes of Reuven and Gad own many cattle and their concern over the maintenance of their property and wealth proves so grave that as the people approach the border to the Land of Israel, the two tribes opt for the land just outside of it: "Your servants have cattle. It would be a favor for us that this land [outside of the Promised Land] should be given to us as a holding. Do not move us across the Jordan" (Num. 32:3).

Hearing this request, Moses only has one thing on his mind—loyalty: "Moses replied to the Gadites and the Reubenites, '*Are your brothers to go to war while you stay here?*'" (Num. 32:4; emphasis added).

Invoking the familial metaphor so familiar to the Genesis Jew, Moses preemptively signals disapproval of any form of self-interest that will supersede collective loyalty. Siblings do not shirk their responsibilities to each other, period. And so, it is only when Reuven and Gad promise that they will join their family in the battle to take possession of their promised homeland—indeed, *lead* them in battle and only return to their land on the other side of the Jordan after everyone has completed taking possession of their inheritance within its borders—that Moses acquiesces:

> Moses said to them, "If you do this, if you lead the troops in battle at the instance of the Lord, and every lead fighter among you crosses the Jordan at the instance of the Lord, until God has dispossessed God enemies from before God's presence, and

the Land has been captured at the instance of the Lord, and [only] then you return [to your families and holdings], you shall be clear before the Lord and before Israel; and this land [on the other side of the Jordan] shall be your holding under the Lord. But if you do not do so, you will have sinned against the Lord; and know that your sin will overtake you. Build towns for your children and sheepfolds for your flocks, but do what you have promised." (Num. 32:20–24)

Loyalty to your national family, Moses admonishes, must take precedence over loyalty to your individual families.

"Fear Your God, That Your Brother Shall Live with You"

These foundational bonds of mutual responsibility are vividly enacted, and institutionalized into law, in the biblical commandment to forgive all loans every seven years:[24]

Every seventh year you shall practice remission of debts. This shall be the nature of the remission; every creditor shall remit the due that they claim from their fellow. One shall not demand payment from one's fellow or kin (*ahikha*), for the remission proclaimed is of the Lord. You may demand payment from the foreigner; but you must remit whatever is due you from your kin.

There shall be no needy among you—since the Lord your God will bless you in the land that the Lord your God is giving to you as a hereditary portion—*if only you heed the Lord your God and take care to keep of this Instruction that I enjoin upon you this day.* For the Lord your God will bless you as the Lord your God has promised you; you will extend loans to many nations, but require none yourself; you will rule over many nations, but they will not rule over you. (Deut. 19:1–6; emphasis added)

The Bible—with God here already functioning, as we will see, in Exodus covenantal mode—posits that those who follow the word of God will be rewarded with blessings of prosperity; by implication, poverty is the consequence of sin, and the persistence of poor people can only be understood as a consequence of their stubborn insistence on continuing to sin. Based on this logic, it would seem perfectly natural to see a poor person and say to oneself, "When this individual repents, God will provide."

Yet this train of thought is nonetheless the antithesis of the obligation of the Genesis Covenant, which requires an unconditional willingness to help members of the tribe. While God can sanction, as fellow members in the Genesis Covenant, we are obligated to assist each other:

> If, however, there is a needy person among you, one of your kin in any of your settlements in the land that the Lord your God is giving you, do not harden your heart and shut your hand against your needy kin. Rather you must open your hand and lend them sufficiently for whatever they need. . . . Give to then readily and have no regrets when you do so, for in return the Lord you God will bless you in all your efforts and in all your undertakings. For there will never cease to be needy ones in your land, which is why I command you: open your hand to your poor and needy kin in your land. (Deut. 15:7–11)

As fellow Genesis Jews, the mere existence of need, regardless of its cause, is sufficient to activate the responsibility of the other.

This loyalty ethos is elaborated expansively in a sequence of verses culminating in the nationwide liberation mandated in the Jubilee Year:

> And if your brother with you becomes poor, his strength fallen into decline, then you shall strengthen him, and let him live by your side as your kinsman. Take no interest or increase from him, but fear your God—that your brother shall live with you. I the Lord

am your God, who brought you forth out of the land of Egypt, to give you the land of Canaan, to be your God.

And if your brother with you becomes poor, and sells himself to you, do not subject him to the treatment of a slave. As a hired servant and a kinsman, he shall be with you; he shall serve with you until the Jubilee Year. Then he shall go out from you, he and his children with him, and shall return to his own family, and to the possession of his fathers shall he return. For they are my servants, whom I brought forth from the Land of Egypt; they may not give themselves over into servitude. (Lev. 25:35–42)

"Your brother . . . your kinsman . . . your brother . . . your kinsman"— the essence of Genesis Judaism is that our religious ethnic narrative creates obligations of mutual care and assistance. Brothers don't use their siblings' misfortune as an opportunity for personal gain; nor do they treat them as slaves. The God who redeemed the Jews from Egypt requires us to walk in God's ways and follow suit by working to redeem each other.

Genesis: Loyalty to the People over Torah

One of Jewish tradition's most powerful examples of loyalty's primacy within its pantheon of values is found in the story of the Golden Calf. While descending the mountain with the Ten Commandments in hand, Moses witnesses the Israelites' illicit, idolatrous feast: "As soon as he came near the camp and saw the calf and the dancing, he became enraged; and he hurled the tablets from his hands and shattered them at the foot of the mountain" (Exod. 32:19). In a moment of fury, Moses rules the people unworthy of the stones that were "God's work, and the writing was God's writing, incised upon the tablet" (Exod. 32:16). Rather than hand them over to the impure, unworthy Israelites, he destroys them.

Yet, here again the midrashic pen weaves a different tale:

This is one of the things which Moses did of his own accord.... He broke the Tablets of the Commandments, and his judgment coincided with God's.... He took the Tablets of the Command- ments and descended and was exceedingly glad. When he beheld the offense which they committed in the making of the golden calf, he said to himself: "How can I give them the Tablets of the Commandments, for if I do so I will be obligating them to major commandments and condemning them to death at the hands of Heaven; for it is written in the Commandments: 'You shall have no other gods before Me'" (Exod. 20:3). He then started back [up the mountain], but the seventy Elders saw him and ran after him. He held fast to one end of the Tablets, and they held fast to the other end, but the strength of Moses prevailed over theirs.... [As he was ascending the mountain] he looked at the Tablets and saw that the words had flown away and ascended from them. How can I give Israel tablets which have nothing on them, he thought; better I take hold of them and break them.[25]

Rabbinic tradition notices that while God commands Moses to descend the mountain, God nevertheless leaves the Commandments in Moses's hands. Moses decides to shatter them—and to the Rabbis, this story is not about anger but about love. Moses wants to return the Torah to God because he realizes that if he gives it to the people in their current idolatrous state, he will be condemning them to death, given the Torah's prohibition against idolatry. Where does Moses's primary loyalty lie? With the word of God, or God's people? Moses chooses the latter, with shocking ramifications: his obligation to the people's well-being takes primacy even over God's Torah.

Of course, there will always be those who believe that religious faith requires a reverse prioritization: loyalty to God's word must always triumph, regardless of case, context, or consequence. In the midrashic narrative this voice is represented by the "seventy elders," who chase after Moses as he heads back up the mountain, presumably to snatch the tablets before he is able to return them to God. In the unfolding drama, Moses ultimately prevails and begins to reascend the mountain to return the Commandments to God—in effect reversing the revelatory event at Sinai. At that moment, God realizes God's mistake—and, learning from Moses, takes the letters back off the tablets, returning them to the ineffable ether. What Moses does for his people, God reciprocates for Moses: instead of shattering the revealed word of God, Moses breaks a set of blank tablets.

As we've seen, through the interpretive lens of the Rabbis, Moses breaks the tablets out of vigilance for the people's well-being. Loyalty cannot be reduced to a willingness to offer financial assistance or to incur financial loss—though it sometimes requires those things. It must entail a willingness to sacrifice even Torah when Torah endangers the people.

Ultimately, then, in the structure and sensibility of the Genesis Covenant, the Torah, whose commandments, as we will see, constitute the bedrock of the Exodus Covenant, follows the Covenant of Genesis, which not only predates it, but in moments of conflict takes precedence over it.

Genesis Loyalty and the Obligation of Tolerance

This idea that loyalty to the Jewish people takes precedence over loyalty to Torah leads to one of the Genesis Covenant's most meaningful and far-ranging implications for Jewish collective life: the obligation to tolerate difference. The foundational Genesis principle that a Jew is a Jew is a Jew, that fellow Jews claim my loyalty and responsibility regardless of what they believe or do, means that the Jewish community will always be inhabited by a wide range of Jews who disagree about the essence of Judaism. Not only is Jewish diversity hardwired into Jewishness itself—according to the Genesis Covenant, there is no basis for anyone to claim to be more of a Jew or a better Jew. A Jew is a Jew is a Jew is a Jew is a Jew. . . .

In the Genesis Covenant, God extends God's grace upon the Jewish people, accepts them unconditionally, and demands of us the same: to emulate this unconditional acceptance in our treatment of each other. A Genesis-centered Jewish community must embody in practice a prominent and distinctive spirit of grace. We can disagree. We can think the other is wrong. But we cannot monopolize or enforce any singular meaning of Jewishness. In fact, what different Jews do and believe, their particular senses and expressions of Judaism, becomes an integral part of our collective story of Jewishness. Genesis itself does not generate any limits to this understanding, as it does not concern itself with what Jews do and believe.

If the Genesis Covenant alone constituted the totality of the story Jews tell themselves about themselves, such radical tolerance could pose a significant challenge. As we will soon see, however, boundaries, limits, notions of good or better Jews and Judaisms are introduced to Jewishness via the Exodus Covenant.

Meanwhile, the Genesis Covenant demands that we relinquish the fantasy of defining, controlling, and validating any one version of our collective Jewish story.

Not a Race—An Imagined Family

Does the story of the Genesis Covenant, of Jewishness without Judaism, define Jews as a race? My opinion is that if it did—whether grounded in the historical narrative of the book of Genesis or not—it would be an idea that has outlived its usefulness, a moral anachronism to be condemned and expunged from Jewish self-understanding.

Jews, as all other peoples, are not immune from racist sensibilities. The idea of election resulting from a belief in Jews' innate superiority does surface in some traditional sources. In its most extreme form, the book of Ezra claims that Jews uniquely embody a "holy seed." Throughout our history, some Jews, especially from within the Kabbalistic and Hasidic traditions, have held fast to versions of this belief.[26] However, as a powerless people for most of our history, these racist sensibilities have remained principally inert. Functionally, one might even argue that in dire times, these notions have helped to buttress Jews' spirit and conviction that God did not abandon the covenant with the Jewish people. As Jews in the twentieth century claimed positions of power, both in Israel and North America, the potential dangers of racism emanating out of a Genesis sensibility has reemerged; overcoming them demands constant vigilance.

That said, in my view the Genesis Covenant and the Judaism it births is ethnic and familial, not racial, and (as we will see) also allows outsiders to join, through conversion, and in the Bible, through marriage. In addition there is no assumption of Jewish superiority. Nehemiah and the book of Genesis could not be clearer: Genesis Jews are nowhere depicted as embodying qualities of moral or spiritual excellence, or in fact any measure of supremacy. Quite to the contrary: it would indeed be strange to claim group preeminence all the while openly elaborating on one's founders' many flaws.

So, what is the first chapter in the story we tell ourselves about ourselves? For our first thousand years, we walked through the world as the Children of Israel—initially a family, eventually a tribe, and finally a nation, embraced by God for who we were, not what we did. Our identity as Jews existed independently of our Jewish practice and faith, having been forged almost exclusively on a narrative of shared ancestry.

And this was not merely a description of who we were; it constituted an ideological assessment of who we *are* and ought to be. Consequently, it calls for a reprioritization of our core values. It demands that we actively embrace our identity as Genesis Jews, accept that a Jew will always be considered a Jew regardless of what that Jew believes or does, and maintain that loyalty to the Jewish people inherently takes precedence over both personal interests and competing religious commitments. More precisely, and more urgently, we are to recognize that to express tolerance and loyalty towards fellow Jews is to mirror God's covenantal commitments—most deeply, a commitment to Jews' roots as Genesis Jews, to Genesis Judaism, and to the forms of religious consciousness to which it gives rise.

To embrace the Genesis Covenant is to assign serious weight to loyalty and tolerance over and above ideological purity. Such tolerance does not imply ideological acceptance, only that each of us assign basic space within the Jewish tent to others' Judaism. How we translate this understanding into practice remains open to multiple considerations, interpretations, and debate.

More significantly, as we will see, the Genesis Covenant constitutes only half of the Jews' story. Once the Exodus Covenant is brought into the equation, balancing the two becomes even more complicated and less easy to define.

2

Exodus Judaism and the Covenant of Commandments

In 2016 a terrorist attempted to kill a group of Israeli soldiers in the West Bank city of Hebron. The soldiers succeeded in thwarting the attack and thought they had killed the terrorist. In fact, he was incapacitated and was lying mortally wounded. Some fifteen minutes later, a soldier from a different unit, Sgt. Elor Azaria, happened upon the scene and saw the terrorist moving slightly. He fired at him and killed him. His superiors—from the minister of defense, through the IDF chief of staff, down the chain of command to Azaria's direct officers—all immediately ordered that Azaria be put on trial for manslaughter and for violating Israel's military code of ethics. The incapacitated terrorist did not pose any danger to those around him, they argued, and could have been controlled with nonlethal means. An Israeli soldier, they posited, even when dealing with a terrorist, has to conduct himself by a higher moral standard.

While the military was clear and unequivocal in its principled stance, the Israeli public, in what in Israel was an unprecedented event, disagreed and openly broke with the army, branding the minister of defense and the chief of staff as traitors. "Who do you love?" became the rallying cry. "Us or them." Evoking Genesis-like loyalty claims, they demanded that the army not abandon "our son in the battlefield." Like Moses with the tribes of Reuven and Gad, they asked, "Your brother is at war? Are you not going to stand with him?" They first demanded that Azaria be let free, and then, after his conviction for manslaughter by a military court, be granted an immediate pardon.

Genesis demands unconditional loyalty to fellow Genesis Jews: to stand together through thick and thin, for a Jew is a Jews is a Jew.

Likewise, the Israel Defense Forces (IDF) code stipulates that "The purpose of the IDF is to protect the existence of the state of Israel, its independence, and the security of its citizens and residents."[1]

But do we solely want to be Genesis Jews, with unconditional loyalty to Jews and no one else? What of our moral obligations to human beings qua human beings?

The Genesis Covenant is a powerful source of identity, but on its own, I believe, it can breed moral mediocrity and even depravity. It is perhaps in recognition of this danger that the IDF code of ethics goes beyond the Genesis Covenant to insist:

> The IDF and its soldiers are obligated to preserve human dignity. All human beings are of inherent value regardless of race, faith, nationality, gender, or status.[2]

Being Jewish must entail more than the Genesis Covenant if the identity is to be worthy of our loyalty.

"Speak to the Children of Israel and Say to Them . . .": Covenant as Calling

The idea of Jews as Genesis Jews is only half of the Jewish collective identity story. The second dimension of this story, what I call the Exodus Covenant, is first fully fleshed out in the book of Exodus, in which God calls the Jews into a new and amended covenant.

As we will see, Exodus introduces the idea that Jewish identity is both a way of life defined by particular behaviors and beliefs and an enduring commitment to live in accordance with God's will. To live with commandments is to never desist from a lifelong project of self-improvement, working to actualize one's many latent potentialities and gifts and live a life increasingly aligned with the Divine.

The essence of this Judaism is perhaps most elegantly expressed in the Bible's most frequently recurring verse, first introduced in Exodus— "And God spoke to Moses, saying, 'Speak to the Children of Israel and say to them . . .'" (Lev. 18:1)—and what immediately follows: a commandment to act, a lived expression of a divine aspiration for humanity. In the response to this calling, Jewish identity is endowed with purpose. It ceases to be something inherited and/or imposed; it is transformed into a choice and responsibility to create a life of value.

Revelation: A Collective "*Lekh-Lekha*"

Heralding this new dimension of Jewishness, the divine bestowal of the Ten Commandments on Mount Sinai (Exod. 20) literally storms onto the scene of Jewish history in an awesome revelatory display. The Ten Commandments announce not only the aspirations engraved on their tablets but the broader declaration that Jewishness is not just an inherited or assumed identity but a way of life comprised of obligations and commitments:

> I am the Lord your God, who took you out of the Land of Egypt, the house of bondage: you shall have no other gods besides me. . . . You shall not make for yourself a sculptured image. . . . You shall not take the name of the Lord your God in vain. . . . Remember the Sabbath day and keep it holy. . . . Honor your father and your mother. . . . You shall not murder. . . . You shall not commit adultery. . . . You shall not steal. . . . You shall not bear false witness. . . . You shall not covet your neighbor's house. . . . (Exod. 20:2–14)

Here the Exodus from Egypt catalyzes a new phase of Jewish collective meaning and identity. The same God "who took you out of the Land of Egypt" because of the relationship and concomitant promises established in the Genesis Covenant with Abraham, now demands something in return—namely faith, loyalty, obedience, and moral behavior. Unlike Genesis Jews, whose covenant is essentially a one-sided manifesto of God's commitments to the Jewish people, Exodus Jews are bound to God—and bound together—by a reciprocal covenant of divine aspiration and human response. This new notion of covenant inaugurates a qualitatively different relationship with the Divine, based not on the past but on the choices we make from Sinai forward.

Now, we might reconsider Abraham in this light. As we saw, his descendants, as Genesis Jews, were required only to *be*. But Abraham himself spent his entire life engaged in a process of *doing* in order to become worthy of God's election and blessings.[3] In essence, Abraham was the first Exodus Jew—just way ahead of his time. Just as God called Abraham on a mission to leave his entire known world—"Go!" (*Lekh-lekha*)—God has called on the rest of us at Sinai to respond as Abraham did, and thereby forge a new path of intimacy with the Divine.

The revelation of the Covenant at Sinai is the collective Lekh-lekha moment of the Jewish people.

Exodus as a Covenantal Framework— Not a Normative Code

The particulars of God's demands within the framework of the Exodus Covenant are given specific form throughout the Five Books of Moses, and are ultimately collated by the Jewish tradition into a code of 613 commandments. This "base layer" of Exodus Judaism is followed by centuries of further synthesis and interpretation, punctuated periodically by new codifications of Jewish law.[4] In the sixteenth century, following in the footsteps of Maimonides's Mishneh Torah (ca. 1170 –80) and Jacob ben Asher's Arba'ah Turim (ca. 1340), Rabbi Josef Karo (1488-1575) authored the Shulkhan Aruch, a codification that aimed to present all of the Exodus Covenant as a clear, concise, "set table" (Heb. shulkhan aruch) of behaviors, (and for Maimonides, beliefs as well),[5] to which all Jews must conform.

When perceived in this manner, Exodus Judaism does not, nor can it serve as a unifying story for Jews tell themselves about themselves. Quite to the contrary, it is a catalyst for divisiveness, with each community and denomination standing firm around their "set table."

However, as used in this work, Exodus Judaism does not denote a specific set of actions or beliefs. Rather, it carries the broader, more adaptive idea that to be in an Exodus covenantal relationship with God is to recognize that one is commanded and obligated, period. As distinct from a Genesis consciousness, Exodus demands that a Jew does and believes something. What this something entails, however, is secondary and subject to diverse interpretations and choices.

Maimonides' commentary on the Mishnah at the end of Tractate Makkot[6] may be read as a positive formulation of this attitude. In it, he posits that the plethora of commandments in the bible is an expression of divine grace, as God does not expect anyone to fulfill them all. Rather, the variety is meant to enable each individual to find one that they can embrace, and fulfil correctly.

One of the core principles of the Torah, is that when a person fulfills one commandment from the 613 commandments properly . . . they merit life in the world to come. And for this Rabbi Hananiah stated, that since the commandments are multiple, it is impossible that a person will not fulfill one of them in their life correctly and completely, and in fulfilling this commandment their soul will be granted life by virtue of that (singular) act.[7]

At the bedrock of this notion of the Exodus Covenant is the belief that Judaism is not a spectator sport. Exodus Judaism is first and foremost the challenge to find your commandment; become an Exodus Jew. What counts is whether you are a player, not how you play and certainly not how someone else assesses the quality of your game.

As such, Exodus Judaism does not privilege any single system of beliefs and practices and can encompass Jews across all ideologies and denominations. It serves as a shared language within which multiple manifestations and potential expressions of doing Jewish can locate themselves.

"If You Will Obey Me Faithfully": The Conditional Covenant

Within this broad framework of potentiality, a number of core features distinguish Exodus from Genesis. The first is the redefinition of the notion of chosenness as conditional upon the fulfillment of God's commandments.

For the Genesis Jew, chosenness is inherited—an unearned and inscrutable status hidden within the infinite will and wisdom of the Divine. Antithetically, in the Exodus Covenant, chosenness is not bestowed but a responsibility and an insistent claim to be realized. To be chosen means to be selected *for* something (like a task), not *as* something (like an elevated status). In this paradigm, a covenantal partnership with God is not simply a permanent function of the past election of Abraham but a variable status that must continually be established and reestablished by one's actions in the present.

The God of the Exodus Jew does not dispense blessings but instead makes them conditional upon Israel's fulfillment of God's designs. The prelude to the revelatory event, when the Children of Israel arrive at the base of Mount Sinai, expresses this idea explicitly. At this moment, God sends Moses an introductory message outlining the basic proposition of the new covenantal relationship:

> The Lord called him from the mountain, saying, "Thus shall you say to the House of Jacob, and declare of the Children of Israel: 'You have seen what I did to the Egyptians, how I bore you on eagles' wings and brought you to Me. Now then, *if* you will obey Me faithfully, and keep My covenant, [*then*] you shall be My treasured possession among all the people. Indeed, all the earth is Mine, but you shall be to me a kingdom of priests and a holy nation.' These are the words that you shall speak to the Children of Israel." (Exod. 19:3–6; emphasis added)

Couched in the elevated register of a love poem we find not merely a clear quid pro quo but a redefinition of the divine covenant itself as reciprocal. *Only in exchange for doing*—"if" the people "keep" and "obey"—will God keep the divine side of the covenant and single out the Jews as a "treasured possession," a "kingdom of priests and a holy nation."

A series of blessings and curses in Leviticus paint the conditionality of the covenant in vivid terms:

> *If* you follow my decrees and are careful to obey my commands, I will send you rain in its season, and the ground will yield its crops and the trees their fruit. Your threshing will continue until grape harvest and the grape harvest will continue until planting, and you will eat all the food you want and live in safety in your land. . . . But *if* you will not listen to me and carry out all these commands, and *if* you reject my decrees and abhor my laws and fail to carry out all my commands and so violate my covenant, *then* I will do this to you: I will bring on you sudden terror, wasting diseases and fever that will destroy your sight and sap your strength. You will plant seed in vain, because your enemies will eat it. I will set my face against you so that you will be defeated by your enemies; those who hate you will rule over you, and you will flee even when no one is pursuing you.
>
> *If* after all this you will not listen to me, I will punish you for your sins seven times over. I will break down your stubborn pride and make the sky above you like iron and the ground beneath you like bronze. Your strength will be spent in vain, because your soil will not yield its crops, nor will the trees of your land yield their fruit. *If* you remain hostile toward me and refuse to listen to me, I will multiply your afflictions seven times over, as your sins deserve. I will send wild animals against you, and they will rob you of your children, destroy your cattle and make you so few in number that your roads will be deserted. (Lev. 26:3–22; emphasis added)

While we retain our national identity as the House of Jacob and the Children of Israel, we can no longer expect to be showered with divine blessing as an inherited birthright. Indeed, if we fall too far out of line, we will be hounded by divine curses.

Furthermore, our Jewishness is no longer solely a passively inherited characterization of who we are. Exodus Judaism casts Jewish identity as a mission. The prophet Isaiah defines the 'nature of that mission with majestic precision: "'In the name of God, my witnesses are you,' declares the Lord, 'my servant whom I have chosen *to the end that* you may take thought and believe in Me and understand that I am He. Before Me no god was formed, and after Me none shall exist'" (Isa. 43:10; emphasis added). Without that sense of mission, the covenant would never have been offered.

Another way of clarifying the distinction between Genesis and Exodus is through the changing roles of God. While the Genesis Covenant is carried by a God who chooses and who bears the brunt of the covenantal responsibility ("*I* will make of you a great nation . . . as numerous as the stars in the sky. . . . *I* will redeem you . . ." [Gen. 22:17]), the God of Exodus Judaism commands, and expects. This shift in God's role finds ultimate expression in the verse, "You shall be holy, for I, the Lord your God, am holy" (Lev. 19:2). God is not merely the source of benevolence and blessing, but also the object of striving and emulation. To enter into the covenant is not simply to be chosen for a reward but to be challenged to become like God.

"Should You Act Wickedly": The Violable, Voidable Covenant

Once mission and conditions are introduced into the equation, the covenant can no longer be seen as inviolable—one of the defining features of its Genesis counterpart. According to the Exodus Covenant, the contract can be breached and God can withdraw:

When you have begotten children and children's children and are long established in the land, should you act wickedly, and make for yourselves a sculptured image in any likeness, causing the Lord your God displeasure and vexation, I call heaven and earth this day to witness against you that *you shall soon perish from the land* that you are crossing the Jordan to possess: you shall not long endure in it, *but shall be utterly wiped out.* The Lord will scatter you among the peoples, and only a scant few of you shall be left among the nations to which the Lord will drive you. There you will serve man-made gods of wood and stone that cannot see or hear or eat or smell. (Deut. 4:25–28; emphasis added)

The Exodus narrative introduces the possibility of God withdrawing from the covenant—and the Jewish people perishing—if their disobedience becomes overly brazen and/or widespread. It raises the danger that failure to observe the covenant can lead to its abrogation.

"Then at Last": The Available Covenant

Does anything remain of the Genesis Covenant's eternal unconditional promise?

Yes. Within the Exodus narrative, the Genesis-based covenant can be found in the bedrock promise that the covenant will remain, while not inviolable, eternally *available*—forever open to being activated by a remnant who chooses to reaffirm their commitment to its precepts. Here the meaning of God being "with us" is that God will always *wait* for us to become . . . Exodus Jews. If we tarry, however, the covenant can remain suspended, indefinitely.

After declaring the covenant violable, for example, Moses promises in a continuation of the Deuteronomy speech quoted above that the covenant will nevertheless remain available to those who seek it out:

But if you search there for the Lord your God, you will find Him, *if only* you seek Him with all your heart and soul—when you are in distress because all these things have befallen you and in the end, return to the Lord your God and obey Him, for the Lord your God is a compassionate God: He will not fail you, nor will He let you perish; He will not forget the covenant which He made on oath with your fathers. (Deut. 4:29–31; emphasis added)

The Torah repeatedly stresses this motif:

Those of you who survive shall be heartsick over their iniquity in the land of their enemies; more, they shall be heartsick over the iniquity of their fathers; and they shall confess their iniquity, and the iniquity of their fathers, in that they trespassed against me, yea, were hostile to me. When I have been hostile to them, and have removed them into the land of their enemies, then at last shall their obdurate heart humble itself, and they shall atone for their iniquity. *Then* will I remember My covenant with Jacob: I will remember also my covenant with Isaac, and also my covenant with Abraham. (Lev. 26:39-42; emphasis added)

When all these things befall you—the blessing and the curse that I have set before you—and you take them to heart amidst the various nations to which the Lord your God has banished you, and you return to the Lord your God, and you and your children heed God's command with all your heart and soul, just as I enjoin upon you this day, *then* the Lord your God will restore your fortunes and take you back in love. He will bring you together again from all the peoples where the Lord your God has scattered you. Even if your outcasts are at the end of the world, from there the Lord your God will gather you, from there God will fetch you. And the Lord your God will bring you to the land that your fathers possessed, and you shall possess it; and God will make you more prosperous and more numerous than your fathers. (Deut. 30:1-5; emphasis added)

The inherited dimension of the covenant promises the *possibility* of blessing, in exchange for observing the commandments. What remains of the Genesis Covenant, then, is the *imprint* of an eternal *possibility* of return: no matter how far one may have strayed from it, the path to the Exodus Covenant is always open.

This idea of the available covenant is the foundation of a famous talmudic debate over the mechanism that will trigger the messianic redemption:

Rabbi Eliezer said: if Israel repent, they will be redeemed; if not, they will not be redeemed. Rabbi Joshua said to him, if they do not repent, will they not be redeemed? But the Holy One, blessed be He, will set up a king over them, whose decrees shall be as cruel as Haman's, whereby Israel shall engage in repentance, bringing them back to the right path.[8]

Both Rabbi Eliezer and Rabbi Joshua reject the comfort of the Genesis Covenant and agree that redemption is always but a *potentiality*, only to become actualized if the Jewish people decide to repent and change their ways. Rabbi Joshua adds that a Genesis/Exodus framing of the relationship does not envision God as a mere bystander awaiting their decision. Once the covenant is essentially suspended in response to the Jewish people's breach, God is on the edge of God's seat, as it were, eagerly encouraging the people to reengage, return, and become who they have the potential to be. Hence, God will create the historical conditions that will force the people's hand, moving them from being Genesis Jews to becoming Exodus Jews.

"It Is Not with Our Ancestors": An Amended Covenant for a New Nation on Their Land

How do Exodus Jews make sense of Judaism's Genesis origins? Since God reconfigures the definition of Jewishness at Mount Sinai, one might reasonably wonder, why didn't God give this covenant originally to Abraham and his immediate descendants?

Exodus proponents in the book of Deuteronomy offer a developmental generational framework for understanding the move from Genesis to Exodus. At the moment the Children of Israel are poised to cross the Jordan and enter the Promised Land of Canaan, Moses summons all Israel and says, "Hear, Israel, the decrees and laws I declare in your hearing today. Learn them and be sure to follow them. The Lord our God made a covenant with us at Horeb. It was not with our ancestors that the Lord made this covenant, but with us, with all of us who are alive here today. The Lord spoke to you face to face out of the fire on the mountain" (Deut. 5:1-4).

The Genesis Covenant, Moses tells the Jewish people as they stand on the precipice of the next phase of their collective evolution, is what has brought them to this stage. "It was not with our ancestors that the Lord made *this covenant*"—but rather the prior covenant, the covenant that binds them to their ancestors, to each other, and to God. Now, it is up to those who are "here today" to receive a new covenant, this new dimension of Jewish collective identity, and carry it forward into the Promised Land—a land intimately tied to the observance of the Exodus Covenant:

> Now this is the Instruction—the laws and the rules—that the Lord your God commanded [me] to teach you, *to be observed in the Land. . . .* These are the laws and rules, *that you must carefully observe in the Land* that the Lord, God of your fathers, is giving you to possess . . . (Deut. 6:1, 12:1; emphasis added)

Living in the land, Moses informs these inchoate Israelites, will require nothing short of an entirely new orientation toward Jewish tradition and community. Residing outside its borders, the Genesis Covenant might have been sufficient. But for you to mature into the next stage of your national existence, a sovereign people living in your own land, you must become Exodus Jews.

Here, Exodus consciousness recasts Genesis Judaism as a temporary reality—an adolescent stage—in the growth of our developing collective identity. Becoming Exodus Jews is the beginning of a new, permanent, fully realized chapter of Jewishness.

"Do Your Ears Hear What Your Lips Are Saying?": Revising Genesis Stories through an Exodus Lens

While the biblical text above came to terms with Judaism's Genesis antecedents, Jewish tradition has also seen a more radical manifestation of Exodus Judaism, in the overwriting and recasting of Genesis narratives within the parameters of Exodus characteristics. Rabbinic proponents of Exodus Judaism established its primacy through a broad reinterpretation of the core sources shaping the identity of Genesis Judaism. Not only did they posit that Exodus Judaism is the real, authentic Judaism of the Jews in their Land but they engaged in a comprehensive effort to reinterpret and retell the Genesis story itself.

First up for rewriting was Abraham. In order to solidify his identity as an Exodus Jew, the Rabbis shaded away the mystery of Abraham's election by reimagining him as a true believer—a fearless and cannily subversive spiritual warrior on behalf of the monotheistic God, whom he chose before God chose him:

> [Abraham's father] Terah was a manufacturer of idols, who once went away and left Abraham to sell them in his place.... A woman came with a plate full of flour and requested, "Take this and offer it to them." So, he took a stick, broke them [the idols] with it, and then put [the stick] in the hand of the largest [idol]. When his father returned, he demanded, "What have you done to them?" "I cannot conceal it from you," he replied. "A woman came with a plateful of fine meal and requested me to offer it to them. One [idol] claimed, 'I must eat first,' while another claimed, 'I must eat first.' Thereupon the largest arose, took the stick, and broke the others."
>
> "Are you making fun of me?" he [Terah] cried out. "Do they have any consciousness?" Abraham responded: "Do your ears hear what your lips are saying?" [Terah] then seized him [Abraham] and delivered him to [the Emperor] Nimrod . . .
>
> "Behold," Nimrod declared, "I will cast you into [the pit], and let your God, whom you adore, come and save you from it."[9]

In this somewhat radical rabbinic expansion of the biblical tale, long before he receives the divine call, Abraham initiates a turn to God on his own, with great courage and at great cost. For this self-generated iconoclasm, the ruling political power, the Emperor Nimrod, exiles Abraham from his homeland. But God soon rewards Abraham's spiritual heroism with the life-altering call to divine intimacy and commitment that is Lekh-lekha (Gen. 12:1): *Come walk with Me. I choose you,* God explains to this unique seeker in the midrashic retelling, *because you alone have chosen Me.*

The rabbinic revision of Genesis stories through an Exodus lens is perhaps most starkly and concisely illustrated in the midrashic commentary on Jacob and Esau—the former chosen to receive the blessing of Abraham, the latter not. With no regard or apparent loyalty or connection to the literal meaning of the verses, the Rabbis justify this selection by painting Esau as an inveterate bloodthirsty liar and sinner and Jacob as living in accordance with classic Exodus Judaism: chosen, like the midrashic Abraham above, for his learning, wisdom, and character. This interpretative legacy begins in Rebecca's womb and extends throughout their lives:

> "And the children struggled in her womb" (Genesis 25:22). When she came near synagogues or schools [of Torah learning], Jacob struggled to come out.... While when she passed idolatrous temples, Esau eagerly struggled to come out.[10]
>
> "The first one emerged red, like a hairy mantle all over; so they named him Esau" (Genesis 25:25). "*Red*": a sign that he would always be shedding blood.[11]
>
> "When the boys grew up, Esau became a skillful hunter, a man of the outdoors; but Jacob was a mild man who stayed in camp" (Genesis 25:27). So long as they were young they could not be distinguished by what they did, and no one paid much attention to their characters, but when they reached the age of thirteen, one went his way to the houses of learning and the other went his way to the idolatrous temples.[12]
>
> "And when Esau was forty years old, he took to wife Judith daughter of Beeri the Hittite" (Genesis 26:34). For forty years Esau used to ensnare married women and violate them, yet when

he attained forty years he compared himself to his father, saying, "As my father was forty years old when he married, so I will marry at the age of forty."[13]

Haman descended from Amalek, who is descended from Esau (Genesis 36:16). It was he who issued the decree to destroy the Jews.[14]

The Holy One, blessed be He, chose Jacob, as it is stated (Psalms 135:4), "For Jacob did the Lord choose." And so [too] it says (Isaiah 41:8), "Jacob whom You have chosen." But He did not bring him close, but rather [Jacob] brought himself close, as it is stated (Genesis 25:27), "Jacob was a simple man that sat in tents."[15]

In these rabbinically slanted midrashic retellings, the Genesis narrative is erased. Projected through the lens of Exodus, Genesis Jews emerge as Exodus Jews.

The Invention of "Good" and "Bad" Jews

Like its Genesis counterpart, the Exodus Covenant's mindset and worldview also generated a distinct Jewish culture and consciousness. But whereas a conceptual bedrock of Genesis Judaism is that God bestows Jewish identity equally, unconditionally, and permanently on every Jew, so there is no basis to judge anyone as more or less Jewish than any other, the Exodus Covenant yields very different attitudes concerning social tolerance, loyalty, indeed identity itself. Once Judaism is conceived in terms of commandments and expectations, members' behaviors and beliefs take on far greater significance. Those who do not conform to required beliefs and practices will find it difficult to remain Jews in good standing. Echoing the whole genre of prophetic literature, Isaiah proclaims, "Hear, O Heaven and give ear, O Earth, for the Lord has spoken: 'I reared children and brought them up, and they have rebelled against me. An ox knows its owner, an ass its master's crib: Israel does not know, my people takes no thought.' A sinful nation, people laden with iniquity, brood of evildoers, depraved children. They have forsaken the Lord, spurned the Holy One of Israel, turned their backs on God" (Isa. 1:2–4).

As the prophets repeatedly testify, Exodus expectations reassess biblical-era Jews as catastrophic failures: "a sinful nation, people laden with iniquity, brood of evildoers, depraved children." Through an Exodus lens, Genesis Jews were bad Jews—Jews who failed at even their most minimal responsibilities.

A later model of this Exodus centeredness and its consequences is found in one of Maimonides's most famous and influential theological essays (ca. 1160–68), where he advocates that Judaism be defined almost exclusively through an Exodus lens—codifying thirteen core principles of faith which, he insisted, define the essence of the Exodus Covenant:

1. Believing in the existence of the Creator
2. The uniqueness of God
3. Denying the corporeality of God
4. Recognizing both the primacy of God and the fact that God is eternal
5. Understanding that God alone is worthy of worship
6. Accepting prophecy
7. Believing in the prophecy, and the unique status of the prophecy, of Moses
8. That the Torah has a divine origin
9. the Torah is a direct replicate of the word of God
10. That God is aware of human behavior and cognizant of it
11. That God rewards the righteous and punishes the wicked
12. That there will be a messianic era in which the world will be redeemed
13. That at that time there will be resurrection of the dead.[16]

For Maimonides, these core principles of faith upon which Judaism is founded are also the gateway through which all Jews *become* Jews:

And when an individual believes in these principles, and their truth is clarified to him, *then* he enters into Israel, and we are commanded to love and to have compassion upon him and to treat him in all the ways that God commanded a human being to treat his or her fellow: with love and compassion.[17]

In Maimonides's Exodus-based theology, one *becomes* a Jew via the gauntlet of a sequence of beliefs. The moment one accepts these beliefs, one is in turn accepted into the community as an insider with all the benefits of membership. But the obverse side of this admittance policy is a strict exclusion policy toward those who deviate from these core beliefs:

But when one of these principles or when a person's faith in one of these principles is corrupted, he has separated from the community. He is a heretic in the essence, he is called a heretic (*min*), an apostate (*apikorus*), and an individual who cuts the plantings. It is a commandment to hate him and to destroy him. And about him it is said, "Your enemy's God I will hate; those who hate you, God, I will hate." (Psalms 139:21)[18]

In Maimonides's view, if individual Jews do not accept, in total, the foundational principles essential to his strictly Exodus-based version of Judaism, their Jewishness is invalid. While in some sense they may still remain Jewish, they have at the very least become "bad" Jews. Since Judaism is a modality of obligatory beliefs and observances, if I have been chosen, as Isaiah posits, to be God's witness, then I must strive with every fiber of my being to embody the testimony as outlined in Exodus Judaism. I must in turn demand the same of every member of my community and distinguish between those who agree and those who refuse.

The Boundaries of Loyalty

As we saw with Maimonides, in Exodus Judaism, loyalty can no longer be taken for granted but becomes contingent upon *what one does* to increasingly align one's life with the covenant.

Embodying this Exodus sensibility, the Rabbis in the Talmud are the first to develop a comprehensive theory of the boundaries of loyalty. "Sacrifices are accepted from Israelite sinners, so that they will repent," the Talmud rules—reflecting both an acceptance that sinners exist as part of the "Israelite" community and an assent that the system allows them the means to repent for their misdeeds.[19] However, the Rabbis then proceed to list three exceptions—three types of "intolerable deviants" who are no longer permitted to bring the penitential sacrifice (*korban hatat*) at the Temple, a primary vehicle for moral and spiritual atonement,: the apostate, the idolater, and the public desecrator of Shabbat (for a more in-depth review of this text and these categories, see chapter 4). In so ruling, the Rabbis effectively block these Jews' path to restoration, forcing them to the margins of communal life.

Notably, here, the prohibition itself reflects the Jewish community's abandonment of responsibility for these Jews' spiritual rehabilitation. Implicitly, but decisively, the community has removed these Jews from the sphere of communal concern. Loyalty to the full community of Israel has become severely attenuated. Even more so, the Talmud, at least in theory, encourages the imposition of an extra-legal death penalty (*moridin ve-lo ma'alin*, lit. "Lowered [into a pit] and not brought out" by fellow community-members and consequently left there to die) upon a class of Jewish deviants who are deemed to personify an extreme rejection of the central principles of Exodus Judaism.[20]

What is perhaps most peculiar about this extreme form of sanction is that it is not implemented by a court of law, which reviews evidence of guilt prior to issuing its judgment. Rather, it empowers regular citizens to take the law into their own hands in order to rid society of deviance deemed to be extreme, subversive, clearly discernible, and public in nature. According to Maimonides, "Anyone who kills one of them has fulfilled a great mitzvah and removed a stumbling block."[21]

While there is no evidence of Jewish communities ever implementing these extreme sanctions, the "story" of this legislation reinforces harsh barriers between Jews based on what they do or believe. In the normal course of communal life, members understand the basic responsibility to protect one another from physical danger and imminent harm. When it comes to these "intolerable deviants," however, this sense of responsibility is eliminated. *The deviant is to be marked and marginalized.*[22]

In the paradigm of Exodus Judaism, some Rabbis even reinterpret the ultimate biblical statement of unconditional communal love—"Love your neighbor as yourself"—to exclude the neighbor who violates the law. Love is only to be afforded to those included in your community of shared religious practice.[23]

Exodus Judaism for the Genesis Jew

Before concluding the analysis of the principles of the Exodus Covenant, it is important to mention that the development of Exodus Judaism, with its myriad of rituals and obligations in the end, also shaped the Jewishness of Genesis Jews. While "being" Jewish as distinct from "doing Jewish" is the hallmark of the Genesis Covenant, once Judaism evolved into a system of particular Jewish behaviors, Genesis-ness also developed its own modality of doing. Under the parameters of Genesis doing, certain aspects of ritual observance and the maintaining of some traditions, also especially those from the extensive Jewish calendar and lifestyle rituals, became expressions of Jewish being. Being a Genesis Jew for many involves the embracing of particular Jewish behaviors and culture, not as an Exodus-like condition for entering the covenant, but simply as a manifestation of one's covenantal identity, a sign of one's affiliation. Prominent examples of Genesis-doing include the Jewish people's almost universal adoption of circumcision, the widespread celebration of bar and bat mitzvahs, getting married under a chuppah and the breaking of the glass at weddings, and participating in a Passover seder. In Israel, this list is even more extensive and includes Friday night Shabbat meals with family and friends, even among those who self-define as secular; not driving on Yom Kippur; lighting candles and eating special fried donuts (*sufganiyot*) on Hannukah; and dressing up children on Purim. All of the above are not necessarily expressions of an Exodus consciousness but simply examples of a social and cultural embracing of being a Genesis Jew, of loyalty to and seeing oneself as a part of a people. I do, not because I am commanded, but because I am a Jew.[24]

A Parallel Evolution

In the end, the covenants of Genesis and Exodus evolve in parallel throughout the Bible. The blessing of a Jewish identity unbound and unbothered by any sense of commandedness—a relationship rooted in God's grace, where Jews are not classified as sinners or nonsinners and are responsible for each other as a result of a story of shared ethnicity—abides hand in hand with the challenge of a Jewish identity predicated on choosing to be worthy to walk with God. In the totality of the biblical story, both modes of covenantal relationships with God and the Jewish people have critical roles to play.

And that is the Bible's real answer to "Who are the Jews?"

3

Conversion and the Rabbinic Synthesis of Genesis and Exodus

As we have seen, the Bible's answer to *Who are the Jews?* is neither the Genesis nor the Exodus Covenant but a call for an ever-evolving synthesis of the two. The biblical imperative is to take both of these seemingly mutually exclusive versions of Jewish identity and engage them in ongoing dialogue—a dialogue that is never resolved, because both shape what it means to be a part of the Jewish people.

And as the ancient Rabbis inherited and transformed the biblical tradition, they accepted the challenge of establishing a difficult synthesis of Genesis *and* Exodus Judaism.

The Rabbis Ask: "Who Are the Jews?"

At its heart, rabbinic discourse on the issue of conversion attempts to answer the question, "Who are the Jews?" Whether and how one officially becomes a Jew is not merely a technical legal question but expresses a theory of who Jews are in the first place. Indeed, the process through which one joins *any* group that permits entry to outsiders is invariably shaped by a concept of the nature of the group itself. In a similar vein, as we will see in the next chapter, setting the boundaries of deviance is similarly representative of a conception of "Who are the Jews?" for there can be no notion of boundaries without a prior notion of what the boundaries are demarcating.

To take a mundane example: anyone can play golf; but at what moment does one transition from golfing to becoming a "Golfer," with a capital "G"? For starters, one cannot become a Golfer without playing golf. But is that the *only* criterion? How often must one play? With what intensity and commitment? Must one own golf clubs? Become a member of a golf club? Own the right outfit? Meet a standard of skill or achievement?

To answer these questions first requires that one has a clear grasp on the concept of what it means, in our culture, to be a Golfer.

Similarly, the decision as to whether someone who wasn't born Jewish and desires to convert and become Jewish has met all of the relevant criteria for the community to consider this person a fellow member is a powerful window into understanding the Jewish tradition's notion of what being Jewish means.

"Just as Israel Entered into the Covenant": The Birth of Conversion

In the Genesis paradigm, one is considered Jewish only by being born into a Jewish family or by marrying a Jewish man. (In the language of the Bible, an Israelite.) Outside of marriage, no mechanism is offered, either in narrative or law, for moving from non-Jewishness to Jewishness. (Even though the rabbinic tradition casts Ruth as a convert, from the Bible's perspective no explicit or formal conversion occurs. This is perhaps why she continues to be referred to as "Ruth the Moabite" throughout the book.)[1]

The Bible's total absence of conversion as we know it fits the essentialist nature of Genesis Judaism. The Genesis Covenant is exclusively for those who are already part of the Jewish people—those who tell a story of their ethnic familial relationship with Abraham.

Of course, the Bible is filled with instances of non-Jews living in the midst of Jews (Heb. *Gerim*, lit. sojourners/strangers)—and with laws regulating and grounding their legal status and ability to participate in the social, economic, and even ritual life of the Jewish community. But this framing, while suggesting a continuum between Jewishness and non-Jewishness,[2] nevertheless enshrines into law the irreducible existential otherness of the latter. Leviticus is clear: the stranger must be treated as a native born (Lev. 19:33–34). But the stranger does not become a Jew; the stranger does not become your brother. Consequently, the stranger can be lent money with interest or sold into slavery, two behaviors that are prohibited toward "your brother" (Heb. *Ahikha*) who came out of Egypt with you (Lev. 25:35–47).

Similarly, the book of Isaiah speaks lovingly about strangers who desire to live in a committed relationship with God: "The aliens that join themselves to the Lord, to minister unto God and to love the name of the Lord, to be God's servants . . . Their burnt offerings and their sacrifices shall be welcomed upon Mine altar, for My house shall be a house of prayer for all peoples" (Isa. 56:6–7).

Notably, even in this messianic vision in which non-Jews can be faithful followers of God, observe the Sabbath, and bring offerings before God—their access to the temple is still grounded in the openness of God's house to "all people." Neither their faith and devotion to God nor their observance of aspects of the Torah are sufficient to transform them into members of the Jewish people.

Likewise, even in the End of Days, when faith in God becomes universal, the nations of the world do not become a part of the Children of Israel but remain members of "all the nations": "In the days to come, the Mount of the Lord's House shall stand firm above the mountains, and tower above the hills. And all the nations shall gaze on it with joy. And the many peoples shall go and say: 'Come, let us go up to the Mount of the Lord, to the House of the God of Jacob. That God may instruct us in God's ways, and that we may walk in God's paths'" (Isa. 2:2–3).

Moved to embark on a pilgrimage to "the Mount of the Lord," they still know to refer to it as "the House of the God of Jacob." When one joins in faith with Israel, the distinct *status* of Israel is not transferred.

The very biblical inconceivability of conversion led Ezra the Scribe—while fighting against intermarriage between Jews returning from Babylonian exile (ca. 458 BCE) and the local inhabitants of Samaria—to decree that all such intermarriages be simply annulled.[3] Had conversion existed, he could have offered an alternative: the demand that non-Jewish spouses adopt the covenant of Israel. But for Ezra, Jewishness is still built on a Genesis-derived (or distorted) notion of a "holy seed" that is Israel's alone, with no recourse for those not born into the covenant.

Only in the second century BCE, during the Hasmonean Period, do we find the first evidence of the possibility of crossing from a non-Jewish identity to a Jewish one. Prior to that, to be a Jew meant to be part of the tribe of Judah, or someone who hailed from the region of Judea—a purely ethnic definition of identity. In the Hasmonean Period, however, "as the metaphoric boundaries separating Judeans from non-Judeans became more and more permeable," historian of Second Temple Judaism Shaye Cohen explains, the definition morphed into both a political and religious identity. "Outsiders could now become insiders."[4]

What gave rise to the idea that birth was no longer a necessary precondition of Jewishness, allowing conversion to emerge as an option? One possibility, attested to by the Rabbis, is that Jews were slowly but surely exhibiting greater fidelity to the Exodus Covenant.[5] By the Hasmonean period, the Jewish community can be seen coalescing around some shared notions of meaning, practice, and belief.[6] This is not to say that the Jews uniformly transformed themselves into a community of committed pietists. But for the first time, most Jews believed in the same God, rested publicly on the Sabbath, circumcised their children, and kept Passover.

As Exodus consciousness transitioned from divine aspiration to communal practice, from theory to lived reality, this living expression seems to have enabled conversion to emerge. If Judaism is no longer experienced as merely an inherited label of regional or familial affiliation but as an aspirational system of beliefs and practices to which one is obligated as well, why limit this covenant to Genesis Jews alone?

Unsurprisingly, then, the quintessential moment of the Exodus Covenant—the giving of the Torah at Sinai—becomes the symbolic template for the Rabbis' new conversion requirements:

Just as Israel only entered into the covenant (at Sinai) by doing three things—circumcision, immersion, and the offering of a sacrifice—so too converts must join through the performing of these three acts.[7]

From this point forward, *Sinai is not just a past event but a model of the pathway into Jewishness.* Anyone who is willing to walk this path may join the people of Israel. Consequently, past ethnic ties as an anchor for identity becomes eclipsed by one's present and future commitments.

Status of the Convert: Synthesizing Genesis and Exodus

How can a system that accepts conversion still then claim to represent Genesis Judaism?

One (deeply problematic) rabbinic answer to this was to accept the legitimacy of conversion but simultaneously uphold certain legal distinctions between converts and born Jews that favor the latter. Take, for example, the biblical law for Shavuot mandating that all Israelites bring their First-Fruits to the Temple as an offering and then recite the confessional formula: "I declare this day to the Lord, your God, that I have come to the land *which the Lord swore to our forefathers to give us*. . . ." (Deut. 26:1–8; emphasis added).

According to one rabbinic opinion, the convert, like all other Jews, is obligated to bring the offering—but is prohibited from the confessional recitation because of the inapplicability of the words "which the Lord swore to *our forefathers* to give us":

> The following bring [the first fruits] but do not recite [the confession]: the convert brings but does not recite, for they cannot say "which the lord our God swore to *our forefathers* to give to us." If one's mother is from Israel, you can bring and recite. When [the convert] prays privately, they should recite "God, the father of Israel" [instead of "the God of our Forefathers"]. And when praying in the synagogue [publicly with other Jews], he should recite, ["the God of *your* forefathers"]. It is only if

one's mother is from Israel that you can recite, "The God of *our* forefathers."[8]

Exodus opens the door to conversion; but Genesis still marks everyone who walks through it with a distinct status.

However, this particular synthesis led to a counteropinion—a countersynthesis, if you will—which was ultimately deemed authoritative with respect to the convert's second-class status:

> It was taught in the name of Rabbi Yehuda, the convert himself may bring the First-Fruit offering and [also, despite being a convert,] recite [the confession]. Why? For God says to Abraham, "I will make you the father of a multitude of nations. Formerly you have been a father of Aram. From now on, you are a father to all of the nations" (Genesis 17:5). Rabbi Yehoshua ben Levi stated: *The law follows R. Yehudah.* The case came before R. Abahu, and he ruled according to R. Yehudah.[9]

Here, Rabbi Yehuda rejects any legal distinction between the convert and one born a Jew—and in doing so recalibrates the relationship between Genesis and Exodus. Without discarding Genesis sensibilities, he radically reinterprets it to *include converts.* Invoking Abraham's midrashic status as the forefather of not just the Jews, but of "all of the nations," he holds that acceptance of Jewish law affords one access not only to being an Exodus Jew but a Genesis Jew as well. Abraham, Rabbi Yehudah argues, is in fact the ultimate synthesis of Genesis and Exodus. Abraham is both the first convert to Judaism (for he must earn his status and does not inherit it), and the generative foundation for the Genesis Jew. He is both the father of Genesis Judaism and the first Exodus Jew.

Therefore, by walking in the way of Abraham, one becomes a member of the Abrahamic family—a family that encompasses not only those born into it but also those from the family of nations who, like

Abraham, chose Judaism.[10] By accepting the covenant, one becomes metaphysically integrated into Judaism's Abrahamic origins and thus an "ethnic" Jew as well. This idea is reflected in the rabbinic statement, "A convert who converts is like a child who is reborn."[11] In the act of conversion, one becomes a Genesis Jew.

This "sprouting" of ethnic roots also explains why converts who want to revert back to their prior status have no remedy under Jewish law. If conversion were limited to the adoption of the Exodus Covenant, then, logically, choosing to walk a different path should constitute an exit from Judaism as well. But because the process entails a permanent binding of one's identity to Genesis Jewishness, the convert who violates it becomes merely another Israelite deviant: an insider forever, for better or worse. For "an Israelite, even though they have sinned, remains an Israelite."[12]

"Even One Small Detail": Conversion through an Exodus Lens

Significantly, the rabbinic grappling over how to synthesize the Genesis and Exodus Covenants also finds compelling expression in the process of conversion itself.

One rabbinic school of thought dismisses the idea of synthesis all together and adopts the dominance of Exodus-like standards in determining the conversion process. Conversion necessitates acceptance of all of Jewish law *in its entirety*. Just as a Jew under the Exodus Covenant is required to accept all of Torah—"If you will obey Me faithfully and keep my covenant, you shall be my treasured possession" (Exod. 19:5)—so, too, one can become a convert only by taking the same holistic oath:

A convert who accepts upon himself all of the Torah with the exception of one word, is not accepted. R. Yossi b. R. Yehuda says: Even [if the exception is] one small detail of Rabbinic law.[13]

Paradoxically, while the idea of the Exodus Covenant opens the door to conversion, this same idea can turn conversion into a prohibitively difficult, if not impossible process, in which even the rejection of one small detail of Jewish law disqualifies one from becoming a Jew. The more dominant the role of Exodus in defining Jewishness, the higher the bar on what counts as Jewish commitment. Since Exodus challenges us to become a "kingdom of priests and a holy nation" (Exod. 19:6), it can be argued that only those who actualize this aspiration should be allowed to join. While a sinning Israelite remains Jewish by virtue of the Genesis Covenant, an aspiring convert who sins is disqualified from the Exodus Covenant—and thus the only Jewishness to which this potential convert could lay claim.

And so, an Israelite who sins is still an Israelite and a convert who sins is also an Israelite—after all, Israel is understood to be a community of sinners: "There is no single good person on earth, who (only) does what is good, and does not sin" (Eccles. 7:20). This, however, doesn't mean that a *potential* convert who sins can *become* an Israelite.

This perspective on conversion ultimately gave birth to the heated "Who is a Jew?" debate of contemporary Jewish life. Since a convert must be an exemplary Jew, each denomination's version of exemplary came to define the conversion process and consequently who counts as a community member in the first place.

"They Accept Him Immediately": Conversion in the Genesis Mode

That said, the rabbinic position that ultimately became settled law synthesized both Genesis and Exodus sensibilities into the conversion process. The Genesis Covenant's view of Jewishness as not what you do but who you are led to an understanding of conversion that prioritizes what one commits to *be*. As a result, the conversion process became far less stringent than the former maximalist requirements of Torah observance:

1. When a prospective convert comes [before the court] to be converted, they say to him: "Why have you chosen to convert? Do you not see that this nation [of Israel] is down-trodden and tortured more than all other nations, and suffer many afflictions?" If he says, "I know, and I am unworthy," the court accepts him immediately [as a convert].

2. They then inform him of some of the minor commandments and some of the major commandments, and the sins of the violation of the laws of gleanings and forgotten sheaf in the corner of the field, and the tithe for the poor. They further inform him of the punishments for the violation of the com-mandments. . . . And just as they inform him regarding the punishments for the violation of the commandments, they inform him of the reward for their fulfillment. . . . In general, they do not speak at length or in great detail.

3. If he accepts, they circumcise him immediately. When he is healed, they immerse him immediately, while two Rabbis stand over him and inform him [again] of a few of the minor commandments and a few of the major commandments. When he has immersed and risen from the water, he is an Israelite in every respect.[14]

This three-stage iteration—first, assessing the convert's awareness of the sociopolitical implications of becoming a member of Israel; second, explicating "some of the major and minor commandments" and the legal consequences of being counted as a Jew; and third, circumcision (for males) and immersion—is a radically different conversion process than that outlined earlier.[15] Whereas previously, the failure to observe any aspect of Jewish law nullifies the conversion process, here, the prospective convert is only taught *some* of the minor and *some* of the major commandments. There is no assumption that s/he needs to know, let alone observe, every detail of the law.

Hence, this source affirms that to be a convert is not merely to observe divine law but to adopt the Genesis covenantal destiny of the Jewish people as his or her own. In essence, the convert is being asked: *Do you recognize that the Jewish covenant with God is not merely a commitment involving beliefs and practices but is a commitment to an all-encompassing communal identity that will influence and shape who you are and your position in the world?* Only if the answer is in the affirmative can one proceed. In fact, one is accepted "immediately."

This first stage of conversion also mirrors the template of the biblical sequence, whereby even before discussing aspects of Jewish law (the Exodus Covenant), the convert must accept upon him/herself the primary Genesis Covenant of familial identity. Because of Genesis, conversion first entails a transformation of one's identity.

Stage two entails the aspiring convert's acceptance that Jewishness is constituted by Exodus as well as Genesis Judaism. Yet the Exodus Covenant at play here entails limited knowledge, the comprehension of *some* aspects of the law—another expression of a Genesis-Exodus synthesis. And, notably, the fact that converts must then express a general recognition that they will be judged by the law—albeit a law they do not as yet know or keep—mirrors the unfolding of the Exodus Covenant in the Bible itself. From the revelation at Sinai, the Children of Israel knew that Jewishness was not limited to Genesis Judaism: it included commandments and expectations for which they would be rewarded or judged. This neither assumed nor required even the knowledge of (much less commitment to) the entirety of the Sinai Covenant as a prerequisite. Rather, it became a framework for the process of their emerging religious identity as newly Exodus Jews. They would gradually be exposed to all the legal requirements over the course of forty years in the desert.

Alternatively, the nature of the Exodus component of this conversion process might reflect a sensibility in which the Exodus Covenant is not a finite set of commandments but rather a framework and form of consciousness. Converts must adopt an Exodus consciousness in which they embrace the idea of being commanded and acknowledge that, in addition to becoming Genesis Jews, they will embark on a journey of Exodus-ness, of doing. Where this journey will end will ultimately depend on them. Just as most of those born Jewish live on a continuum of Exodus behaviors and aspirations, so too can the convert.

"The Rest Is Commentary": Conversion into a Genesis Jew Alone

Another rabbinic strand calls for a "radical-Genesis" approach to conversion: converting a prospective convert into being a Genesis Jew alone. After all, the thinking goes, if Genesis allows a born Jew to be a full Jew regardless of acceptance of Exodus, why should a convert be held to a different standard?

The famous Hillel the Elder is credited with this innovation. A popular talmudic tale recounts how three prospective converts first approach Hillel's counterpart and ideological opponent, Shammai. The first wants to convert on condition that he can reject the whole Oral Tradition—basically 90 percent of Jewish law as Hillel and Shammai have come to know (and help to create) it. The second is willing to convert only on condition that he is taught the whole Torah while standing on one foot—thus seemingly exhibiting insincerity, if not outright mockery, toward both the process and his commitment to fulfilling even some expectations of the Exodus Covenant. The third desires to convert without any interest in the Exodus Covenant but exclusively out of a materialistic desire to profit from what he sees as the financial benefits of becoming a member of the Jewish priestly clan. Shammai summarily rejects them all, deeming their conditions unacceptable, even offensive. All three then turn to Hillel.

Hillel, by contrast, converts each of them on the spot, without any questioning, argument, or even a word. Only then, after they have become Jews, does Hillel begin to engage their conditions and educate them about the teachings of the Exodus Covenant and its Torah: "What is hateful unto you, do not do unto others," he instructs the convert who asked to be taught the entirety of the Torah while standing on one foot. "That is the whole Torah, and the rest is commentary. Now, go study."[16]

Here, Hillel is positing something deceptively radical: the primary condition for conversion is simply one's willingness to be a Jew. In other words, individual choice is the most significant criterion for becoming Jewish. How that Jewishness is defined is secondary.

To be clear, Hillel is not disregarding Exodus Judaism. His stature throughout the Mishnah, where he is recognized as one of the greatest legal authorities of the Jewish legal tradition; his appointment as *Nasi*, head of the Sanhedrin; and his legacy in the ensuing tradition all speak to his being the embodiment of commitment to its flourishing and dissemination. Yet, for Hillel, conversion represents a different way to synthesize Genesis and Exodus: the Exodus Covenant enables the notion of conversion, but it is Genesis that determines the process itself. (The Rabbis in the Talmud did not discuss Hillel's position further; later authorities did, but that is beyond the scope of this discussion.)

How do these two divergent understandings of the Jewish story coexist within a single religious system?

In general, when setting guidelines for conversion, the Rabbis refuse to frame a notion of Jewishness that absents either Genesis or Exodus consciousness. For some Rabbis, one approach is more dominant than the other. Nonetheless, each rabbinic strand honors the divergent voices of both living covenants.

4

Good Jews and Bad Jews and the Art of Boundaries

I first became sensitive to the importance of communal boundary policies thirtysomething years ago, when I started my rabbinic career working as the scholar-in-residence for a Jewish community center (JCC) on the East Coast. It was a teaching pulpit, and in that capacity I instituted a weekly Torah study seminar for the JCC board members and leaders, many of whom also served in leadership roles on a Jewish national level.

One year into my position, the head of a national Orthodox movement contacted me. Knowing that I, an Orthodox rabbi, was working at the JCC, he asked if I would be willing to partner with him and his organization to run a weekend study retreat for my leadership. I gladly agreed, but under one condition. Given the JCC's mandate as a community organization, we needed to respect the ideological diversity of the community. As such, we could not run any program that was exclusively affiliated with one denomination. I explained that I would be happy to expose my leaders to his organization and ideology, as long as the weekend was also open to rabbis of different denominations.

Upon reflection, the rabbi agreed to these terms—but under one further condition. He explained that as an Orthodox Jew he had his red lines—in the lexicon of the Talmud, his *yehareg ve-al ya-avor*, things he would die for rather than transgress. Literally translated as, "Let him be killed and not violate (the law)!," this principle traditionally served to demarcate the ultimate boundaries of Jewish life: idolatry, incest, and murder.

As a young rabbi, I recognized the significance of the moment: a leading figure in Orthodox Judaism was about to outline his position on Judaism's core, on lines beyond which no compromise was possible. The rabbi then informed me that he could participate in the retreat with other denominations as long as all prayer services segregated men and women with a physical divider, or *mechitzah*.

I was astounded by his answer. Nowhere in Jewish law is gender-segregation via *mechitzah* elevated to some exceptional significance, and certainly not to the extent that one should be prepared to martyr oneself rather than transgress it. It is a familiar hot-button issue within modern Judaism, but nowhere does it warrant boundary-generating status. Furthermore, even if one were to accept the dubious premise of *mechitzah*'s religious gravity, was it more important than observing the Sabbath? Keeping kosher?

Only later, as I reflected on his answer, did I understand the sophisticated and subversive rationale behind this peculiar choice. The significance of *mechitzah* lay not in its inherent importance but specifically in its role as a dividing mechanism, not only between men and women during prayer services but between Orthodoxy and non-Orthodoxy. This rabbi knew that non-Orthodox Jews, although willing to compromise on many other matters, would not countenance segregated seating in a synagogue. By demanding that all prayer be divided by gender with a *mechitzah*, the rabbi was signaling his intent to either run the weekend exclusively under Orthodox auspices or cancel the weekend altogether.

While indispensable for social cohesion, boundaries can also be abused and used to undermine the possibility of shared communal life. The purpose of his boundary was not to define the core features of his beliefs, or to challenge others to join him therein, but to divide the community along denominational lines, with Orthodoxy standing alone behind its new nonnegotiable red line. For this rabbi, the *mechitzah* served not merely to divide men and women during prayer but to divide the Jewish people.

Upon reflection I understood that if we wish to realize Jewish collective life—meaning a Jewish peoplehood that can transcend denominational lines and include all factions of the Jewish community—we need to develop an approach to boundaries that is self-consciously focused on cultivating as inclusive a social space as possible.

"Shared Cultural Space": The Necessity of Boundaries

Why are boundaries necessary in the first place?

There is no such thing as a monolithic or ideologically uniform community. Whether we choose our fellow members or inherit them, the only certainty is that over time we will find ourselves in profound disagreement with them. Difference is a prevalent and permanent feature of all social structures.

For this reason, social boundaries become an indispensable force for societal cohesion. By demarcating what is unacceptable, a society can achieve a measure of unanimity among its members despite their differences. Rather than attempt to achieve agreement about what is legitimate—a notoriously difficult point for communities to coalesce around—the society works instead to create consensus around those behaviors that everyone can agree are *illegitimate*. Through these boundaries and the consensus they generate, a mere collection of individuals is transformed into a community with a particular shared "cultural space" that distinguishes their values from others.[1] So, for example, individual Americans or Israelis might disagree about the core quality or value that constitutes the essence of being an American/an Israeli, but they are likely to agree that assisting an enemy of America or Israel in times of war is a line that no one advocating for Americanness or Israeliness can accommodate. Even if we cannot agree on who we are, through boundary policies we can agree on who we are *not*—and in this way create a basis for a sense of communal selfhood.

When it comes to the Jewish community, we too must concede that communal consensus on questions like "What does Judaism mean?," "What are the most important things that a Jew should do?," and "Which values are more important than others?" are forever out of reach. The question then becomes, "Are shared boundaries also out of reach?" Even if we are destined to disagree about the content of the Exodus Covenant, might agreement about its boundaries be a feasible aspiration?

Pluralism, Tolerance, and Deviance: The Art of Boundaries

To fully respond to this challenge requires a bit of background. In establishing boundaries that determine how differences are approached—which are respected, which tolerated, which ostracized—societies utilize three primary categories and sensibilities: pluralism, tolerance, and deviance.

Pluralism assigns equal value to (certain) opposing positions. It means being cognizant of difference without asserting hierarchical claims. Pluralism does not necessitate the acceptance of *all* positions (it should not be equated with relativism), but it does recognize the possibility of equally valuable goals that cannot be "graded on one scale."[2] It allows us to see others' very different viewpoints as being just as authentic as our own. The classical statement of pluralism in Jewish tradition is the talmudic axiom about the starkly opposing philosophies and legal rulings of the schools of Hillel and Shammai. For three years the students of Hillel and the students of Shammai argued with each other, one saying, "The law follows us," the other, "The law follows us." A voice came forth from Heaven and declared, "These and these are the words of the living God."[3]

Yet nowhere is it suggested that *every* opinion qualifies for this divine stamp of pluralistic approval.[4] For those that fall outside of "these and these," beyond the communally sanctioned spheres of discourse, we require other categories—namely, tolerance and deviance.

Tolerance comes into play when we encounter behaviors or differences we believe to be wrong. As the renowned moral philosopher Bernard Williams explains, "If there is to be a question of toleration, it is necessary that there should be something to be tolerated; there has to be some belief or practice or way of life that one group thinks (however fanatically or unreasonably) wrong, mistaken, or undesirable."[5]

We can sense a paradox here. Why should I tolerate, much less allow my community to accommodate, something I believe is wrong? Why not just reject it?

One reason is epistemological. Notwithstanding what I know or believe, I may recognize some issues as sufficiently complex that I cannot claim certainty over the truth. I am humble about what I (or any one person) know(s) and thus allow for the possibility of another opinion.

In *On Liberty*, John Stuart Mill bases the case for tolerance on the expanded perspective dictated by the progressive unfolding of human advancement. While I believe I may know something to be the truth at this moment, I cannot be certain that this will remain the case for all time. Maintaining this awareness is critical for a community's long-term viability—for only societies that tolerate a diversity of opinion can allow future generations to adapt and evolve.

The Rabbis of the Mishnah in Tractate Eduyot similarly adopted this argument: "Why do we retain the record of a minority opinion alongside that of the majority, given the fact that the law always follows the majority? So that a future court can learn the minority opinion and base their opinion on it."[6] If we were to erase those opinions that rabbinic authorities once rejected as nonauthoritative, we would be shrinking the pool of knowledge from which future generations can draw.

There is also a compelling sociopolitical case for tolerance. I share my community with a multiplicity of individuals with different worldviews who have an equal claim to shape the public sphere. While I may believe that I know "the" truth, I make no claim that my opinions should exclusively determine which ideas and policies will be acceptable within, much less govern, our shared cultural space.

The third category, *deviance*, comes into play when we encounter positions or practices that are simply too destructive for us to allow them to influence or define the character of our shared communal structure. At this juncture, our commitment to community demands that we limit the application of tolerance.

In other words, deviance is the classification societies use to describe the difference that crosses a communal red line, the intolerable "conduct about which 'something should be done.'"[7] It denotes "behavior, beliefs, and characteristics that violate society's, or a collectivity's, norms, the violation of which tends to attract negative reactions from audiences. Such negative reactions include contempt, punishment, hostility, condemnation, criticism, denigration, condescension, stigma, pity, and/or scorn."[8]

Through the category of deviance, a community distinguishes between the forms of variability and diversity it conceives as outside the parameters of its shared identity, and those it is able to accommodate. In an important sense, tolerance and deviance define one another: difference not deemed deviant is treated with tolerance, while difference deemed intolerable is labeled as deviance.

And yet, not all deviant behavior triggers societal boundaries. One of the most critical sensibilities and sensitivities in boundary discourse is the notion of "tolerable deviance." The seeming oxymoron of "tolerable deviance" describes behaviors or beliefs that we reject as legitimate within the confines of our communal life, without rejecting the *individuals* who perform them or instituting measures of social punishment and marginalization against them. For example, driving fifteen miles above the speed limit, while illegal and subject to sanction, does not generate social censure. After paying a fine, one is free to resume one's journey as both a driver and a community member in good standing.

Intolerable deviance, on the other hand, is when society responds by not only rejecting the act but by sanctioning the offender. Sometimes the distinguishing criterion between tolerable and intolerable deviance is the perceived severity of the deviance. Continuing the example, driving under the influence of alcohol or drugs is perceived to be far more dangerous in putting the lives of others at risk than merely driving over the speed limit. Consequently, the driver is taken off the road and in some cases serves jail time. The first drove too fast; the second is a drunk driver. The deviant act redefines the offender's identity.

Often, however, the distinction between tolerable and intolerable deviance is a function neither of the severity of the act nor of its danger to others but rather of its relative frequency and prevalence in the society at large. Simply put, a social group cannot designate something as intolerably deviant that a significant number of its members do or believe in. Legislating a boundary in this situation would only fracture the community's collective identity. The behavior in question may be condemned but not legislated as a boundary.

Joking about Adultery (and Other Signs of Tolerable Deviance)

One of the most familiar examples of tolerable deviance pertains to laws against adultery—which, precisely because of its perennial prevalence in society, never coalesces as a societal boundary at all. While universally condemned in almost every moral system, it nevertheless remains unsanctioned, not just legally but socially.

One of the telling indicators of deviance that has become tolerable is the culture of jokes that builds up around it. Intolerable deviance is never a laughing matter. The permissibility of humor betrays a communal consensus that the deviance is either not that severe or has become normative. Similarly, intolerable deviance cannot be flaunted publicly with little or no shame. Political figures and celebrities can be serial adulterers but not violators of incest taboos.

By a similar token—as we have seen play out in the struggle for acceptance by those with alternate sexual and gender identities—as long as "deviant" behaviors remain closeted and socially invisible, intolerable-deviant status (including the ascription of pathologizing stigmas like moral turpitude and mental illness) is more easily enforced. Yet once a critical mass of group members stage an exodus from the closet's confines, the damaging implications of casting a large segment of the community as intolerable start to be felt throughout the society. Reestablishing the social equilibrium necessitates a negotiation, which inevitably results in some shift in their categorization. Some community members may continue to view the behavior as deviant, but the society no longer classifies the individuals as intolerable or subjects them to communal sanctions. In some cases the acts or beliefs come to be redefined as tolerable, or even fully accepted under the rubric of pluralism.

From Intolerable to Tolerable and Back

In the Jewish community, one of the most universally accepted social boundaries from the rabbinic period through the mid-twentieth century focused on marriage between Jews and non-Jews. During that time, intermarriage was defined almost exclusively as intolerable deviance and marginalized to the extent that the parents of Jews who intermarried were mandated to sit shivah, a heart-rending act of symbolic mourning that declared not merely their children's exclusion from family and community but their expulsion from the land of the living.

However, with the steady increase of interfaith marriage in North America toward the end of the twentieth century, a natural outcome of Jews' newfound complex identities and acceptance into the mainstream of North American life, parents stopped sitting shivah, and instead family members started attending the weddings. With the settling awareness that we had become an intermarried community came a growing acceptance of intermarriage, and some rabbis began to perform intermarriages out of a desire to ensure the Jewishness of the family. For most Jews in North America, as the decades passed, attitudes toward intermarriage shifted as well, from deviance to tolerance—if not pluralism.

In Israel, intermarriage is statistically insignificant and thus can maintain its traditional classification as an uncrossable boundary for Israelis across the religious and ideological spectrum. However, with the influx of hundreds of thousands of formally non-Jewish immigrants from the former Soviet Union (who qualified for citizenship under Israel's Law of Return, which defines and regulates the right to automatic citizenship by virtue of having a Jewish father or one Jewish grandparent or being married to Jew), the lines have begun to blur. The immigrants are considered part of the broader Jewish community, but without being formally recognized by any official Israeli rabbinic body. The fact that no scalable conversion option is available for Israeli Jews (because of the monopolistic Orthodox rabbinate's opposition to converting people who aren't committed to an Orthodox lifestyle) has led to an increase of intermarriage between the Russians and the larger Israeli Jewish community. In these cases, we are already seeing a societal shift of reclassifying such marriages as "tolerable."

The move from intolerable to tolerable also occurs in the reverse. One of the most prominent contemporary examples is sexual harassment. For centuries it was considered a normal feature of male-female social intercourse. As abuses began to be litigated and new laws passed, in the latter part of the twentieth century, the violation moved from pluralism, to tolerance, to tolerable deviance. Some publicly argued that such restrictions are unnatural, preventing "normal" gender relations, and unenforceable to boot. As a result, even as the law designated clearer boundaries and regulations, and even though behavior slowly began to change, it nevertheless remained commonplace and de facto culturally tolerable. Only as a result of the #MeToo movement did society begin to catch up with its self-proclaimed boundaries, enforce its sanctions, and reclassify such behavior as intolerable.

Balance: A Categorical Imperative

A healthy society is one that uses all of the categories—pluralism, tolerance, tolerable and intolerable deviance—at different times and in different circumstances, to conceptualize, integrate, and reject different forms of difference. The overutilization of a single classification has profound negative social implications. In times of intensified ideological debate and difference, for example, communities often fall into the trap of building their social structures almost entirely around either pluralism or intolerable deviance. But if pluralism is used too broadly, with all boundary conversations jettisoned for the sake of communal solidarity, it will tend to devolve into relativism, which instead of ascribing the possibility of the existence of equally valid truths discards those categories altogether—thereby disintegrating the possibility of a society of particular identity and meaning. At the opposite extreme, the reclassification of anything to which one cannot ascribe equal value and truth as intolerable deviance suppresses free expression and thought and encourages mutual suspicion among members, yielding social factionalism and alienation.

While every society requires both pluralism and intolerable deviance to survive, the primary engines for assimilating difference are tolerance and tolerable deviance. These encourage our ability to live with each other.

In the long run, however, a society *must* achieve consensus on the category of intolerable deviance—on its red lines, its boundaries. Without that consensus, its members will be engaged in constant political, legal, and cultural crises, leading to the inevitable undermining of social cohesion and communal identity.

An example of precisely such a moment is the current growing schism between Israeli and North American Jews around their differences in classifying non-Orthodox forms of Judaism. In Israel, where the Conservative and Reform denominations are a minority, many Orthodox, traditional, and even secular Jews perceive them as intolerably deviant expressions of Judaism. Their intolerable status is inscribed into laws that formally reject the validity of Reform, Conservative, and many modern Orthodox marriages and conversions.

This marginalized status quo was clearly visible in the lack of Israeli public interest, much less support, for the designation of a pluralistic, non-gender-segregated prayer section at Jerusalem's Wailing Wall. In North America, where Conservative and Reform Jews constitute at least half of the Jewish community, this kind of marginalization, even on the part of Orthodox Jews, would be self-evidently incoherent. In fact, around areas of broad communal consensus for North American Jews (e.g., Israel's survival and antisemitism), cooperation among Orthodox, Conservative, and Reform Jews is common.

This bitter boundary debate reflects an ever-deepening ideological wedge between Israeli and North American Jews in which Israelis feel alienated from their North American counterparts and North

Americans feel stigmatized and rejected (see chapter 10). If we are to overcome some of our divides, Israeli and North American Jewry will have to be unified not merely around issues of survival but around the boundaries that help give shape and purpose to our communal life.

Boundaries of Genesis and Exodus

Notably, one of the baseline necessities of collective social life—formulating a consensus on what acts constitute intolerable deviance—is incompatible with the Genesis Covenant, which says there is no such category: there are no better or worse Jews, just Jews. God stayed with Abraham's children and the Children of Israel throughout their desert wanderings and their years in the Land of Israel, despite the people's constant rejection of God's commandments. Anyone who fails to fulfill the criteria of the Genesis Covenant is not an "intolerable deviant" but simply a nonmember.

Only with the Exodus embrace of Jewishness as a framework of expectations and obligations does the matrix of better/worse Jews becomes possible, and "intolerable deviance" become a coherent category (with the multitude of commandments constituting fertile ground for an extensive field of intolerability). Membership, too, becomes conditional: "Now, *if* you shall obey me faithfully and keep my covenant, you shall be my treasured possession . . ." (Exod. 19:5; emphasis added).

These sharp distinctions give rise to an urgent question: given their near-symmetrical opposition on boundary delineations, are Genesis and Exodus "synthesizable" into a coherent boundary policy?

Good Jews and Bad Jews

As with conversion, when it came to boundaries, the rabbinic tradition refused to choose between the two competing covenants. On the one hand, it accepted the Exodus notion that some actions ought to classify their perpetrators as intolerable. On the other, it accepted as axiomatic the Genesis principle that a Jew is a Jew is a Jew. Nowhere does the rabbinic tradition punish a violator of its boundaries with the loss of status as a Jew. Thus, as alluded to earlier, even a convert who is Jewish merely for a few minutes and immediately reverts back to the prior faith is nevertheless classified as an "*Israelite* Deviant."[9]

Genesis's unwavering loyalty and tolerance for Jews who are different lies at the gravitational center of the rabbinic theory of boundaries. As a result, the Rabbis expanded the application of tolerance for difference in general, while placing severe limits on intolerability. They proceeded to classify most violations of the commandments as tolerable deviants: "sinning" or "criminal" Israelites. As we will see, under rabbinic influence, "an Israelite who sins is still an Israelite" became "an Israelite who sins remains, in most instances, a tolerable deviant."

Destroyed People and Enemy Heretics: Defining Intolerable Deviance

What boundary violations, then, render an Israelite intolerable?

Incorporating aspects of both covenants, the Rabbis defined the core condition for intolerability as the complete and total separation from and rejection of the Genesis Covenant and/or the Exodus Covenant. If either the Jewish people are still your people, or some facet of Torah still obligates you, you are not intolerable. If you violate parts of this Torah, you are a sinning Israelite, but not intolerable. But if you sever covenantal bonds, you are a *meshumad*—a destroyed person.[10]

Converting Out of Judaism

The paradigmatic *meshumad* is the Jew who converts out of Judaism, rejecting all of Torah and aligning oneself with another community.[11] Such an individual is ultimately called "one-who-is-destroyed-with-respect-to-the-whole-Torah," or simply a "whole-Torah *meshumad*" (*meshumad le-kol ha-Torah*).

Idolatry

Outside of the wholesale rejection of all Jewish law and identity embodied in the decision to convert out, in rabbinic literature, only three acts are considered sufficiently covenant-severing to qualify one as a whole-Torah *meshumad*: (1) idolatry; (2) public desecration of the Sabbath; and (3) individual acts of deviance performed out of spite.[12] To the Rabbis, each in its own way constitutes an act of total covenant betrayal.

The classification of idolatry as covenant-breaking is not surprising: in the Bible, within its Exodus narrative, idolatry constitutes *the* deviance, *the* act that breaks or suspends the covenant. Picking up on the biblical centrality of this prohibition, the Rabbis declared, "Whoever accepts idolatry is as if they reject the entire Torah. Whoever rejects idolatry is as if they accept the entire Torah."[13] By the rabbinic period (unlike in the Bible), a foundational implication of the Exodus Covenant is that one cannot embrace God and Torah and worship idols simultaneously. Under this covenant, idolatry is tantamount to converting out. Conversely, "Whoever rejects idolatry is called a Jew."[14]

Public Desecration of the Sabbath

The branding of the public desecration of the Sabbath as intolerable deviance, on the other hand, is both surprising and complex. There is no obvious basis for this status in the biblical canon. Of all the Ten Commandments, only idolatry and violating the Sabbath are singled out as equivalent to rejecting the whole Torah, while murder, adultery, theft, and dishonesty in business play far more dominant roles in the prophetic castigation of Israel's sins. In a further twist, only the *public* violation of the Sabbath is classified as intolerable, unlike idolatry, which is intolerable whether performed in public or private.

To understand the elevated status of Sabbath desecration as a covenant-breaker, we would best recall the cultural and historical context in which the Exodus Covenant took root toward the end of the Second Temple Period, at the beginning of the Common Era. By then, idolatry had ceased to be a factor in Israelite society, and the Jewish community was largely living in accordance with the public rituals obligated by the Torah—most significantly, observing the Sabbath. At the time Jewishness came to be explicitly identified with the practice of resting on the seventh day.

In this milieu, private desecration of the Sabbath was deemed no more severe than the violation of any other commandment; having no symbolic resonance beyond itself, it remained a tolerable act. Public desecration, however, was different. Just as idol worship in the rabbinic era implied ipso facto the rejection of the essence of the Exodus Covenant, so too the public desecration of the Sabbath declared the realignment of one's identity outside of the Jewish community and the Genesis Covenant.

The Genesis Covenant, after all, came with one condition: the choice to belong. In the Bible, the central expression of this choice, *the* sign (*ot*) of the covenant, was the act of circumcision. Now, however, in rabbinic discourse—which became constitutive in Jewish law—public desecration of the Sabbath served as *the* new sign of rejecting Genesis. In publicly abstaining from acting like the rest of the Jewish community, one essentially was proclaiming, "The Jewish people are not my people."[15]

Interestingly, by the mid-nineteenth century, when the Sabbath ceased to be widely observed and no longer defined Jewish communal identity, its public desecration ceased to be considered a boundary violation and was reclassified as equivalent to a private desecration.[16]

Intolerable Spite

While the Rabbis were unanimous in regarding idolatry and public Sabbath desecration as intolerable acts, some rabbinic figures added the more conceptually nuanced category of "deviance-out-of-spite."[17]

The classic paradigm for such deviance is eating the carcass of a kosher animal not killed in accordance with Jewish law when an otherwise identical piece of kosher meat—defined as having the same taste, aesthetics, and price—is equally available. Without the mitigating factor of desire/preference, if one still habitually chooses the nonkosher option, and is publicly known to do so, the criterion of "deviance-out-of-spite" is activated.[18] Similar to idolatry and the public desecration of the Sabbath, spite is read as indicative of a more intentional and broad-based identity transformation: a self-conscious decision to withdraw oneself from the Exodus Covenant. When that occurs, the boundary of intolerability is crossed.

In practice, "intolerable deviants" may not be kicked out of the Jewish community. Instead, they may be stigmatized as a member in lesser standing unworthy of communal compassion or concern or barred in humiliating and alienating ways from fully participating in (at times even attending) holiday festivities, lifecycle events, daily religious services, and other key sites of communal celebration, reflection, and bonding.

The Tolerance of a Limited Red Line

The radical nature of this understanding of intolerability rises into sharp relief when we consider its implications. By limiting the definition of intolerable deviance solely to these extreme cases in which one rejects the whole Genesis and/or Exodus Covenant *in total*, then any other deviance—any number or configuration of sins—renders one at the very worst, a *tolerable* deviant. Thus the Rabbis revolutionized what it means to be a "bad" Jew.

Passionate advocates of the Exodus Covenant, the talmudic rabbis could have articulated a much more extensive list of red-line triggers of Whole Torah Meshumad intolerability—similar to what Maimonides later did with his Thirteen Principles of Faith. While the Rabbis did identify a category of commandments that they posited as equivalent to the whole Torah, and formulated and numerated lists of "the" essential commandments, they refrained from referencing these categories or lists when it came to articulating their red lines.[19]

As we have seen, the deep purpose of boundaries is to attain communal consensus on who we are *not*, rather than on who we are. Communal clarity on broad baselines of collective identity—who we are *not*—enhances a community's bonds of shared purpose, whereas emphasis on particular baselines—who we are—magnifies nonconsensus and division. In an aggressively inclusionary Genesis-inspired move—not dissimilar to Moses's breaking of the tablets so that his Golden Calf-worshiping followers could not be judged for their sins—the rabbinic tradition chose the route of communal cohesiveness, severely limiting the red line of intolerability and rendering the vast majority safely tolerable "Good Jews."

Intolerability of the Enemy-Heretic

The Rabbis also delineated a second category of covenant-breaker: the enemy-heretic (*min*). Here again, the essential feature is not the particular act of deviance but the fact that the enemy-heretic is actively campaigning to undermine fidelity to communal norms.

As developed in rabbinic literature, the danger of the enemy-deviant is not subjective—"I feel threatened" does not meet the standard of *min* classification. Only when one is found openly and overtly campaigning against others' understanding and application of the Exodus Covenant does one open oneself to an intolerability designation and sanctions.[20] In a sense, the Rabbis' position can be concisely distilled as: *As a deviant, you'll be tolerable as long as you accept my right to pursue my understanding of Judaism, even if you reject it for yourself. When you do not respect my ability to do so; when we're not engaged in a debate, but you're waging a cultural war against me; when you're actively working to destroy my Judaism* you will be classified as *min* and ruled intolerable.[21]

Perhaps unsurprisingly, the enemy-deviant category has typically emerged when two sides are battling for hegemony and control and one side attempts to subvert the status of the other. One such moment, the (ca. second to fourth century CE) conflict between Rabbinic Judaism and early Christianity for the mantle of Judaism, encompassed most of the rabbinic cases where the category was applied.[22] In somewhat like vein, in the early nineteenth century, traditional and liberal forces fought publicly for representation of post-Emancipation Judaism (see chapter 6).[23] Today, while various denominations and ideologies challenge each other, public attempts to actively undermine the viability of others are rare (with the principal exception of certain Orthodox policies meant to monopolize Israeli Judaism, which liberal Jews could justifiably classify as expressive of enemy-deviant status; see chapter 9).

An Israelite Who Sees Oneself as an Israelite Is an Israelite: The Self-Imposed Boundary

As we've seen, then, for the Rabbis, intolerable deviance is invoked exclusively as a response to members who completely remove themselves from either the Genesis or Exodus Covenants, Jewishness being an amalgamation of the two.

In setting this line, the Rabbis are essentially establishing it as a self-imposed category. If you openly separate yourself from the community, we then designate you as an outsider. As long as you do not sever ties with one of the covenants, you remain a member in good standing. Intolerability is basically a legal ruling to accept and formalize a deviant's self-classification, rather than a prescriptive punishment for an extreme transgression.

The foundational rule of the Genesis Covenant is that an Israelite who has sinned is still an Israelite. In the synthesis of Genesis and Exodus sensibilities, the Rabbis generated a new foundational rule: an Israelite who sees oneself as an Israelite, no matter how much they've sinned, is still an Israelite in good standing.

Implications

The distinct lenses of Genesis and Exodus could have led to profound, irreconcilable consequences. Without an Exodus corrective, the Genesis Covenant could have created a notion of Jewishness devoid of mission and purpose. Without a Genesis corrective, the Exodus Covenant inevitably creates multiple distinct and competing Jewish communities, dealing a death blow to any larger sense of Jewish peoplehood.

Furthermore, Exodus Jews like the Rabbis could have easily erected boundaries around an elite subcommunity that excluded Jews of radical and diverse levels of practice and belief: essentially the majority of the Jewish people. However, because of their commitment to Genesis—because of their understanding that Jewishness must be far more tolerant and expansive than the sub-boundaries accepted by their community of fellow rabbis—the Rabbis developed another category for those (like themselves) committed to striving toward exemplary aspirations: the community of *Haverim* (literally "friends" in religious aspiration).[24] Significantly, they never succumbed to the temptation of defining Jewishness or Jewish legitimacy, much less tolerability, according to the aspirational standards they set for themselves. To thus set Jew against Jew would be to forge a culture of division and toxicity.

By integrating the sensibilities of both Genesis and Exodus, the Rabbis established boundaries, an essentially Exodus move; however, inspired by Genesis, these boundaries allow a diverse community of meaning to flourish within the lived reality of the Jewish people.

5

Maimonides, Champion of Exodus

The biblical and rabbinic periods endowed their inheritors with a legacy and a challenge: to maintain the vital dialogue between the Covenants of Genesis and Exodus. Eschewing ideologues and extremists who sought to make one voice dominant, subsequent generations formulated and modeled a Judaism that viewed each as an authentic representation of God's will. Over the ensuing centuries and into the Middle Ages, this commitment to a vibrant and inclusive Jewish community based on a strong Genesis-Exodus synthesis was largely—but not completely—maintained.

Two formative shifts—Maimonides's redefinition of Jewishness as essentially an Exodus sensibility and the diminishing of Genesis Judaism in nineteenth-century Western Europe as a result of Emancipation and denominationalism—would challenge this commitment. And Jews today are still building on the new conceptual frameworks of Jewish identity that would emerge, for better and for worse.

"From Moses to Moses": Maimonides and the Embrace of a Philosophic Exodus

Centuries after the completion of the Talmuds in Palestine and Babylonia (modern-day Iraq), much had changed in Jewish life. In the Middle Ages, the Jewish diaspora spread westward, throughout Europe and Northern Africa, and encountered fellow monotheistic faiths—in particular Islam—that challenged Judaism with new ideas. At the time, Islam had become the cultural center of "modern" intellectual, scientific, and cultural thought and innovation: a model of how a tradition could incorporate the best of "contemporary" philosophical thought

(Aristotelianism and Neoplatonism) into its religious and theological thinking. Its vital example offered an implicit challenge to other religious formations.

The figure whose life's work was most singularly dedicated to—and successful at—ensuring that Judaism could compete intellectually in this rarefied, high-stakes marketplace of ideas was Moses Maimonides (1135–1204).

Engraved on Maimonides's tombstone in a cemetery in Tiberias, Israel, is the epitaph: "From Moses [of Biblical fame] to Moses [Maimonides] there was none like Moses." *The* greatest philosopher and halakhic authority of the Jewish tradition, Maimonides proceeded to transform Jewish thought and law in his time and henceforth. His teachings were never perceived as the personal opinions of a particular scholar. To the contrary, they immediately became analogous in canonical standing to the Bible and Talmud: constitutive, authoritative, bedrock elements of *the* Jewish story; elements that any new narrative of the whole had to contend with from then on.

My Maimonides

Maimonides played a constitutive role in my own life as well. From an early age, I was bothered by the biblical narrative of reward and punishment whereby the obedient are promised long and prosperous lives while the deviant are destined to hardship and death, all at the hands of the judging God. I believe in God, but having grown up in the decades following the Holocaust, I could not accept the notion of a God who intervened in history. I was torn by the question of whether I could remain an observant Jew within the "system"—the parameters of a normative Orthodox lifestyle and worldview.

At age sixteen, while attending a seminar on Maimonides that my father was teaching at Hebrew University, I encountered the following words: "One who wishes to serve God out of love . . . should believe that wisdom exists, and that this wisdom is contained in the Torah . . . which teaches us virtues which are the commandments, and vices which are the sins. As a decent person, one must cultivate the virtues and avoid the sins, and in so doing, will perfect the specifically human qualities which reside within them."[1]

For Maimonides, to worship God out of love is to be motivated by a commitment to one's humanity and striving to follow the dictates of decency. Reward and punishment are not part of the equation. I remember saying to myself, "Now that is a Judaism I can be committed to." The sentiment was solidified when Maimonides continued:

"Do not be like the horse or the mule, which have no understanding, whose mouth must be held in with bit and bridle." (Psalms 32:9) . . . With humankind, that which should restrain them is their inner control of self. When a person achieves human perfection, *it* [their inner control of self] restrains them from doing those things which are called vices, and which undermine their perfection. *It* urges and impels one toward those things which are called virtues, and which bring one to full perfection.[2]

The highest level of loving God is achieved when one is compelled by an inner motivation to live a virtuous life. The commandments are a map of this life, not a series of dictates to follow in blind obedience. Consequently, for Maimonides, the ultimate religious life is not one in search of God's favor and reward but rather a journey to fulfill the human mission of living a life of virtue.

Most Jews never read this text, and even fewer understand it. When I share it with others, many perceive it as alien to a life with God, let alone an expression of the highest form of worship. For me, however, it was the oxygen I needed in order to live a committed Jewish life. Once Maimonides articulated it, it did not matter who agreed with me. I had Maimonides on my side and as a result, was, by definition, within the story.

Throughout my life, as I encountered challenges both personal and theological, Maimonides empowered me to find my path *within* Judaism, to change and reinterpret that which would alienate me from my tradition. Because of him, I came to believe that the more I strive to approximate decency and to fulfill my humanity, the closer I am to God, and the more in sync I am with Judaism and its expectations of me.

As I delved deeper into his writings, I discovered that this framework was not only *my* Maimonides. His own life's work centered around the same mission: to try to save his own commitment to Judaism by reinterpreting that which he found alienating within the tradition he'd inherited.

The Great "Reframing": Truth before Tradition

In articulating his approach to Jewish thought and law, Maimonides was guided by two distinct, and often contradictory, commitments: to Jewish law as handed down in the tradition and to the truth as it had come to be known through the teachings of the philosophers. A compromise on either was unacceptable to him. As Maimonides explained in his *Guide of the Perplexed*:

> [This book's] purpose is to give indications to a religious man for whom the validity of our Law has become established in his soul and has become actual in his belief-such a man being perfect in his religion and character, and having studied the sciences of the philosophers and come to know what they signify. . . . He must have felt distressed by the externals of the Law [and simple reading of Scripture which contradict what he knows to be true]. . . . He would remain in a state of perplexity and confusion as to whether he should follow his intellect and renounce [the teachings of Scripture] . . . and consequently consider that he has renounced the foundations of the Law. Or should he hold fast to [the simple meaning of scripture] . . . and not let himself be drawn on by his intellect, and rather turn his back on [the truth], and in doing so perceive that he has brought loss to himself and harm to his religion.[3]

Maimonides faced a challenge: the tradition he inherited included precepts that contradicted what he knew to be objective philosophical truth. The attribution of physical and emotional attributes to God; the Bible's apparent indifference to the pursuit of knowledge and the contemplative life; and the focus on purely physical rewards for righteousness—for Maimonides, Aristotle had the better of Judaism on all these topics.

The dilemma of the Jewish religious philosopher was what to give up—tradition or truth. For Maimonides, a Judaism out of sync with the truth was an inferior religion, and a commitment to truth without Judaism would disconnect him from his religious identity. Sacrificing either was not only inconceivable but both existentially and religiously incoherent. Ultimately, Maimonides came to believe, tradition *cannot* contradict that which philosophical reflection knows to be true.[4]

His life's work was to forge a third path, within which he would not be forced to choose.[5] To achieve this, he embarked on a massive and comprehensive reframing of the "simple" or surface meanings of both biblical scriptures and rabbinic statements, offering definitive reinterpretive resolutions to all apparent conflicts.

This commitment to aligning tradition and truth would lead him to redefine the respective significance of Genesis and Exodus Judaisms. And, given Maimonides's stature in the Jewish story, once he shifted the Jewish value system definitively in favor of the latter, our collective-identity discourse was irrevocably altered.

"When All These Foundations Are Perfectly Understood": Redefining Judaism as an Exodus Covenant

Maimonides's Jewishness grew out of and was nourished by the core belief that Judaism's purpose is to create individuals and communities capable of reaching the highest levels of human actualization. In his strict Aristotelian worldview, this could mean only one thing: Jews becoming knowers of God. Never one to mince words, he begins his codification of Jewish Law announcing this aspiration as the first of the Ten Commandments:

> The basic principle of all basic principles, and the pillar of all sciences, is to realize that there is a first being who brought every existing thing into being. . . . If it could be supposed that He did not exist, it would follow that nothing else could possibly exist. If, however, it was supposed that all other beings were nonexistent, He alone would still exist. . . . To acknowledge this truth is an affirmative commandment, as it is said, "I am the Lord your God." [Exod. 20:2][6]

For Maimonides, what distinguishes humanity from all other creation is that it alone shares with Divinity the capacity for intellectual cognitive endeavor. This is what the Bible means when it speaks of human beings created in the image of God.[7] The telos of a human life is to actualize this capacity, to become as close to one-with-God as possible through the perfection of one's cognitive faculty, one's "knowledge." To live a full Jewish life is to be constantly engaged in pursuit of this intellectual aspiration.[8]

As a result, Maimonides found little to value in Genesis Judaism. Idling in Genesis's "Being Jewish" sensibility was tantamount to failing in both one's Jewish and human purpose. Demanding no aspiration, Genesis offered no meaningful connection or contribution to Judaism's raison d'être. Thus, it was unworthy of a primary place within the tradition.

By contrast, his "Thirteen Principles of Faith" (as outlined in chapter 3) together comprised *the* essential gateway to Jewishness: "When all these [thirteen] foundations are perfectly understood and believed in, *then* this person enters the community of Israel. And one is obligated to love and pity him and to act towards him in all ways in which the Creator has commanded that one should act towards his brother with love and fraternity."[9]

In this remarkable and pivotal source, Maimonides still uses the Genesis-based model of family ("brother") to characterize the relationship between fellow Jews. But in sharp contrast to the Genesis framework, membership in this family is no longer based on birth: one joins by learning, accepting, and holding fast to its principles of faith. Indeed, Maimonides explicitly states that this is how one "enters the community of Israel."

The reverse holds equally true. Someone who "denies that which is fundamental" cannot be part of Maimonides's Israel. "[If] a man doubts any of these foundations, *he leaves the community*."[10] The individual becomes marginalized as a "sectarian heretic [*apikorus*]," and Jews in good standing are "required to hate him and destroy him."[11]

There is no clearer definition of Judaism as essentially an Exodus Covenant.

"And He Implanted in Their Hearts This Great Idea": Abraham the First . . . Philosopher?

Furthermore, in a full-spectrum campaign to reshape Judaism in his vision of Exodus, Maimonides rewrote Genesis-inflected biblical narratives, removing all vestiges of Genesis-consciousness and transforming the texts into Exodus understandings.

Abraham, for example, is not the founder of Genesis Judaism but the world's first philosophical monotheist and founder of a community created around embracing his version of the Exodus Covenant:

He arose and declared in a great voice to the whole world and extolled to them that there is only one God for the whole world, and to God alone is it worthy to worship. And he would walk and call and gather the people from city to city, from kingdom to kingdom, until he entered the Land of Canaan, as it is said, "And he called there in the name of God, the God of the world." And as the peoples would gather around him and ask him regarding his words, he would teach each and every one of them in accordance with their intellectual capacity, until he brought each to the path of truth; until there gathered around him thousands and tens of thousands. *And these are the ones who are called the People of the House of Abraham.*

And he implanted in their hearts this great idea, and he composed books. And he taught this to Isaac his son. And Isaac in turn sat, taught, and brought people to this idea. And Isaac taught his son Jacob and appointed him to teach. And he sat and taught and brought this idea to all those who accompanied him. And Jacob taught his sons, all of them, and separated Levi to be the head of the yeshiva, to teach the way of God and to keep the commandments of Abraham. And he commanded his children that they should not stop appointing somebody from the House of Levi, one appointment after another, so that the teachings will not be forgotten. And this idea grew amongst the sons of Jacob and all those who accompanied them. *And there came to be in the world a people who know God.*[12]

Going much further than the rabbinic tradition, Maimonides doesn't merely redefine Abraham; he redefines *the Jewishness his covenant gave birth to*. What Maimonides's Abraham passes down through the generations *is not his seed—it is an idea*. The House of Abraham no longer comprises biological family members; rather, it is a spiritual "family" of all who join him in accepting the Maimonidean Exodus Covenant. The Children of Israel (*Bnei Yisrael*), the first Jewish community, are no longer merely the sons of Jacob. Israel are the "*people who know God.*"

"And He Taught This in Great Length": Conversion with an Exodus Twist

The focus on Jewishness as essentially a manifestation of one's commitment to the Exodus Covenant also guides Maimonides's approach to the conversion process. Whereas the rabbinic conversion tradition struck a delicate synthesis between Genesis and Exodus, first challenging converts to recognize they are joining a community of Genesis Jews and then introducing them to select elements of the Exodus Judaism framework, Maimonides adds a significant condition to the process that changes its essential nature.

At the outset he ostensibly follows rabbinic precedent, asking the candidate: "Why do you want to convert? Don't you know that Israel at this time are severely oppressed and attacked?" If the person says, "I know and I am unworthy," they are accepted immediately.[13]

But then, right before proceeding with the next process outlined in the Talmud—"And they are taught some of the major and some of the minor commandments"—Maimonides rules:

> He is then taught the fundamentals of the Jewish religion—the oneness and uniqueness of God, and the prohibition against idolatry. And he is taught this *in great length*.[14]

For Maimonides, there simply is no becoming a member of the Jewish people without embracing what he defines as the central premise of its Exodus Covenant: substantive knowledge of God. Without it, one fundamentally remains an idolater, rendering conversion meaningless.

Maimonides then continues and essentially follows rabbinic precedent: "We inform him about some of the minor commandments and some of the major ones. We do not elaborate on this matter."[15] Here Maimonides has added the explicit guideline not to "elaborate" on the teachings of the commandments. This move, however, is the result not of a Genesis sensibility but of Maimonides's assessment that these are not the essence of Exodus Judaism. That distinction belongs exclusively to knowledge of God.

With this revision of the conversion process, Maimonides dispenses with the rabbinic tradition's Genesis-weighted formulation and initiates an Exodus-dominated conversion that persists to this day. His approach set the stage for later authorities to reject future conversion processes deemed lacking in a specific Exodus content demand, or falling short of narrow standards of knowledge and behavior. Nowadays, each modern denomination has its own agenda around what must be taught "in great length." A potential convert is required to know and accept what the converting rabbi believes is essential to Exodus Judaism before qualifying for conversion.

"Anyone Who Kills Him Has Fulfilled a Great Mitzvah": Exodus Boundaries

Maimonides reverses rabbinic precedent to advance his Exodus-centered ideology in Jewish boundary discourse as well. This leads him to question the essential Jewishness of the person who does not embrace his notion of what Jewishness requires:

> An Israelite who worships idolatry: he is like an idolater in all respects, and he is not like an Israelite who violated a capital transgression.[16]
>
> The public desecrator of the Sabbath is like one who worships idols, and both are like non-Jews in all matters.[17]

Additionally, he expands the parameters of the intolerable to include infidelity to his Thirteen Principles of Faith, asserting that joining the Jewish people is contingent on accepting all of them: "And when an individual believes in these principles, and their truth is clarified to him, *then* he enters into Israel."[18]

By implication, failure to do so leaves one outside the Jewish people.

Up until Maimonides, this kind of language was extremely rare in Jewish-legal discourse, which was suffused with the ethos of the Genesis Covenant as encapsulated in "*An Israelite, even though they have sinned, is still an Israelite.*" Nonetheless, full steam ahead, Maimonides articulates some of the most extreme sanctions known to Jewish tradition:

> But when one of these principles or when a person's faith in one of these principles is corrupted, he has separated from the

community. He is a heretic in the essence, he is called a heretic (*min*), an apostate (*apikorus*), and an individual who cuts the plantings. It is a commandment to hate him and to destroy him. And about him it is said, "Your enemy's God I will hate; those who hate you, God, I will hate." (Psalms 139:21)[19]

Whoever repudiates the Oral Torah is one of the heretics whom any person has a right to put to death. . . . [He is] *not a part of Israel* and does not require witnesses, prior warning, or judges before being put to death. Rather, anyone who kills [him] has fulfilled a great mitzvah and removed a stumbling block.[20]

There is seemingly no place in Maimonides's Jewish world for one who denies essential principles of faith or renounces core commandments. That person is ejected from Israel, and all believers are encouraged to remove the heretic from their midst—including via extrajudicial capital punishment.

The Captive Child: Maimonides's Acknowledgement of Genesis Bonds

That said, even Maimonides could not completely expunge the Genesis Covenant from his formulation of Jewish identity. Rather, in a radical innovation, he *repositioned* it. He confined the relevance of Genesis solely to considerations of membership status, while leaving the content of Jewish life under the exclusive jurisdiction of Exodus:

(This ruling of extra judicial capital punishment only applies to) one who repudiates the Oral Law as a result of his reasoned opinion and conclusions. . . . However, their children and grandchildren who are misled by their parents and who were born into heresy or apostasy and were raised and trained upon their heretical views, are like a child who was taken captive amongst the heathens. . . . He is like one compelled to sin against his will, for they raised and trained him according to their mistakes. . . . Therefore, effort should be made to bring them back in repentance, to draw them near with paths of peace, until they return to the strength-giving source of the Torah, and a person should not hurry to kill them.[21]

And so, with a turn of the mind and a stroke of the pen, all the severe legal sanctions will henceforth be applied only to the extremely rare self-made ideologue, the one who wakes up one day and knowingly repudiates a nourishing educational environment. By contrast, any and all individuals raised in a home that did not fully imbue them with the knowledge of Exodus Judaism and bring them into its covenantal expectations—which, it can be argued, applies to almost every home *even within the Jewish community*—are to be considered blameless. Instead of being sanctioned, they are to be embraced with compassion and love.

In essence, through a dramatic expansion of the law of the Captive Child—which traditionally applied only to a person raised in idolatrous captivity—Maimonides radically defangs and circumscribes all of his severe threats towards heretics to a theoretical realm. In so doing, he establishes a new balance between the Covenants of Genesis and Exodus, their respective applications in Jewish Law, and, perhaps most significantly, their cultural valence. On the one hand, Maimonides amplifies the Genesis Covenant, legally annulling the entire category of intolerable deviance by rendering (nearly) *all* deviants tolerable, so long as their inadequate education has coerced them into such a position. At the same time, Maimonides narrows the scope of the Genesis Covenant by refusing to allow Genesis commitments to limit the content, sphere, or authority of his Exodus Judaism. Genesis limits the sanctions that can be applied when Exodus lines are transgressed, but in no way alters the lines themselves.

In short, Maimonides breaks from rabbinic tradition. Rather than draw communal boundary lines unified around a broad engagement with the frameworks of Genesis and Exodus, and thus inclusive of most Jews, he establishes red lines that remain pure articulations of Judaism as he believes it ought to be—unadulterated by the "dirty" reality of the Jewish choices Jews often make.

Maimonides is willing to forgo the sanctions associated with intolerability. What he will never allow is for any Jew he deems intolerable to influence, adulterate, or dilute the content of the Judaism he believes in. And these two things are clearly related: precisely *because* he frees himself from dirtying his own legal hands with practical sanctions, Maimonides is able to maintain his focus on core Jewish principles in their most ideal form. The only definition of Judaism that really matters is the pursuit and understanding of God to the utmost extent possible. No sanctions also means no need to accommodate or adjust toward or compromise with those who do not understand or agree with his particular, unique reading of the Exodus Covenant.

Genesis Jews and Exodus Judaism

Even more fundamentally, Maimonides cannot follow his rabbinic predecessors in *synthesizing* Genesis and Exodus into his system. For him, what makes Judaism *Judaism* is neither a mythic bond to a common ancestry nor a minimal or general Exodus commitment. Judaism is a very particular set of beliefs and aspirations, most significantly the pursuit and understanding of God to the utmost extent possible. This is the only definition of Judaism that really matters, the unique feature that invests it with its essential value. So while Maimonides does *integrate* Genesis and Exodus, a *synthesis* proves impossible. It would require accepting an end product with features of each covenant—in particular, the non–God centered reality of Genesis Jews.

His code of law for all Jews begins with an elaboration on the required knowledge of God.[22] No conversion to Judaism is possible without the convert studying this in great length.[23] Furthermore, even one who is born a Jew only becomes fully Jewish by embracing all of his Thirteen Principles of Faith.[24]

In Maimonides's worldview, both Genesis and Exodus have their own place (parallel to the modern distinction between Judaism as a national identity and Judaism as a religion). The embedded duality is resolved by allotting to each its own "kingdom." Jews are members of a nation by birth—the inheritance of Genesis. Genesis, however, does not shape who Jews ought to be—that is exclusively an Exodus domain. As a result, one must embrace Jews of all stripes and attempt to bring them back into the fold of "true Jewish beliefs."

This lack of synthesis, and subsequent elevation of Exodus within the Jewish story, has many implications. A positive one is the removal of any racial vestiges to Jewishness as a byproduct of its Genesis roots. In his famous Letter to Obadiah the Convert, who wondered whether, given his convert status, he was permitted to recite in his prayers, like all other Jews, words like, "*our* God," "the God of *our* forefathers," or "who has sanctified *us* though Your commandments," Maimonides offers the following remarkable response:

> Yes, you may say all this . . . in the same way as every Jew by birth. . . . In the same way that he [Abraham] converted his contemporaries through his words and teaching, he converts future generations through his testament. . . . *There is no difference whatsoever between you and us.* . . . Do not consider your origin as inferior. While we are the descendants of Abraham, Isaac, and Jacob, you derive [your Jewishness directly] from God through whose words the world was created.[25]

Even though converts do not share in the ethnocentric narrative implied by the Genesis Covenant, they are full and equal members in the Exodus Covenant. And since the latter ultimately defines Jewishness, there is no difference whatsoever between one born a Jew and one who chooses to become one.

That said, in time, Maimonides's demand that faithful Jews practice tolerance of Jews while endeavoring to reorient those who have seemingly been misdirected would prove to be inherently unstable and unsustainable. Without a more inclusive definition of Judaism, and/or a more nuanced notion of boundaries, the centrifugal forces of Exodus changes not only one's definition of Judaism but of Jews as well. As we will see in the next chapter, this is precisely one of the consequences of denominationalism in the Exodus-centered Jewishness of emancipated Western European Jewry.

6

Emancipation from the Genesis Covenant

While a Genesis sensibility is not defined by tragedy, it is often rein-forced by it.

One of my strongest experiences of its covenantal pull is at the military cemetery every year on Yom Hazikaron, Israel's Memorial Day, when I stand with my sister and our family around her husband's grave, together with thousands of other Israelis, all mourning their loved ones. The cemetery in Ra'anana, a small city near Tel Aviv, is not large—fewer than a hundred soldiers are buried there. As the years pass, the families have expanded, and each soldier's group of visitors grows. Today, there is not a square inch to spare.

The military ceremony itself is dull and alienating. But, at 11 a.m., when the countrywide two-minute siren pierces the air, humbling everyone into a mournful silence, the experience of being with my people is profound. In cemeteries across the country, in every home, business, and street, even on the highways, the whole country comes to a stop. Jews of every color, nationality, denomination, and ideology stand still together, bound not only by shared tragedy but by a sense of shared identity that transcends, at least for that moment, all of our divisions.

Well, almost every Jew. Some Jews, principally from within the Haredi community, do not stand during the sounding of the siren, do not stop walking, working, learning, talking.

Granted, there are ideological explanations for their actions founded in Haredi understandings of Exodus. Some explain that the ceremonial moments of silence and standing at attention during the siren are not the way Jews traditionally mourn, and it is forbidden to emulate non-Jewish customs. But does this concern outweigh the obligation of loyalty demanded by Genesis? Even if Haredi Jews don't serve in the army, aren't they obligated to acknowledge some level of solidarity with our soldiers and families who sacrificed everything?

Refusing to stand silently on Israel's Memorial Day paints much of Haredi society as fully detached from Genesis's covenantal bonds. They are Exodus Jews without the foundation and counterweight of Genesis.

It is important to understand, however, that this Exodus-imbalanced Judaism is not a twentieth or twenty-first-century phenomenon. It did not begin with the advent of Zionism and the creation of the State of Israel. Its roots are planted in the debates and denominations deriving from Jewish Emancipation in late eighteenth-century and early nineteenth-century Western Europe.

"One Must Refuse Everything to the Jews as a Nation": Western Europe and the Condition of Citizenship

Throughout the Middle Ages, Jews were afforded different levels of autonomy and self-governance but were almost never accepted as equals anywhere they lived. Status and rights, if there were any, were directly tied to one's faith, and "Jew" was always the wrong box to check, guaranteed to leave one on the outside looking in.

With the formation of modern nation-states in parts of Western Europe, however, this reality began to shift. No longer vassals of a lord and servants to his dictates, within the nation-state all could now make an ostensibly equal claim to "citizenship"—a form of belonging defined not only by religious or ideological factors but physical borders and adherence to the laws of the state. The process of including Jews as citizens in Western Europe was termed Emancipation.

One of the leading centers of Emancipation was France, which as early as the 1780s began to discuss the issue of citizenship for Jews. It did so, however, in the context of a stark zero-sum game: one could either continue to be a part of the Jewish nation or become a full-fledged citizen of France. The two, the French nobleman and politician Count Clermont-Tonnerre declared in 1789, were mutually exclusive:

We must refuse everything to the Jews as a nation and accord everything to Jews as individuals. . . . They must be citizens. . . . If they do not want to be citizens, they should say so, and then, we should banish them. It is repugnant to have in the state an association of non-citizens, and a nation within the nation. . . . In short, Sirs, the presumed status of every man resident in a country is to be a citizen.[1]

To Clermont-Tonnerre, the Jews' outsider status was the byproduct of their own self-alienation and loyalty to Jewish national identity. His stipulation that Jews could acquire citizenship by terminating their distinct national affiliation and integrating into the French nation-state as individual Jews contained both an exciting opportunity (to break the isolation and otherness that defined Jewish existence) and a significant challenge for Jews (at what price?). Could they be Jews as individuals, separate from their national identity?

Or, to use the categories put forth in this book—could they limit their Jewishness to embracing the aspirational framework of the Exodus Covenant as individuals, while adopting French citizenship as their primary collective identity? To do so would mean untethering the ethnic ties and loyalty bonds that foster a collective Jewish national identity. The Genesis Covenant demands unconditional loyalty to the Jewish people; could the Jewish people set aside their Genesis identity and become unconditionally bound and loyal to their fellow Frenchmen instead?

"Can a Christian Marry a Jewess, or a Jew a Christian Woman?": The Genesis of French-Jewish Identity

In 1806 Emperor Napoleon convened a group of Jewish communal representatives (The Assembly of Jewish Notables) to address a series of queries designed to clarify the suitability of Jews for citizenship. He sent official commissioners to this assembly to investigate the extent to which Jews in France were willing to, and capable of, becoming Frenchmen:

His Majesty, the Emperor and King, having named us Commissioners to transact whatever relates to you [the Jewish community], has this day sent us to this assembly to acquaint you with his intentions. . . . Far from considering the government in which you live as a power against which you should be on your guard, you will assist it with your experience and cooperate with it in all the good it intends; thus you will prove that, following the example of all Frenchmen, you do not seclude yourself from the rest of mankind.

Our most ardent wish is to be able to report to the Emperor that amongst individuals of the Jewish persuasion, he can reckon as *many faithful subjects, determined to conform in everything to the laws and to the morality, which ought to regulate the conduct of all Frenchmen.*[2]

The ghetto walls could be dismantled. The extreme limits imposed on Jews (where they could live, how they could support themselves) might be traded in for the dignified mantle of equal citizenship. For the first time in the many centuries of the diaspora, Jews could be defined not as "outsiders" but as Frenchmen. A "Jew of the Prussian Empire" could now—finally—become a "French Jew."

Before that could happen, however, the assembly had to address Napoleon's telling questions: Can a Jewess marry a Christian, or a Jew a Christian woman—or has the law ordered that Jews only marry among themselves? In the eyes of the Jews, are Frenchmen considered as brethren or strangers? In either case, what conduct does their law prescribe toward Frenchmen not of their religion? Do the Jews born in France, and treated by the laws as French citizens, consider France their country? Are they bound to defend it? Are they bound to obey the laws and to follow the directions of their civil code?[3]

Napoleon's questions were designed to elicit a clear answers to fundamental matters: the nature of Jewish collective identity, the place and relative prominence of French identity by comparison, and the implications of this new configuration for their shared social life. To paraphrase Napoleon: *I am willing to accept you as Frenchmen, but can you join us fully and unequivocally as Frenchmen, or does your commitment to your fellow Jews define you principally as a member of the Jewish nation, thereby creating insurmountable boundaries and dual loyalties?*

"Frenchmen Professing the Religion of Moses": Citizenship Supplants Genesis

In response to Napoleon, the Assembly of Jewish Notables articulated an answer that radically recalibrated the relationship between the Covenants of Genesis and Exodus:

> The assembly, impressed with a deep sense of gratitude, love, respect, and admiration for the sacred person of His Imperial and Royal Majesty, declares, in the name of all *Frenchmen professing the religion of Moses*, that they are fully determined to prove worthy of the favors His Majesty intends to give them.[4]

Employing the logic of Maimonides and extending its implications for their own age, members of the assembly argued that the essence of Judaism is its Exodus Covenant—the aspirational framework of "the religion of Moses"—and therefore they were free to reformulate a new "non-Jewish Genesis-type covenant" with their fellow Frenchmen, henceforth identifying as Frenchmen of Jewish persuasion. Jews were members of a religion, not a separate nation. Furthermore, they argued, Judaism's Exodus ethos was *itself* fully aligned with and adaptable to the fundamental laws and principles of the French nation-state—thus enabling the Jews to unequivocally embrace their newfound French identities.

In order to actualize the citizen rights and benefits of the modern nation-state, the very idea of the Genesis Jew—an identity connecting fellow Jews to a story of shared ethnic roots and bound to each other by unconditional familial ties—was relegated to the past, and the Exodus Covenant expanded to eclipse it as *the* central aspect of Jewish identity.[5]

Assimilation and the Demise of Exodus Commitments

This drift away from the collective bonds of the Genesis Covenant, initially triggered by the opportunity of citizenship, was dramatically accelerated by a second byproduct of Western European Emancipation: denominationalism.

As Jews were increasingly welcomed into their local communities, not only in France but in Germany and elsewhere, they did not merely trade out their Jewish Genesis identities for a French or German one. They also began to "assimilate" the dominant culture's ethos—its values, aspirations, and practices—while jettisoning many elements of the Exodus Covenant, especially aspects of Jewish law that reinforced a particularistic identity. Jews wanted to speak the language of their fellow citizens and be educated on the terms of their adopted homelands. Dietary laws, which prevented Jews from breaking bread with the "outside" world, were deemed onerous and counterproductive. Sabbath restrictions on work, which undercut Jews' ability to compete in the marketplace, were deemed untenable self-sabotage.

Judaism could now be held up against the larger culture, a world still perhaps "outside" but no longer beyond the pale; the world in which they had begun, after nearly two millennia in exile, to live. In this newly open marketplace of identity, could Judaism compete? For many Jews, the answer was a resounding no. Having already discarded their limiting Genesis identities, they began to relinquish their Exodus Covenant responsibilities as well.

The Reform Movement: Anti-Assimilationist Trailblazers

The Reform movement proffered the first response to this assimilationist trend. One of the first "outreach" (*kiruv*) movements in modern Jewish history, it sought to solve the conundrum, *How do we create a Judaism that the new emancipated enlightened Jew of Western Europe would want to belong to?*

Initially, their suggestions were relatively minor. To lower the barriers to participation and put their more assimilated coreligionists at ease, they created forms of worship that would feel cultured, akin to those attended by the Jews' Christian peers. They repositioned the synagogue altar (*bimah*) from the middle to the front of the synagogue, facing the congregation; they prayed in the vernacular and enhanced the Sabbath service with musical instruments (though in that era, only played by a non-Jew).

Other changes were both more pointed and more sweeping. One of the most significant liturgical shifts involved the removal of prayers for messianic redemption and the return of God's Temple to Jerusalem. For the modern, emancipated Jew, such aspirations were embarrassingly primitive. Moreover, such Genesis-inspired nationalist aspirations to "return" to Jerusalem could be taken as a sign of disloyalty to the nation-state that had welcomed them as full citizens.[6]

The essential impulse of this extensive, coordinated communal effort to keep Jews Jewish in the new environment was to reformulate an Exodus Covenant that the new Jewish citizens of France, Germany, or Hungary could accept. Given that these Jews had widely rejected their Genesis identities in favor of their newfound national citizenship identities, Reform movement leaders wanted to guard against further slippage under the Exodus Covenant. But this accommodating move unleashed profound critical backlash from more traditional Jews, giving rise to a phenomenon that would further entrench the centrality of the Exodus Covenant at the expense of Genesis: Jewish denominationalism.

"They Living Their Lives and We Ours": Denominationalism Goes Sectarian

In response to the Reform movement's innovations, the prominent Hungarian halakhic authority Rabbi Moshe Schreiber (known as the Hatam Sofer) composed a furious array of legal responsa that rejected not only the legitimacy of the Reform movement's positions but the legitimacy of Reform Jews themselves. In the 1820s he proclaimed:

> If their [Reform Jews'] fate were in *our* hands, I would be of the opinion to separate them from *our* midst, to desist from giving *our* daughters to their sons, and their sons to *our* daughters, so as to prevent *our* being drawn after them. . . . They living their lives and we *ours*.[7]

With his introduction of a distinction between "their" fate and "ours" (meaning his own followers), Schreiber stripped the Genesis Covenant of its raison d'être. The same could be said of Maimonides, but Schreiber crossed into territory Maimonides never approached. In Schreiber's formulation, once one identified as a Reform Jew, one has functionally exited the Jewish paradigm and become a member of a different religion.

His ideology had Genesis-breaking consequences. In the latter part of the nineteenth century, Schreiber's students formally applied to the Hungarian government to have their community be recognized as a Jewish religion distinct from Reform Judaism. From that point on, they petitioned, there should no longer be a single unified Jewish collective, but rather two separate entities: the Reform and the Orthodox.[8] While formally rejected, they went on to form their own denomination, what is known today as Haredi or ultra-Orthodox Judaism. Thus Jewish denominationalism replaced Jewishness as the singular collective.

While denominationalism had initially emerged out of an overactive Exodus consciousness, Orthodoxy's increasing insularity led it to develop a de facto exclusive Genesis Covenant of its own. Basic Jewishness was now contingent on denominational affiliation: if you don't share my denomination's core Exodus commitments, we don't share a Genesis Covenant at all. Instead of *Israel even though they have sinned, are still Israel*, the ideology now posited that the *Orthodox, even though they have sinned, are still Orthodox*.[9]

The End of Genesis?

In the same era, the Reform movement in America was also driving Exodus consciousness to an even more extreme conclusion: dropping Genesis from its definition of Jewishness altogether. As its pivotal inaugural Pittsburgh Platform of 1886 declared:

> We recognize, in the modern era of universal culture of heart and intellect, the approaching of the realization of Israel's great Messianic hope for the establishment of the kingdom of truth, justice, and peace amongst all men. We consider ourselves *no longer a nation, but a religious community*, and therefore expect neither a return to Palestine, nor a sacrificial worship under the sons of Aaron, nor the restoration of any of the laws concerning the Jewish state.[10]

For Reform Jews beginning to experience hints of a promised American Dream, the traditional messianic hope had become partially realized—and the remainder rendered obsolete. The idea of a distinct people, bound unconditionally to each other by a Genesis Covenant, seemed anachronistic against the backdrop of modern universalism and reason whose seeds were currently bearing the palpable messianic fruit of "truth, justice, and peace amongst all men" in American society. As a result, they declared both the end of Judaism's ethnically grounded Genesis Covenant and the founding of Jewishness on a universalist religious rendering of the Exodus Covenant. Jews were no longer a nation with particular ties of loyalty and concern, but a subcommunity within America, defined by shared spiritual and moral aspirations for the world.

By the end of the nineteenth century, for possibly the first time in postbiblical Jewish history, the two-thousand-year dance between Genesis and Exodus seemed in jeopardy in many mainstream Ashkenazi Jewish communities in Western Europe and North America.

Instead of the Genesis Covenant defining Jewishness as an expression simply of who you are—a member of a community chosen by God and bound together by a story of shared ethnic roots—Jewish identity was grounded exclusively in the Exodus Covenant: a system of beliefs, practices and now denominational affiliations.

Thus, Emancipation's dramatic promise to radically transform the status and condition of the Jews also significantly shifted the meaning of Jewishness and threatened its collective nature. Had it actually been fulfilled, there would be no answer to the question, *Who are the Jews?*, for the Jewish people as a singular collective would have ceased to exist, replaced by multiple Jewish denominations and communities of faith.

Paradoxically, Jewishness was saved from this predicament by European Emancipation's failure.

"A Certain Cultured Idea": Legally Emancipated, Culturally Enchained

The hope of Emancipation in Western Europe, with its promise of social equality, was soon squelched with the resurgence of a stubbornly virulent antisemitism whose brief latency had been temporarily mistaken for a cure. As the Zionist leader Max Nordau put it, Jews were legally emancipated but remained culturally enchained:

> In order to produce its full effect, Emancipation should first have been completed in sentiment, before it was declared by law. But this was not the case. . . . The Emancipation of Jews was pronounced, not through a fraternal feeling for the Jews, but because logic demanded it. . . . In this manner, Jews were emancipated in Europe, not from an inner necessity, but in imitation of a political fashion; not because the people had decided from their hearts to stretch out a brotherly hand to the Jews, but because leading spirits had accepted a certain cultured idea which required that Jewish emancipation should figure also in the Statute book.[11]

Legally—on paper—Jews were offered the possibility of full citizenship; culturally they remained outsiders. Even as they worked to relinquish their Genesis-Jewish bonds and integrate their religious identity with newfound citizenship in their nation-states, antisemites held tight to viewing them as non-Frenchmen, non-German, non-English. Moreover, the category of antisemitism itself, which entered European parlance at the end of the nineteenth century, categorized Jews with an essentialist Genesis hue—as a group with a distinct *Semitic* origin, destined to be forever stateless foreigners in Europe.[12]

7

Zionism and the Resurrection of Genesis

In my capacity as president of the Shalom Hartman Institute, I frequently travel to the United States and Canada to give lectures about Jewish identity, Jewish thought, and Israel. When I mention that I am a Zionist, I am sometimes challenged: why use that term? After all, some people say, Zionism's central aim, to create a homeland for the Jewish people in Israel, has been fulfilled, so the Zionist movement has no contemporary significance. Recently, when teaching a group of Judaic scholars in the United States, I was asked to not use the term for a different reason: it connotes a justification of Israel's oppressive occupation of Palestinians in Judea and Samaria.

As I hope to show in this chapter, Zionism is neither a movement exclusively relegated to the past nor a reflexive endorsement of the Israeli government's policies. It primarily and most meaningfully represents an expanded vision of Jewishness for modern Jews: a far more dynamic and inclusive vision than the asymmetrical, Exodus-heavy imbalance initiated by Maimonides and reenforced by nineteenth-century denominationalism. As such, Zionism is essential for Jews worldwide. To engage with Zionism and Israel is not merely a question of loyalty to a country: it involves, rather, embracing the critical place both Genesis and Exodus continue to play in the story we tell ourselves about ourselves.

"One People": Herzl Revives Genesis-Jewishness

For Theodore Herzl, the founder of the modern Zionist movement, Europe's seemingly insatiable appetite for antisemitism brought home with searing clarity that the hope and aspiration of Emancipation would not be fulfilled. Christian Europe would never assimilate Jews as equal citizens. While Jews might have been willing to change their core loyalties, antisemites were not.

His solution to the "Jewish Problem" was a logical outgrowth of this insight: relinquish the aspiration for acceptance and instead "create for the Jewish people a publicly and legally assured home in Palestine."[1] As Herzl argued in his foundational Zionist manifesto, *The Jewish State*:

> [I]n vain do we make the same sacrifices of life and property as our fellow-citizens; in vain do we strive to increase the fame of our native land in science and art, or her wealth by trade and commerce. In countries where we have lived for centuries we are still cried down as strangers. . . . Everything tends, in fact, to one and the same conclusion, which is clearly enunciated in that classic Berlin phrase: "*Juden Raus!*" (Out with the Jews!).
>
> I shall now put the question in the briefest possible form: are we to "get out" now, and where to? Or may we yet remain? And, how long? . . . We are one people—our enemies have made us one without our consent, as repeatedly happens in history. Distress binds us together, and, thus united, we suddenly discover our strength. Yes, we are strong enough to form a State, and indeed, a model State. . . . Let the sovereignty be granted us over a portion of the globe large enough to satisfy the rightful requirements of a nation; the rest we shall manage for ourselves. . . . We shall live at last as free men on our own soil, and die peacefully in our own homes.[2]

For Herzl, the Emancipated aspiration to replace a Genesis Jewish identity with a particular European national one had failed. Jewish survival would require an honest reckoning with a reality always understood by the antisemites of history: in others' eyes, we were, and always would be, a separate, irreducible community with our own distinct national identity. Herzl elaborated, "I think the Jewish question is no more a social than a religious one, notwithstanding that it sometimes takes these and other forms. It is a national question, which can only be solved by making it a political world-question to be discussed and settled by the civilized nations of the world in council. *We are a people—one people.*"³

With this re-embrace of the Genesis Jewish identity—one of Jewish history's great U-turns—Herzl and other early Zionists restored this conception of Jewishness to the center of our collective self-understanding. In doing so, they also imbued it with a particularly modern twist. Inspired by the emerging nation states spreading across Europe in the nineteenth century, the secular political wing of Zionism separated Genesis from its religious covenantal roots and translated it into modern nationalist terms. In this framework, the Jewish people were not primarily a collective in a covenantal relationship with God but members of a nation with historical bonds to each other and a right to a sovereign state in their ancestral homeland.

The conceptual wedding of Genesis Jewishness to the modern political invention of the nation-state—what I call "Genesis Zionism"—was neither necessary nor self-evident. Indeed, it was the essential innovation of Political Zionism, which aimed to create a sovereign Jewish state.

While of course a Genesis sensibility had long existed independent of Political Zionism, the reverse was not possible. At its core, Political Zionism was a Genesis Zionism, an ideology that viewed Jews as essentially one people, a nation, by virtue of shared destiny. "We are one people—our enemies have made us one without our consent, as repeatedly happens in history. Distress binds us together."⁴

Thus the Genesis Covenant served as the foundation for the idea of a homeland for the Jewish people—a place where Jews could simply be. Be safe. Be free from persecution. Be normal.

"Declaration of Sympathy": The Balfour Paradox

The Zionist idea continued mainly as an internal Jewish aspiration until after World War I—when the British, who received the Mandate over then-Palestine, embraced the synergy between a Genesis Jewish identity and Jewish nationalism and gave it legitimacy in the international political arena. In the landmark Balfour Declaration of 1917, the British government essentially accepted not only the core aspirations of the Zionist movement but its reasoning as well:

> Dear Lord Rothschild, I have much pleasure in conveying to you, on behalf of His Majesty's Government, the following declaration of sympathy with Jewish Zionist aspirations which has been submitted to, and approved by, the cabinet. His Majesty's Government views with favour the establishment in Palestine of a national home for the Jewish people.[5]

This "sympathy" with the Zionist aspiration became internationally accepted with the League of Nations Mandate for Palestine of 1922.[6]

It is important to notice, however, that the success of Zionism in Europe was founded on a bitter paradox: its embrace entailed an official recognition of the fundamental alien status of the European Jew. Emancipation, built on the premise of full political and social integration, should have made a statement like Balfour's incoherent, obsolete. How could a nation-state (Britain) that had formally accepted these members of a faith minority as full citizens still conceive of the idea of an independent national homeland for them? Britain's answer to the Zionist movement's claims should have been: *There is no need for a national homeland for the Jewish people: Jews, you are full citizens where you are.*

Yet despite Emancipation (and precisely aligned with Zionist reasoning), this was not Britain's response. The reaction betrayed that Britain had never stopped seeing Jews through a Genesis lens, as foreign nationals within its midst. If the Jews *want* to leave . . . wouldn't it be better for everyone?

Not surprisingly, British cabinet member Edwin Montagu, a textbook "Englishman of Jewish persuasion," found this development profoundly upsetting: "Zionism has always seemed to me to be a mischievous political creed, untenable by any patriotic citizen of the United Kingdom,"[7] he argued. His logic made sense. Zionism was accepted as a national movement of the Jewish people—first by the British Empire and then ultimately by the League of Nations—precisely because of Emancipation's failure. Vis à vis Western civilization, the Jews were still "them."

Genesis Zionism and Exodus Zionism

While initially Zionism challenged Judaism and the Jewish people to reengage with their Genesis sensibilities and often called for a prioritization of Genesis over Exodus, it would not be correct to see it as an exclusively Genesis-based movement. A broad, rich, radically innovative religious and secular "Torah" developed within Zionist thought, offering diverse visions of the new Jews and Judaism that a return to the homeland would enable. Both Genesis and Exodus sensibilities became integral to the broader Zionist project. The former was channeled into a political Zionism that prioritized the work of establishing a homeland for the Jewish nation. The latter was translated into cultural Zionism, which I refer to as "Exodus Zionism"—emphasizing the renaissance in Jewish life that could/would be effectuated once the Jewish state was established.

Yet, even as Genesis-Political Zionism and Exodus-Cultural Zionism prioritized different dimensions of the Zionist movement, they developed side by side and often coexisted in the same person. The Cultural-Zionist wing was founded by Ahad Ha'am (Asher Zvi Hirsch Ginsberg), known as the "secular rabbi of Zionism." "It is not only the Jews who have come out of the ghetto," he famously declared. "Judaism has come out too."[8] In his view, the task of a Jewish community living in Palestine (a community, and not necessarily a sovereign nation) was to effectuate its spiritual redemption. Emancipation, meanwhile, presented a new and powerful threat to the Jewish people's spiritual and collective identity:

When it [the Jewish people] leaves the ghetto walls, it is in danger of losing its essential being or, at the very least, its national unity. It is in danger of being split up into many kinds of Judaism, each with a different character and life, as there are countries of the dispersion. Judaism is, therefore, in a quandary: It can no longer tolerate the *Galut* form [i.e., ghetto existence] which it had to take on, in obedience to its will-to-live, when it was exiled from its own country; but, without that form, its life is in danger. So, it seeks to return to its historic center. . . . Then, from this center, the spirit of Judaism will radiate to the great circumference, to all the communities of the Diaspora, to inspire them with new life and to preserve the over-all unity of our people. When our national culture in Palestine has attained that level, we may be confident that it will produce men in the Land of Israel itself who will be able, at a favorable moment, to establish a State there—one which will not merely be a State of Jews but a really Jewish state.[9]

For Ahad Ha-Am, the principal goal of Zionism was to breathe new life into Judaism's Exodus Covenant by reconnecting it to its Genesis roots (in his words "national unity") by creating a cultural center in Palestine that would in turn reconnect all of Jewish life worldwide to its national culture. This was not, however, to the exclusion of political Zionism; to the contrary, he too hoped for a Jewish state:

Hibbat Zion, [the pre-Zionist movement which advocated for Jewish settlement in Palestine] no less than "Zionism," wants a Jewish state and believes in the possibility of the establishment of a Jewish state in the future. . . . "Zionism," therefore, begins its work with political propaganda; Hibbat Zion begins with national culture, because only *through* the national culture and *for its sake* can a Jewish State be established in such a way as to correspond with the will and the needs of the Jewish people.[10]

For Ahad Ha'am, the nation state was not necessary for solving the Jewish problem of excessive denominationalism: the Jews' return to their homeland was sufficient. Still, it remained an ideal. But if there was to be a Jewish nation state, it could not "merely" be a state of Jews; it had to be a Jewish state with a Jewish national cultural agenda. For this agenda to succeed, it had to forge a new bond between Genesis and Exodus.

Similarly, Herzl, the leader of the Political Zionist wing, also avoided an either/or approach, developing his own vision of Exodus Zionism while doggedly pursuing his primary political-Genesis agenda. In addition to *The Jewish State*, his political manifesto, Herzl penned *Altneuland* (*The Old-New Land*), a utopian novel depicting life in the future Jewish State. Not merely the embodiment of Genesis sensibilities, *Altneuland* envisioned an aspirational Exodus renaissance as well:

> Friedrich's first visit to the Temple was on a Friday evening. David had engaged rooms for the party at one of the best hotels near the Jaffa Gate, and at sundown invited his guests to go with him to the Temple. Friedrich walked ahead with Miriam, David and Sarah following. The streets which at noon had been alive with traffic were now suddenly stilled. Very few motor cars were to be seen; all the shops were closed. Slowly and peacefully the Sabbath fell upon the bustling city. Throngs of worshipers wended their way to the Temple and to the many synagogues in the Old City and the New, there to pray to the God whose banner Israel had borne throughout the world for thousands of years.

> The spell of the Sabbath was over the Holy City, now freed from the filth, noise and vile odors that had so often revolted devout pilgrims of all creeds when, after long and trying journeys, they reached their goal. In the old days they had had to endure many disgusting sights before they could reach their shrines. All was different now. There were no longer private dwellings in the Old City; the lanes and the streets were beautifully paved and cared for. All the buildings were devoted to religious and benevolent

purposes—hospices for pilgrims of all denominations. Muslim, Jewish, and Christian welfare institutions, hospitals, clinics stood side by side. In the middle of a great square was the splendid Peace Palace, where international congresses of peace-lovers and scientists were held, for Jerusalem was now a home for all the best strivings of the human spirit: for Faith, Love, Knowledge.[11]

True to his Genesis Zionist priorities, however (and unlike Ahad Ha'am), for Herzl, this renaissance of Judaism and the development of an Exodus Zionism were only possible through the establishment of a Jewish national state that redeemed the Jews from their diasporic physical enslavement:

> Jews had prayed in many temples, splendid and simple, in all the languages of the Diaspora. The invisible God, the Omnipresent, must have been equally near to them everywhere. Yet only here was the true Temple. Why? Because only here had the Jews built up a free commonwealth in which they could strive for the loftiest human aims. They had had their own communities in the Ghettos, to be sure; but there they lived under oppression. In the *Judengasse*, [Jewish Quarter/Lane] they had been without honor and without rights; and when they left it, they ceased to be Jews. Freedom and a sense of solidarity were both needed. Only then could the Jews erect a House to the Almighty God whom children envision thus and wise men so, but who is everywhere present as the Will-to-Good.[12]

For Herzl, Genesis and Exodus Zionism were integrated, but with Genesis dominant and Exodus conditional upon it.

"Rather the Character of Luxury": The Necessity of Genesis

Herzl's position ultimately prevailed. And the more it trained its focus on the actual work of settling and protecting the Jews who made aliyah to Palestine, and forming a state, the more dominant it became. As Ze'ev Jabotinsky, the leader of Revisionist Zionism—which insisted upon the Jewish right to sovereignty over the whole of Eretz Yisrael, equated to Mandatory Palestine and Transjordan—famously declared in his address before the British Palestinian Royal Commission in London in 1937:

> The conception of Zionism which I have the honor to represent here is based on what I should call the humanitarian aspect. By that I do not mean to say that we do not respect the other, the purely spiritual aspect of the Jewish nationalism, such as the desire for self-expression, the rebuilding of a Hebrew culture, or creating some "model community of which the Jewish people could be proud." All that, of course, is most important: *but as compared with our actual needs and our real position in the world today, all that has rather the character of luxury.*[13]

In brief, in the face of the immediate need to provide refuge for the persecuted Jews of Europe, all discussion of Exodus Zionism was a luxury the Jewish people could not afford.

What was true in the 1930s became doubly true in the '40s as the Nazi plan to exterminate European Jewry unfolded, and after World War II, when the future Jewish nation state strove to serve as the place of refuge for the survivors. The need for this prioritization continued into the 1950s, as the state stretched itself to accommodate the flood of Jews fleeing persecution in Arab and Muslim lands and struggled to become economically, politically, and militarily viable in the midst of continuous wars against seemingly impossible odds. Even today, when pursuing Exodus Zionism in the State of Israel arguably no longer qualifies as a luxury, a great many Israelis insist that the range of threats to the existential viability of the state require Jews' complete, sustained vigilance.

This sensibility ultimately gave rise to the ascendency of Israel's political right—for whom security issues and state borders are foremost concerns—toward the end of the twentieth and beginning of the twenty-first century. No modern politician has embodied and addressed these concerns more than Benjamin Netanyahu, the longest serving prime minister in the history of Israel. On January 23, 2020, for example, he spoke at the World Holocaust Forum:

> I wish to assure again our people and all our friends, Israel will do whatever it must do to defend our state, defend our people and defend the Jewish future. Ladies and gentlemen, as the Prime Minister of Israel, I promise that the words "Never again" will be no empty slogan but an eternal call to action. With this call to action, we will continue our marvelous journey of the revival of our people that emerged from the valley of dry bones. From bones [*atzamot*] to independence [*atzmaut*], and from independence to strength [*otzmah*], from Auschwitz to Jerusalem, from darkness—to light.[14]

For the majority of Israelis, the words Jews have recited at Passover seders across the millennia, "Bechol dor va-dor kamim aleynu lehalotienu"—in every generation there arise those who want to destroy us—feel as relevant today as at any other point in Jewish history. This is why the dominant sentiment of a wide spectrum of Israelis regarding Netanyahu's October 2015 address to the UN General Assembly was that he was speaking truth—*their* truth—to world powers:

> Seventy years after the murder of six million Jews, Iran's rulers promise to destroy my country. Murder my people. And the response from this body, the response from nearly every one of the governments represented here has been absolutely nothing! Utter silence! Deafening silence. . . .
>
> But throughout our history, the Jewish people have learned the heavy price of silence. And as the Prime Minister of the Jewish State, as someone who knows that history, I refuse to be silent. . . .

I'll say it again: The days when the Jewish people remained passive in the face of genocidal enemies—those days are over. . . .

I know that preventing Iran from developing nuclear weapons remains the official policy of the international community. But no one should question Israel's determination to defend itself against those who seek our destruction. For in every generation, there were those who rose up to destroy our people. . . .

So, here's my message to the rulers of Iran: Your plan to destroy Israel will fail. Israel will not permit any force on earth to threaten its future.

And here's my message to all the countries represented here: Whatever resolutions you may adopt in this building, whatever decisions you may take in your capitals, Israel will do whatever it must do to defend our state and to defend our people.[15]

Israel has many diverse aspirations for its Exodus Zionism, but, aligned with Herzl and Jabotinsky's original Zionist vision—because of an acute awareness of the Jews' history of fighting near constant battles in a region that perceives it as colonial conquerors and aliens and continues to call for "Juden raus"—it sees its first and primary task to survive and serve as a place where every and any Jew can simply Be: be safe, be welcome, be at home with the Jewish people.

This commitment is further exemplified in the speech every IDF chief of staff delivers at Auschwitz at the culmination of the March of the Living, an annual event bringing young Jews from around the world together with Israeli soldiers, first to Auschwitz and then to Israel. The March of the Living is designed to signify the core role of Israel as *the* antidote to the Holocaust—both the one that already occurred and any the future may hold:

With hundreds of "Witnesses in Uniform" by my side—joining the thousands of representatives of the IDF who come here every year . . .—the defending force of the Jewish people, reborn in its land—with tight lips, a hoarse voice and tears in my eyes, yet still standing tall, I salute to the ashes of our people and vow: "Never Again." . . . Never again shall we stand helpless, crying for the mercy of others. Never again shall we beg to be defended. Never again shall we allow our sons and daughters, our parents and grandparents to be erased from the face of the earth. . . . I vow to uphold the responsibility of the Israel Defense Forces—never again to allow Jewish blood to be spilled in vain.[16]

The job of the Israel Defense Forces is to be the *Jewish people's* defense forces, if and when the time comes. Changing this priority, for many, *has rather the character of luxury*.

Emerging out of Exodus-centered European-Enlightened Jewry, Zionism reminded Jews what the antisemites of history never forgot: Jews are "a people who dwells apart, not reckoned among the nations" (Num. 23:9), with distinct bonds of loyalty and care for each other. Embracing this reality, Zionism reestablished Jewish identity on its Genesis bedrock.

Zionism hoped to bring Genesis back to the center of Jewish identity alongside a reimagined discourse around the Exodus Covenant. It hoped to solve the problem of Jewish collective existence so that Jews could reach new heights of reimagining the content of Exodus Zionism. But a large segment of Israel society has postponed this synthesis to a tomorrow that has yet to arrive.

8

The North American Homeland between Europe and Zion(ism)

For much of Jewish history, Jews prayed for "Next Year in Jerusalem," yearning for redemption from their tortuous, meandering diasporic existence. The Zionist movement sought to actualize the millennia-old dream to—next year—be a free and independent people in Jerusalem.

For Europeans, the need for a homeland for the Jewish people was coherent since that homeland was not to be found on the European continent. By contrast, to grasp the North American Jewish experience is to feel in one's bones that the long-delayed Jewish redemption could occur in North America. Unlike most European Jewish communities, the American Jewish experience did not come to an end with the Holocaust. America appeared to uphold the promise—of Jews being at home as a minority—that Europe could never fulfill.

In a broad sense, the American Jewish experience has been fundamentally not one of diaspora, but of home. For much of its history, America was the place one made aliyah *to*, not a place one made aliyah *from*. "Next Year in Jerusalem" referred to—best case—a family vacation, a Federation mission, a summer trip, a gap-year experience.

Nowhere is this unique sense of Jewish "at-home-ness" more evident than in one of the signature modern institutions of American Jewish life: AIPAC. By the end of the twentieth century, and continuing into the first part of the twenty-first, the largest Jewish convocation had been the AIPAC Policy Conference in Washington, which brought over fifteen thousand Jews annually to lobby Congress on behalf of Israel. Not a foreign intervention, AIPAC is built on the notion that strong political, economic, and military bilateral ties between Israel and America are in America's interest.[1] As such, the Jews who attended the conference and support AIPAC, and who lobby Congress on Israel's behalf, are saying: our interests are America's interests, and we have a voice in deciding and shaping what is in America's interests. America is home, *our* home.

In this second Jewish homeland, Genesis and Exodus became intertwined in a uniquely North American Jewish story.

"We Consider Ourselves No Longer a Nation, but a Religious Community": The Genesis of Jewish Americans

The Zionists were not the only doubters that Emancipation could ever come to full fruition in Christian Europe. A much larger constituency of Jews shared this sentiment: the over two million who moved from Europe to North America from the end of the nineteenth century before the formation of the State of Israel in 1948.[2]

In reality, only a small percentage of the Jewish people embraced the political Zionist ideology that the only solution to Jewish alienation was the creation of a Jewish national homeland. By 1930 fewer than 175,000 Jews had immigrated to Palestine.[3] (By the time the State of Israel was founded, 650,000 resided there.)[4] The vast majority of European Jews who gave up on Christian Europe sought salvation not in Israel, but the United States. For them, the solution to antisemitism was a more welcoming Western host-society in which they might find acceptance.[5]

In its alternative to the nationalist Zionist option, the North American model emulated European Jewry's emancipatory aspirations, now in a new setting. To cite the Reform movement's 1885 Pittsburgh Platform, the success of the North American Jewish experiment would entail replacing a Genesis-Jewish collective identity with an American one: "We consider ourselves no longer a nation, but a religious community."[6]

"A Two-Way Street": Genesis Americans and Support for Israel

At first, the majority of North American Jews either rejected or were indifferent to the Zionist project. But as it grew in prominence after the 1917 Balfour Declaration, and especially after the State of Israel's establishment in 1948, expressions of a new kind of engagement began to emerge.

North American Jews were Exodus Jews: America was home, and Judaism was their religion. Support for Israel took the form of either *tzedakah*—charity from the powerful and established North American Jewish community to the politically and financially challenged Jews of Palestine and the nascent Jewish State—or the framing of Zionism as a liberal ideological movement whose mission was very much aligned with that of mainstream American Jews' Exodus Judaism.[7]

Two years after the formation of the State of Israel, one of the most prominent North American Jewish leaders of the time, Jacob Blaustein, dialoguing with Israel's Prime Minister David Ben-Gurion, gave powerful expression to the tzedakah-oriented form of this American "pro-Israel" sentiment:

> As to Israel, the vast majority of American Jewry recognizes the necessity and desirability of making it a strong, viable, self-supporting state. This, for the sake of Israel itself, and the good of the whole world. The American Jewish Committee has been active, as have other Jewish organizations in the United States, in rendering, within the framework of their American citizenship, every possible support to Israel. . . .
>
> While Israel has naturally placed some burdens on Jews elsewhere, particularly in America, it has, in turn, meant much to Jews throughout the world. In Europe, Africa, and the Middle East, it has provided a home in which *they* can attain their full stature of human dignity for the first time. In all Jews, it has inspired pride and admiration, even though in some instances, it has created passing headaches. . . .
>
> But we must, in true spirit of friendliness, sound a note of caution to Israel and its leaders. . . . It must recognize that the matter of good will between its citizens and those of other countries is a two-way street: that Israel has a responsibility in this situation—a

responsibility in terms of not affecting adversely the sensibilities of Jews who are citizens of other states by what it says or does. . . .

American Jews vigorously repudiate any suggestion or implication that they are in exile. American Jews—young and old alike, Zionist and non-Zionist alike—are profoundly attached to America. . . . *To American Jews, America is home.* They believe in the future of a democratic society in the United States under which all citizens, irrespective of creed or race, can live in terms of equality. They further believe that, if democracy should fail in America, there would be no future for democracy anywhere in the world, and that the very existence of an independent State of Israel would be problematic. Further, they feel that a world in which it would be possible for Jews to be driven by persecution from America, would not be a world safe for Israel either.[8]

For Blaustein, America was *more* than home: it was the best solution for Jews' "outsiderness" and the primary guarantor of their safety. Zionism and the rebirth of Israel provided a service especially to non-American Jews but had little or no significance to Blaustein's version of American Exodus Judaism. For him, Israel was somewhat of a burden, a bothersome relative constantly in need of assistance. It was a responsibility he was willing to bear because of Jews' mutual religious ties and historical tradition and pride. However, if Israel undermined his sense of home and belonging in America by claiming to be *the* exclusive homeland of *all* Jews and serving as the base for a worldwide Jewish Genesis Covenant, he—and most American Jews—would withdraw their support. Much like other Jewish communities in need around the world, Israel claimed him. But it was a limited claim that did not touch the deeper nature of American Jewish identity.

"Noblest Aspirations": A New American Exodus Zionism

Nonetheless, even before the emergence of the State of Israel, American Jews *could* be inspired by the new types of Jewishness Zionism was already producing in Palestine. They could be Genesis Americans, and Exodus Zionists and Jews.[9]

This stance was powerfully articulated by Louis D. Brandeis, a leader of the nascent American Zionist movement after World War I—soon to be appointed to the U.S. Supreme Court:

> Every American Jew who aids in advancing the Jewish settlement in Palestine, *though he feels that neither he nor his descendants will ever live there*, will likewise be a better man and a better American for doing so. . . . There is no inconsistency between loyalty to America and loyalty to Jewry. The Jewish spirit, the product of our religion and experiences, is essentially modern and essentially American. Not since the destruction of the Temple have the Jews in spirit and in ideals been so fully in harmony with the noblest aspirations of the country in which they lived.
>
> America's fundamental law seeks to make real the brotherhood of man. That brotherhood became the Jewish fundamental law more than 2500 years ago. America's insistent demand in the 20th century is for social justice. That also has been the Jews' striving for ages. Their affliction as well as their religion has prepared the Jews for effective democracy. . . .
>
> Indeed, loyalty to America demands rather that each American Jew become a Zionist. For only through the ennobling effects of [Zionism's] strivings can we develop the best that is in us, and give to this country the full benefit of our great inheritance.[10]

The Zionist Jews of Palestine did not merely claim Brandeis; they inspired him, representing the best expression of a contemporary Exodus Covenant. He wrote, "In the Jewish colonies of Palestine there are no Jewish criminals; because everyone, old and young alike, is led to feel the glory of his people and his obligation to carry forward its ideals. The new Palestinian Jewry produces instead of criminals, scientists . . . pedagogues . . . craftsmen . . . (and) the Jewish guards of peace who watch in the night against marauders and doers of violent deeds."[11]

Zionism did not undermine Brandeis's understanding of Judaism as a religion founded on the Exodus Covenant—to the contrary, in his view it was a new and vital expression of this covenant. He argued that one of the unique features of American identity was the notion that embracing multiple loyalties can make one a *better* U.S. citizen: "Let no American imagine that Zionism is inconsistent with [American] patriotism." For Brandeis, being Jewish and being American were not mutually exclusive—the two identities had a shared vision, and indeed tradition, of values and ideals. Zionism's great innovation was not its renewed emphasis on a Genesis Jewish identity but its resurrection of a profound and inspiring version of the Exodus Covenant.

"Judaism Is the Soul of which Israel Is the Body": The Israeli Restoration of North American Genesis Sensibilities

Perhaps it was inevitable that as the twentieth century progressed, the increase in North American Jewish support for Israel led to a heightened affinity with Genesis Jewishness. Jews spoke broadly of Jewish Peoplehood, a category that cast Jews qua Jews as a collective independent of what they did or believed.[12]

This notion of Genesis peoplehood took root independent of Zionism. Many American Jews embraced Israel without endorsing the nationalist platform of Political Zionism, which continued to be seen as antithetical to the American Jewish ethos.[13] While never supplanting America as home, Israel nevertheless evolved into a vital catalyst for Jews in America to connect more deeply with Jews worldwide through their Genesis roots.

Evidence of this deep shift is found not just in the writings of prominent American Zionists like Stephen S. Wise and Mordechai Kaplan but even in the previously anti-Zionist Reform movement.[14] As we saw, pre-Zionism, the Reform movement had expunged the Genesis Covenant—and with it, any aspiration for the rebirth of Jewish nationalism. The messianic era would usher in not Jewish redemption, but universal enlightenment.

While this aptly describes the zeitgeist of pre-Zionist North America, by 1937, when the Reform movement articulated its updated ideology in its Columbus Platform, significant changes had already taken hold. By then, the Balfour Declaration and the League of Nations had assigned Zionism a place of respectability, indeed prominence, in Jewish discourse. A battle was being waged in Palestine, and the Jewish community around the world—anchored by an increasingly affluent and successful American Jewry—felt called upon to support the weak and endangered Jewish settlement in Israel.[15] Rearticulating its ideology in—and for—this new historical moment, the Reform movement's platform now included an entire subsection about "Israel" under the broader subject heading, "Judaism and Its *Foundations*." Within five decades, Israel had ascended from irrelevant nonstatus to being viewed as one of Judaism's foundations.

The 1937 platform proclaimed that "Judaism is the soul of which Israel is the body"—a striking metaphor in which Diaspora Judaism remained identified with the Exodus Covenant, but Israel was the carrier of a resurgent sense of Genesis sensibilities. The same Zionist aspiration that had been cast off fifty years prior was now reintegrated into the structure of Reform identity—albeit still in a junior role:

> Living in all parts of the world, Israel has been held together by the ties of a common history and, above all, by the heritage of faith. *Though we recognize in the group loyalty of Jews who have become estranged from our religious tradition, a bond which still unites them with us*, we maintain that it is by religion and for its religion that the Jewish people have lived.[16]

For the Reform movement in the 1930s, its Exodus Covenant, aka "our religious tradition" and "the heritage of faith," remained the essence of Judaism. Zionism, however, was compelling the movement to make room for "the group loyalty of Jews who have become estranged from our religious tradition": Genesis Zionists for whom Jewishness was principally a national affiliation.

With Zionism, a Genesis consciousness returned to the fore. Jewishness again meant being bound to each other not only because of what we do or believe but also, simply, because of who we are.

"Haven of Refuge, Center of Culture": The New American "Pro-Israel" Balance

Nevertheless, the central thrust of Reform ideology vis à vis Zionism remained grounded in Exodus terms. Again, the 1937 Columbus Platform:

> In all lands where our people live, they assume and share loyally the full duties and responsibilities of citizenship and to create seats of Jewish knowledge and religion. In the rehabilitation of Palestine, the land hallowed by memories of hopes, we behold the promise of renewed life for *many* of our brethren. We affirm the obligation of all Jewry to aid in its upholding as a Jewish homeland by endeavoring to make it *not only a haven of refuge for the oppressed but also a center of Jewish culture and spiritual life.*[17]

In this early twentieth century North American reformulation, the future Israel was not (à la the Balfour Declaration) *the* homeland of the Jewish people—but *a* homeland. While not necessarily for all Jews, it was sufficiently pivotal to resurrect the Genesis Covenant: all Jews are required to stand with, protect, and help those who choose to move to Israel and intertwine their fate with the Jewish State.

At the same time, the relationship with Israel extended beyond Genesis loyalties. The new "pro-Israel" Reform Jews were challenged to ensure that Israel not serve merely as "a haven of refuge for the oppressed but also a center of Jewish culture and spiritual life"—in other words, not merely to support Genesis Zionism but to serve as advocates and catalysts for a new Exodus Zionism as well. With this statement, the Reform movement represented what was and remains a central aspect of the pro-Israel Jewish community's relationship with Israel. To support Israel is to also be invested in the nature of the Exodus Jewish life created there.

Nuremberg Rules: The Post-Holocaust Mobilization of Genesis Consciousness

At the same time, and nearly single-handedly, Hitler reinforced the centrality of Genesis consciousness as a pillar of Jewish life. In what became almost a truism for North American Jewry, the Nuremberg Laws' definition of a Jew knew only of Genesis Jews and excluded any Exodus sense of Jewishness:

1. A Jew is an individual who is descended from at least three grandparents who were, racially, full Jews. . . .
2. A Jew is also an individual who is descended from two full-Jewish grandparents if:

   (a) he was a member of the Jewish religious community when this law was issued, or joined the community later;
   (b) when the law was issued, he was married to a person who was a Jew, or was subsequently married to a Jew;
   (c) he is the issue from a marriage with a Jew, in the sense of Section I, which was contracted after the coming into effect of the Law for the Protection of German Blood and Honor of September 15, 1935;
   (d) he is the issue of an extramarital relationship with a Jew, in the sense of Section I, and was born out of wedlock after July 31, 1936.[18]

In Nazi Germany Jews were so defined by their Genesis roots that even if they converted out of Judaism and severed ties with their community, if they had ancestry going back three generations—or through marriage—they were still Jewish. According to Nazi ideology, a *Jew even though they have sinned, is still a Jew.*[19]

This had a profound influence on post-Holocaust North American Jewish life, and indeed on Jewish life worldwide. The prevailing sentiment was that if Hitler made no Exodus-based distinctions among Jews, neither should we. A Jew is a Jew is a Jew. Thus, in the postwar years, Jews everywhere mobilized around their shared Genesis Covenant.[20] "*Never Again*" became an essential commandment. Never again would a Jew stand idly by when another Jew was in danger.

"Everything Changed for Us": The Six-Day War and the Ascent of Jewish Peoplehood

In as much as the Holocaust jolted North American Jewry's self-understanding with an infusion of Genesis sensibilities, Israel's dramatic victory in the Six-Day War solidified peoplehood's predominance and transformed it into a central feature of North American Jewish identity.[21] After the 1967 war Israel was no longer the poor and needy cousin dependent on North American Jews for support. Israel itself became the locus and exemplar of Jewish power, exuding strength, dignity, and success. As such, it became—almost overnight—a source of adoration, inspiration, and Jewish pride.[22]

For religious Zionists, the victory bore profound religious and spiritual implications that injected their view of Exodus Zionism with new life: the liberation of the Temple Mount and historic Judea and Samaria ignited a new messianic fervor around God's imminent return to history and Israel.[23] However, for the majority of Jews both in Israel and the Diaspora, the miraculous-seeming victory was a triumph of Genesis sensibilities for the Jewish people, binding Jews together worldwide. In short, Israel's success had made Jews everywhere the winning team. Nathan Sharansky gave powerful voice to this sentiment as he recounted the impact of the victory on his Jewish identity from beyond the Soviet Iron Curtain:

We knew all too well the anti-Semitic stereotypes about greed, parasitism, and cowardice—but about what Judaism stood for, we knew nothing. . . . Then, in six dramatic days, everything changed for us. The call that went up from Jerusalem, "The Temple Mount is in our hands," penetrated the Iron Curtain and forged an almost mystic link with our people. And while we had no idea what the Temple Mount was, we did know that the fact that it was in our hands had won us respect. . . . We belonged to something, even if we did not yet know what, or why. . . . Instinctively and without any real connection to Judaism, we became Zionists.[24]

A similar sentiment emerged across North America. While still firmly committed to an American Exodus Judaism, the Genesis Covenant began to claim American Jewry and play an increasingly central role in its consciousness. "*We are One*" became a dominant Jewish slogan, *Jewish Unity* a dominant communal directive.[25] Caring for Israel and remembering the Holocaust regularly polled as an important part of being a Jew.[26] Nondenominational communal organizations anchored in Genesis consciousness—such as Federations, JCCs, AJC, the Conference of Presidents, and AIPAC—led North American Jewish life and discourse.[27]

Support for Israel was no longer a factor of Jewish life, but arguably the central agenda.[28] A Jew could violate any aspect of the Exodus Covenant and still remain a Jew in good standing. However, a Jew could not abandon, or for many, even criticize, Israel. As Rabbi and philosopher Eugene Borowitz so eloquently articulated in 1968:

I am left with one major problem with regard to the entire question of our relationship to the State of Israel. I think the worst thing that Zionism and the State of Israel have done for us is to give us another topic in America which cannot be debated. We now have a subject on which no arguments are allowed, no criticism. A new sacred cow is introduced. Open your mouth in a Jewish audience to raise a question critical of the State of Israel, critical of Zionism, and if you're talking with Israelis, that's all right; if you're in the State of Israel and getting into an argument, that's all right; but to an American Jewish audience you are not allowed to say any-thing bad about the State of Israel. It is assumed either that you are a paid agent of Mao Tse-tung or of the American Council for Judaism or that there is something the matter with you as a Jew.[29]

North American Jewry, deeply fractured among myriad denomi-nations, was now united around Israel. A newfound sense of shared Jewishness transcended the partisanship of Exodus-inspired denom-inational Judaism.[30]

A direct outgrowth of this denomination-transcending Israel-based peoplehood development is Birthright Israel. The premise of this sweep-ing project, which gives every eligible young Jewish adult worldwide, especially the less connected, the opportunity to visit Israel, is that a Jew's principal birthright is not the synagogue or Jewish summer camp experience, not day school or Hebrew school education—it is a chance to come to Israel free of charge.

While Birthright was originally marketed as the solution to assim-ilation, targeting eighteen- to twenty-six-year-old Jews who might otherwise be lost to Judaism, the trip is not designed to enhance or expand participants' Exodus consciousness or commitment/s. At its core, it is an experiential journey into our shared Genesis roots—a covenant that its supporters believe is experienced most powerfully in the modern State of Israel.[31]

The Renaissance and Potential of North American Exodus Judaism

During this same period of increased Genesis consciousness, and often under the influence of the same events, North American Jews remained deeply engaged in the evolution of their own emergent internal Exodus discourse, refusing to adopt the either/or model of nineteenth-century Europe. For the remainder of the twentieth century, they worked to revitalize their religious and communal institutions, engaged in formal and informal Jewish education at unprecedented levels, and embarked on an extensive effort to renew and deepen the ways in which Jewish life was lived in North America. They built thousands of synagogues as well as hundreds of day schools, camps, and JCCs; created multiple rabbinical and cantorial schools for every denomination; built Judaic studies departments in universities large and small; inaugurated Jewish newspapers and magazines, teacher training schools, theater and culture, book clubs, and on and on.[32]

Even Israel and the Holocaust, previously drivers of Genesis consciousness, came to be recast through an Exodus covenantal lens. In 1967 the philosopher Emil Fakenheim (a Holocaust survivor) exemplified this move through his articulation of the "new" Jewish commandment, of equal status to the 613 found in the Bible:

> There emerges what I will boldly term a 614th commandment: the authentic Jew of today is forbidden to hand Hitler yet another, posthumous victory.[33]

Hitler, Fakenheim conceded, achieved a powerful victory by successfully murdering six million Jews. We the survivors, he posited, therefore have a new Jewish obligation—to not grant Hitler a second victory by leaving our people and our tradition:

> If the 614th commandment is binding upon the authentic Jew, then we are, first, commanded to survive as Jews, lest the Jewish people perish. We are commanded, second, to remember in our very guts and bones the martyrs of the Holocaust, lest their memory perish. We are forbidden, thirdly, to deny or despair of God, however much we may have to contend with Him or with belief in Him, lest Judaism perish. We are forbidden, finally, to despair of the world as the place which is to become the kingdom of God, lest we help make it a meaningless place in which God is dead or irrelevant and everything is permitted. To abandon any of these imperatives, in response to Hitler's victory at Auschwitz, would be to hand him yet other posthumous victories.[34]

To truly respond to the Holocaust, Jews had to embrace Jewish life—and this embrace in turn obligated each Jew to embark on the Jewish journey of reengaging with the Exodus Covenant.

Writing from Israel, where he moved our family after the Six-Day War, my father, David Hartman, worked to reframe the way both Israelis and North American Jews understood Zionism and the reality of a Jewish State in Israel—particularly with respect to its potential role in the formation of a vital Exodus-focused Jewish identity for Jews worldwide:

> I live with the guarded hope that out of this complex and vibrant new Jewish reality will emerge new spiritual directions for the way Judaism will be lived in the modern world. Israel expands the possible range of halakhic involvement in human affairs beyond the circumscribed borders of home and synagogue to the public domain. Jews in Israel are given the opportunity to bring economic, social, and political issues into the center of their religious consciousness. The moral quality of the army, social and economic disparities and deprivations, the exercise of power moderated by moral sensitivity—all these are realms that may engage halakhic responsibility. From this perspective, the fact that Israel enables us to make the whole of life the carrier of the covenant is in itself sufficient to ascribe profound religious significance to the secular revolt that led to Israel's rebirth.[35]

To paraphrase Ahad Ha'am, for my father, Israel did not only save the Jews—it had the potential to save modern Judaism. Through an expansion of the parameters of Jewish concern and responsibility, the Exodus Covenant could be revitalized and imbued with new relevance and significance for Jews around the world:

> Israel should not be understood merely as a haven for the persecuted and the wandering Jew or as a guarantee against assimilation. It is shortsighted to use the Holocaust as a justification for the need

for a Jewish national home. Israel from my perspective provides a new direction for Judaism's confrontation with modernity. It opens up the possibility of renewing the covenantal drama of Sinai in a vital new way. The rebirth of Israel marks the repudiation of the halakhic ghetto as the means for guarding Jewish survival in history. Israel not only argues against the ghettoization of Judaism, but is also a rejection of the mistaken universalism that characterized the assimilationist tendencies that affected many Jews as a result of the breakdown of the ghetto. The birth of the third Jewish commonwealth teaches all of Jewry that being rooted in a particular history and tradition need not be antithetical to involvement and concern with the larger issues affecting the human world.[36]

North American Judaism: The Synthesis

In this story of twentieth-century Jewry, North American Judaism, like Zionism and much of Jewish life over the millennia, can be understood as an attempt to engage with both Genesis and Exodus and forge to a balance between the two. Genesis and Exodus talk with each other, play off each other, but never eclipse or suppress one another.

A powerful illustration of the complexity of the American Jewish experience can be found in the next official shift of the Reform movement's ideological stances. In light of the previously discussed 1937 Columbus platform, consider the Reform rabbinate's 1976 San Francisco platform:

We continue to probe the extraordinary events of the past generation, seeking to understand their meaning and to incorporate their significance in our lives. The Holocaust shattered our easy optimism about humanity and its inevitable progress. *The State of Israel, through its many accomplishments, raised our sense of the Jews as a people to new heights of aspiration and devotion* . . . We have learned that the survival of the Jewish people is of highest priority and that in carrying out our Jewish responsibilities we help move humanity toward its messianic fulfillment . . .

2. *The People Israel*—The Jewish people and Judaism defy precise definition because both are in the process of becoming. Jews, by birth or conversion, constitute an uncommon union of faith and peoplehood. Born as Hebrews in the ancient Near East, we are bound together like all ethnic groups by language, land, history, culture, and institutions. But the people of Israel is unique because of its involvement with God and its resulting perception of the human condition. Throughout our long history, our people has been inseparable from its religion with its messianic hope that humanity will be redeemed . . .

4. *Our Religious Obligations*: . . . The past century has taught us that the claims made upon us may begin with our ethical obligations but they extend to many other aspects of Jewish living, including: creating a Jewish home centered on family devotion; lifelong study; private prayer and public worship; daily religious observance; keeping the Sabbath and the holy days; celebrating the major events of life; involvement with the synagogues and community; and other activities which promote the survival of the Jewish people and enhance its existence.

5. *Our Obligations*: The State of Israel and the Diaspora—We are privileged to live in an extraordinary time, one in which a third Jewish commonwealth has been established in our people's ancient homeland. We are bound to that land and to the newly reborn State of Israel by innumerable religious and ethnic ties. We have been enriched by its culture and ennobled by its indomitable spirit. We see it providing unique opportunities for Jewish self-expression. We have both a stake and a responsibility in building the State of Israel, assuring its security, and to not grant Hitler a second victory by leaving our people and our tradition.[37]

The revised platform bears witness to a deep dual-covenantal commitment: a comprehensive vision of Judaism and Jewish life encompassing Genesis and Exodus. Gone is the earlier language of zero-sum dichotomy: "We consider ourselves no longer a nation, but [exclusively] a religious community." Jews are both "bound together like all ethnic groups" and unique because we are not exhausted by our ethnic identity. Jewishness as Genesis-ness is emphasized in the construction of Jews as an ethnic group united by language, land, history, culture, and institutions. Jewishness as Exodus-ness is expressed through commitments to God, study, prayer, and daily ritual observances on both familial and communal levels. Jews have two core obligations: to build a way of life upon ethical and spiritual obligations and devotions and to be bound to the Jewish people and their ancient homeland.

In essence, the 1976 platform embodied a new understanding of the relationship between the American Reform movement and Israel. The subsequent Reform movement platform (and the final one to date), "A Statement of Principles for Reform Judaism" adopted in Pittsburgh in 1999, upholds the 1976 shift in the Israel-Diaspora relationship as well.

Once Genesis and Exodus coexist within the fullness of a Jewish identity, Israel and Diaspora are no longer in competition. Both are critical for Jewish life, as a Jewish community that bears witness to how a "people transcends nationalism even as it affirms it."[38] Jews can affirm nationalism as an integral part and consequence of our Genesis Covenant but recognize that it can never be an end unto itself. The call of Exodus—"You shall be unto Me a kingdom of priests and a holy nation"—demands that we concern ourselves not only with issues of survival but also with the question of survival for what end.

PART TWO

A Zionism for
the Twenty-First
Century

9

Foundations for a Twenty-First Century Liberal Jewish Story

Having identified the shared metanarratives of Genesis and Exodus and their respective roles in shaping the story of Jewishness, now, in part 2, we move to application. As the living inheritors of this tradition, we are neither empty vessels nor uninterested emissaries of the stories that we have told ourselves about ourselves. It is up to us to decide which stories to continue telling about ourselves and how to tell them; to determine who we can and ought to be; to formulate and practice our era's vision of Jewishness with each other and with the generations that follow us; to synthesize Genesis and Exodus into workable versions of a collective identity for their respective times.

Based on the broadly liberal sensibility shared by the vast majority of contemporary Jews in North America and at least 60 percent of Israeli Jews (who vote for liberal parties or coalesced against the judicial reform), I will outline a new paradigm for how a revitalized synthesis of Genesis and Exodus can spark critical insights and transformative solutions in some of the key areas of communal dysfunction playing out in and between Israel and North America in the twenty-first century.

In the process, I hope to start a new kind of conversation about how the next chapter of the Jewish story might be told.

The Complexity in the Synthesis

While Genesis and Exodus generate core sensibilities, how the synthesis between the two plays out in the real world is not subject to simple, clear-cut directions. On a basic level, Genesis demands loyalty to Jews, Exodus to Torah. What if they conflict? Does the tolerance obligated by Genesis demand that we accept each other's conversions? Pray in each other's synagogues? Accept intermarriage and the intermarried?

Conversely, Exodus advocates for an aspirational Judaism. But where should our Exodus priorities be: in the moral or ritual realms? Does a commitment to the Exodus Covenant allow for the designation of major swathes of the Jewish people as intolerable? For controlling the religious observances of Jews in the State of Israel? For overriding the Genesis-based concerns for Israel's viability?

And how do we achieve a Genesis-Exodus synthesis? How do we balance concern for the welfare of Jews with concern for the responsibilities of Jews? In Israel, what impact does a Genesis and Exodus synthesis have on issues of state and religion, or war and security? What is a Genesis/Exodus-synthesized Torah of power?

I believe there is no singular Jewishly authentic answer to any of the above questions and that adopting Genesis and Exodus as meta-narratives of Jewishness does not lead to a new Shulhan Arukh for our times, a singular and unambiguous guide for how to apply one's dual covenantal commitment. Diverse, good, and committed Jews, who embrace both Genesis and Exodus, can reach very different conclusions regarding their practical implications, and embracing both Genesis and Exodus neither erases differences nor privileges one version of the story over others.

Ultimately, as long as one self-identifies as a Genesis Jew and is a player in Exodus, one is a part of the shared Jewish story. How the chapters of this story shape each person's individual or communal choices and policies will inevitably vary. We can share in the frameworks of Genesis and Exodus while recognizing that good and committed Jews can disagree as to how to express each covenant and synthesize them in their lives.

Toward a Particular Synthesis Founded in a Modern Liberal Genesis/Exodus Judaism

That said, in parts 2 and 3 I do give preference to one particular synthesis—guided by a particular understanding of modern liberal Jewish sensibilities. I contend that in our current multidenominational context, a broad spectrum of Jews encompassing a wide range of observances and beliefs—Modern Orthodoxy, Conservative, Reform, Traditional, Renewal, Reconstructionist, postdenominational, and secular among them—share in the framework of Genesis and Exodus, that is, a dual commitment to (1) belonging to the Jewish people (the Genesis Covenant) and (2) accepting some aspect of Torah (Exodus Covenant), however broadly construed as constitutive in one's Jewish life. But in addition, we also share a particular set of common values and principles—those of "Liberal Judaism," which

1. Encourages a synthesis between our three-thousand-year tradition and modernity and incorporates many of modernity's teachings into contemporary expressions of Torah.
2. Cultivates human autonomy and the right to know and decide what is best for oneself, and to have one's Jewish choices generally respected in the community's marketplace of ideas.
3. Views the Jewish religious tradition (the Exodus Covenant) as diverse and multivocal. Disagreement for the "sake of heaven" is necessary, for no single position can exhaust the "word of the living God."[1]
4. Adopts pluralism and tolerance as the default tools for navigating Jewish and ideological difference.
5. Establishes boundaries and limits to pluralism and tolerance, albeit with varying approaches to the nature, location, and consequence of particular boundaries and red lines.
6. Embraces the multifaceted nature of Judaism as a system balancing elements of ethics, faith, rituals, learning and

culture, all the while asserting—in the spirit of the prophetic tradition—that ethics must always take primacy in our individual and communal lives, and in national policies.[2]

7. Calls for a religiously and ideologically diverse public sphere (including in Israel) in which the state makes no law respecting the establishment or preference of one religion or denomination over others, or prohibiting the free exercise thereof.[3]

8. Stands for human rights and a Judaism dedicated to the inalienable freedoms of all human beings regardless of religion, nationality, sexual orientation, gender identity, or race.

9. Demands that all "others" be treated as we Jews have wanted to be treated throughout our history to be treated. "What is hateful unto you do not do to others,"[4] the cornerstone of Jewish ethics, applies to all of humankind, for all are created in the image of God.

This list is not exhaustive, and certainly not engraved in stone. Some might add principles; others might remove some. That said, I believe they are constitutive for a broad segment of the modern liberal multidenominational Jewish community—my "denomination," the community to which I belong and to which I address the remainder of this book. Within this community, there are still many disagreements, conflicts, and rivalries. Yet, when we set aside the details of the particular dietary and Shabbat laws we do or don't keep, the synagogues we frequent or not, the God we pray to or believe in or not, there is significant consensus on much of the above.

As for my ideological opponents, those who do not share in the above principles and are liable to find the subsequent chapters foreign, irrelevant, even alienating at times, I recognize that your synthesis of Genesis and Exodus leads to very different conclusions. I might disagree, and even abhor, some of the choices you make and the Judaisms you represent. There are some synagogues I will never pray in, and some political parties I will never vote for. Moreover, in the midst of what I believe is now a critical cultural war over the future of Judaism, the Jewish people, and Israel, I will debate you and fight over whose Torah and synthesis will capture the imagination of the Jewish people and Israel and determine our policies. Nonetheless, as long as you embrace the Covenants of Genesis and Exodus as cornerstones of your Jewishness, I believe that we are partners and fellow members in the same story, and I acknowledge your Exodus sensibilities as authentic and legitimate parts of Jewishness. At the end of the day, I take seriously the Genesis mandate that "Israel even though they have sinned, are still Israel."

As to my fellow modern liberal Jews: the chapters that follow present an opportunity to activate some of our core principles in order to reshape the story we will tell ourselves about ourselves, both in Israel and North America. Ultimately, we are the sum of the stories we tell ourselves about ourselves, and our generation is at a critical inflection point. Through a renewed synthesis of Genesis and Exodus, I hope we can find important insights and direction and infuse newfound meaning and vitality into our story of Jewishness.

10

Recalibrating the Religion-State Status Quo

A number of years ago, I delivered a lecture on the challenges and contradictions in Israel's state and religion policies to a group of colonels in the Israeli army. Afterward, an officer who had spent two decades commanding elite combat units asked if he could speak with me privately.

In my office, he presented his dilemma. Five years ago, after years of trying to conceive, he and his wife adopted a child from Eastern Europe. Upon bringing her home to Israel, they contacted the Rabbinate to convert her to Judaism and learned that the conversion would be dependent on him and his wife observing a semi-Orthodox lifestyle, including keeping Shabbat and a kosher home, and agreeing to send the child to an Orthodox school.

The officer and his wife were secular Jews, and they wanted to raise their child as a good secular Jew. With the possible exception of a kosher home, none of these conditions were acceptable to them. Thus they discovered that while they were Jewish enough to serve and die for their country, in Israel they could not convert their child to be Jewish the way they were. In the Rabbinate's eyes, they were inferior "non-kosher" Jews.

Shocked at the chutzpah of the Rabbinate, they committed to the conditions until their daughter's conversion process was complete. Then they proceeded to ignore the stipulations, reasoning correctly that no one would come and check after the fact, and once the conversion was finalized, it wouldn't matter anyway.

The story did not end there. Because, the officer explained to me, in one month's time he and his wife were going to adopt their second child, and he knew he couldn't game the system again. The Rabbinate would see that his eldest daughter was not registered in an Orthodox school and refuse to convert the new baby on those grounds. He and his wife faced the inconceivable reality that their new child would not be Jewish.

How could it be that in the homeland of the Jewish people, secular Jews cannot convert their children to be like them? How was it possible that secular Israelis have allowed Orthodoxy such control over their lives?

The problem, however, goes beyond the national legislative level, to the personal one, wherein a wide segment of non-Orthodox Jews are disempowered and disenfranchised from their Jewish identity. Being "religious" (*Dati*) in Israel is broadly accepted by secular, traditional, and Orthodox alike as being synonymous with Orthodoxy, leaving the non-Orthodox majority as nonreligious (non-Dati), conceptually and psychologically without a place in their own religion.

Recently, like many liberal rabbis in Israel, I again experienced the depth of this phenomena when I received a call from a vendor whose store I frequent near my house. Her grandson was to be of bar mitzvah age in six months, and being a traditional Jew, she was deeply troubled by her son, daughter-in-law, and grandson's lack of planning and interest in having a bar mitzvah celebration. Neither parent was interested, and her grandson, while open to the idea, had no direction. She asked me if I could be of help in recommending someone to teach her grandson to read from the Torah. I told her that if he is not interested and his parents are not on board, no teacher, no matter how skilled, could succeed. I sent her to lay the groundwork and explore if there was any interest. She got back to me a few weeks later, despondent. As a family they couldn't talk about it. I then told her to ask her family if they would meet with me. They agreed.

Instead of starting with the upcoming bar mitzvah, I asked the parents to speak of their relationship with Judaism. The mother, an immigrant from the former Soviet Union, shared that for her Judaism is not an identity but something more akin to a philosophy, a system with wisdom from which one can learn. I asked if she saw herself as principally a Jew or an Israeli and she answered unhesitatingly, "Israeli." Her husband, upon hearing her response, said, "I see myself as principally a Jew." It was clear that this was not a subject that they had ever broached together. "I was raised with tradition," he continued, "but I no longer keep any of them in my family." Before I could engage him further, he said, "But, of course, every week, we always have a Friday night diner at home with the children, and I recite the Kiddush." When I told him that this makes him one of the more observant Jews in the world, he looked at me incredulously. I asked his wife if she participates, and she responded, "Of course. Shopping, preparing the Shabbat dinner, sitting and talking together, etc." I then asked her, "It seems that in your life Judaism is not just a philosophy?" She too looked at me, not understanding what I was saying.

Finally it was the bar mitzvah boy's turn. Unhesitatingly he said, "I am a Jew."

I then explained to the family that when it comes to a bar or bat mitzvah there are no rules that the family must follow, as one becomes a bar mitzvah (lit. obligated by the commandments) automatically when one turns thirteen. As a result, the family was free to choose to celebrate and commemorate the moment in any way that fit their Jewish values and comfort level: for instance, reading from the Torah or not, whether at a synagogue or at the Kotel, having a party, or engaging in a learning project or a tzedakah project. The boy responded again, unhesitatingly: "I want to read from the Torah." I asked him why and he responded, "Because that is the tradition, and it makes it serious." I asked the family if they had a synagogue they were comfortable with and they said no. "Are you comfortable at the Kotel?" I asked, turning to the mother. And she responded, "Of course."

"Do you prefer an egalitarian service?" I asked, thinking that they might find this welcoming as secular Jews, but they didn't know what I was talking about and had never heard of the egalitarian section of the Kotel. I explained both options. The mother seemed to be neutral as long as she could observe her son reading. I asked the bar mitzvah boy and he said, "I want my mother there." "Where?" I asked. "Watching or standing next to you?" He paused and said, "Either." A few minutes later he said, "Next to me."

As the conversation continued, the whole family embraced the idea of a tzedakah project and began talking excitedly about volunteer options near their home and about family members who worked in social welfare institutions who could be helpful.

I don't know what the family will decide in the end. I gave them contact information for both a traditional Orthodox and an egalitarian teacher and committed to assisting them further if needed. As they left, the parents thanked me for framing for them what a bar mitzvah means and entails and empowering them to begin thinking about it.

But what is it about Jewish life and education in Israel that has produced such a profound sense of disempowerment in their Jewish lives? Why, despite their myriad Jewish commitments, did they perceive themselves as spectators, incapable of assessing their Jewish identities as meaningful and important and shaping their roles as players in the Jewish arena?

State and Religion: The Original Sin

As Zionism was embarking on one of the greatest collective enterprises in Jewish history, the Jewish people united in their Genesis focus on creating a new Jewish homeland were hopelessly divided on how the Exodus Covenant should be expressed within it. Among the multiple ideological groups who had to build this homeland together were:

Religious (Orthodox) Zionists, for whom the Exodus Covenant was defined by fidelity to traditional Jewish law. Their Exodus Zionism led them to believe that national sovereignty in the historical homeland claimed ultimate religious significance. In the Land of Israel, and in the context of Jewish nationalism, the Jewish people would finally fulfill the aspirations of Exodus, to be a kingdom of priests, and usher in the Messianic Era.[1]

Ultra-Orthodox Jews, whose Exodus Covenant was also defined by fidelity to traditional Jewish law, albeit more conservatively than for their Religious Zionist counterparts. Their understanding of the Exodus Covenant conversely led them to reject assigning any religious significance to Jewish nationalism. They viewed Zionism as a secular revolt against God and Torah—but nevertheless wanted to preserve their Jewish way of life in the Holy Land.[2]

Secular Jews, for whom a new secular Exodus Covenant was central to their identity individually and collectively and who saw in Jewish nationalism the foundations for this new Exodus Covenant. For them, Exodus was not based principally on fidelity to Jewish ritual but on the obligation to work the land, defend the Jewish people, and nurture Jewish values, culture, and language.[3]

Secular Israelis—as distinct from Secular *Jews*, this group saw in Israeli nationalism an opportunity to free the Jewish people from its *Jewish* covenants and to embrace a new national secular one in which Israel would be a normal nation, similar to France or Italy. In their understanding, Israeliness replaced Jewishness as the essence of collective identity.[4]

Traditional Jews (Mesorati), predominantly but not exclusively of Sephardic/Mizrahi origin, who were at home with the traditional manifestations of Exodus Judaism's laws and rituals; saw authentic Exodus Judaism as exclusively Orthodox, even while they did not observe many Orthodox practices themselves; and supported an Israel where such Jewish observances were expressed and fostered in the public sphere.[5]

How does one construct a shared homeland under these conditions?

The majority of Jews in Israel at the founding of the state, including the vast majority of its leadership, were principally Ashkenazi Jews drawn from the Secular Jewish and Secular Israeli groups. These two groups regarded religious ritual and law with discomfort and often antipathy and wanted to either abolish its claim on Israel or free Israel and the Jews from its traditional diasporic, ritual-centered manifestations. Nevertheless, given the size of the *Yishuv* (Jewish settlement in pre-state Palestine) and the precariousness of the nascent Jewish state, this majority needed the partnership not only of the Religious Zionist and Mesorati camps, who had very different notions of Exodus Zionism, but even of the Ultra-Orthodox, for whom Exodus Judaism and Zionism were mutually exclusive. To achieve a measure of consensus and construct governing coalitions, the Jewish Secular and Israeli Secular majority adopted state and religion policies founded on numerous internal contradictions and compromises.

On the one hand, as we will see in the Declaration of Independence, Israel's founding secular leaders desired a Jeffersonian wall of separation between religion and state.[6] They hoped to essentially restrict the Jewishness of the public sphere to Genesis Zionism: a collective identity defined in broad national terms, leaving each group to express its distinct conception of the Exodus Covenant privately at home. But in the process of coalition-building with religious factions, and apparently believing that the need for concessions would be temporary since Orthodoxy would inevitably dissipate over time through its exposure to secular Zionist enlightenment, these secular leaders conceded first to some Orthodox demands for overt expressions of Judaism in the public domain and ultimately allowed for significant aspects of Orthodoxy's Exodus Judaism to determine public policy for the whole polity. Thus the Secular Zionist ethos of an Exodus-neutral public domain in the Jewish state would not be fulfilled.

I call this misguided strategy of abdicating the Exodus Zionism of the public domain the "original sin" of Israeli state-religious identity.

The Declaration of Independence: Genesis Zionism

Initially, the secular founders of the state envisioned Israel as a liberal Western democracy, interpreting the meaning of a Jewish state—as referred to by the United Nations—as essentially a state for the Jewish people, a sovereign national homeland and refuge, with almost no reference to any particular Exodus manifestations.

This approach is repeatedly expressed in Israel's Declaration of Independence. Its opening paragraphs emphasize the Jewish people and their relationship with the Land of Israel:

> The Land of Israel was the birthplace of the *Jewish people*. Here *their* spiritual, religious and national identity was formed. Here *they* achieved independence and created a culture of national and universal significance. Here *they* wrote and gave the Bible to the world. . . .
>
> Impelled by this historic association, *Jews* strove throughout the centuries to go back to the land of their fathers and regain statehood. In recent decades, *they* returned in their masses. *They* reclaimed a wilderness, revived *their* language, built cities and villages, and established a vigorous and ever-growing community, with its own economic and cultural life. *They* sought peace yet were ever prepared to defend themselves. *They* brought blessings of progress to all inhabitants of the country.[7]

God, Jewish tradition, and Jewish law have no part in the founding narrative of the declaration. Jewish statehood is about returning the Jewish people to their homeland, the place where their peoplehood was born and the place to which they have always yearned to return. The Jewish settlement, the nineteenth- and twentieth-century emigration to Palestine, was about reclaiming a land that lay fallow, reviving the Hebrew language, and economic and cultural revitalization. There is no mention of the religious and ritual significance of the land, nor of any religious renewal by the settlers. When the phrase "Jewish State" is mentioned, it is immediately characterized in Genesis terms, as a state of the Jewish people: "On the 29th of November 1947, the United Nations General Assembly passed a resolution calling for the establishment of a *Jewish State* in the land of Israel; the General Assembly required the inhabitants of the Land of Israel to take such steps as were necessary on their part for the implementation of that resolution. This recognition by the United Nations of the right of the *Jewish people* to establish *their State* is irrevocable."[8]

A Jewish State without an Exodus Covenant

This clear intention to separate the state from its Exodus Covenant emerges most noticeably in the declaration's seminal singular paragraph outlining the policies that will govern the nascent Jewish state:

> The State of Israel will be open for Jewish immigration and for the ingathering of the exiles, it will foster the development of the country for the benefit of all of its inhabitants, it will be based on freedom, justice and peace as envisaged by the prophets of Israel. It will insure complete equality of social and political rights to all its inhabitants, irrespective of religion, race, or sex, it will guarantee freedom of religion, conscience, language, education and culture, it will safeguard the holy places of all religions, and it will be faithful to the principles of the charter of the United Nations.[9]

In the day-to-day life of the country there was to be complete equality between Jew and non-Jew, freedom of religion safeguarded for all, and equal protection for the holy places of all religions. There is *almost* no mention of the Jewish nature of the state.

Almost, for in fact there are two ways this paragraph of the declaration breaches the firewall between Jewishness and the state. The first is the encouragement and facilitation of Jewish emigration—a manifestation of Genesis Zionism and the idea that a Jewish state is first and foremost the state of the Jews. There is no Jewish state without Jews and a Jewish majority; as a result, the first policy statement of the declaration involves facilitating this through a focus on Jewish emigration.

The second can be found in its biblical invocation, "as envisaged by the prophets of Israel." Note, however, that the reference to the prophets has been tempered to include only the universal values of freedom, justice, and peace. The full prophetic agenda was of course far more robust, calling for, for example, the abolishment of idolatry, a return to faith and devotion to God, the defeat of Israel's enemies, and the coming of the Messiah. The framers of the declaration did not see these prophetic aspirations as obligating them; indeed, they had no place in the nascent state's agenda. Exodus Judaism/Zionism was exclusively an embodiment of universal moral values and the prophets served not as a source of authority but to provide a Jewish language and framework within which to couch universal values.

In this formulation basically free from Exodus commitments, the State of Israel becomes an almost mirror opposite of its Western European Jewish communal antecedents. In emancipated Europe, Jews were citizens of their nation-state and members of the Jewish faith. They were Frenchmen of Jewish (Exodus) persuasion. In this version of a Jewish state, Jews would be citizens of a Jewish state with a Western secular identity: Genesis Jews bound to a liberal universal covenant.

Who Is the "Rock of Israel"?

As the declaration was being produced, Ben-Gurion found himself under pressure to attain the support and backing of the Orthodox community.[10] The latter insisted that in Israel's Declaration of Independence, God's name must appear. This posed a serious problem for the secular leaders, many of whom refused to sign a document that referred to a diasporic God in whom they did not believe.

For secular Israelis, God was a source of neither authority nor comfort. Nor was faith terminology a unifying cultural reference. In fact, Secular Zionists viewed European Jews as exhibiting self-destructive passivity largely because of their faith in God, to whom they prayed for salvation instead of taking personal responsibility for their destiny.[11] Liberating the Jew from Europe required liberating the Jew from God. Laws of nature and realpolitik had to displace Jews' misplaced faith in the supernatural and miraculous. An essential aspect and innovation of these leaders' new secular vision of Exodus Zionism was teaching Jews that the source of comfort and protection was to be found within themselves.

Yet the Orthodox would not sign the declaration without a reference to *their* Exodus Covenant and source of authority and comfort: God. A compromise language was found, one that seemed innocuous at the time, but which in fact was a harbinger of patterns to come:

> Placing our trust in the *Rock of Israel* [*Heb.* "*Tzur-Yisrael*"], we affix our signatures to this proclamation at this session of the provisional Council of State, on the soil of the Homeland, in the city of Tel-Aviv, on this Sabbath eve, the 5th day of Iyar, 5708 (May 14th, 1948).[12]

Who is "the Rock of Israel?" As is often the case with linguistic compromises, the answer depends on whom you ask. For the secular Israeli, the term refers alternately to Israel, the Jewish people, or the army. For the Orthodox, the term is one of the ways the Bible refers to God; its use thus injected the declaration with a needed dose of tradition.[13]

Ultimately, rather than achieve consensus on the nature and ideal expression of Exodus Zionism, this compromise allowed each side to speak only to itself. It also set a precedent of secular accommodation to a religious sensibility, and not vice versa, that would messily spill over, again and again, into policy issues facing the country. Its impact on policy proved not unifying but mutually alienating—with Orthodoxy's dominant, coercive version of public Exodus Zionism crowding out the possibility for any other vision to emerge.

Ben-Gurion's "Status-Quo" Two-Step: Relinquishing Exodus Zionism to the Orthodox

In 1947, before the declaration was finalized, Orthodox demands regarding both their community's religious rights and the place of Judaism in the state led Ben-Gurion to pen a seminal policy letter. The

"Status Quo Agreement," as it came to be known, outlined a position on issues of state and religion issues in a somewhat self-contradictory two-step. First, it pushed back against the Orthodox agenda, declaring that Israel could not become a theocracy:

> The establishment of the state requires the approval of the United Nations, and this is impossible unless freedom of conscience in the state is guaranteed to all its citizens, and unless it is clear that there is no intention of establishing a theocratic state. The Jewish state will also have non-Jewish citizens, Christians and Muslims, and, evidently, it will be necessary to ensure in advance full equal rights to all citizens and the absence of coercion or discrimination in matters of religion or in any other matter.[14]

Seemingly drawing his marker in the sand, and echoing the principles later formulated in the Declaration of Independence, Ben-Gurion declared that Exodus Jewish commitments were antithetical to a liberal democracy with a multireligiously affiliated population. Yet, what he marked with one hand, he blurred with the other. Expressing sympathy with Orthodox concerns, he continued:

> Still, the Executive appreciates your demands, and is aware that these are matters that worry not only the members of [leading ultra-Orthodox political party] Agudath Israel, but also many of the religious faithful in all Zionist parties or in no party, and it is sympathetic to your demands.[15]

As a result of this sympathy, Ben-Gurion agreed to allow a number of glaring exceptions:

Sabbath. It is clear that Sabbath will be the legal day of rest in the Jewish state. Permission will naturally be given to Christians and to those practicing other religions to rest on their weekly day of rest.

Kashrut. All means should be pursued to ensure that every
   state-run kitchen for the use of Jews serves kosher food.
Marital Law. . . . The Agency's Executive will do whatever possible to satisfy the deep need of the religiously observant in
   this matter, lest the House of Israel be divided in two.
Education. Full autonomy will be guaranteed to every education network . . . and the state will not infringe on the religious philosophy or the religious conscience of any part of
   the Jewish people.[16]

Assigning the official day of rest for Jews on the Sabbath—and later
formalizing the national calendar around the Jewish one—does not in
itself necessarily represent a significant breach of church-state separation. In fact, the end of Israel's Declaration of Independence explicitly
recognizes both calendars in its closing words—"in the city of Tel-Aviv,
on this Sabbath eve, the 5th day of Iyar, 5708 (May 14th, 1948)."[17] It is
similar to the use of the "prophets of Israel" in the declaration: a day
of rest from work needs to be assigned, and in the State of the Jews, for
Jews, their cultural heritage will determine its parameters; therefore,
in the language of the agreement, it is "clear" that the choice for the
day of rest for Jews will be the Sabbath. That said, there are no "Blue
laws" mandating rest for Jews on the Sabbath, and more importantly,
there is no designation of how it will be observed in the public sphere.

Similarly (and perhaps at first glance not obviously), the kosher food
clause for state-run institutions, principally the military, is a byproduct
of Genesis Zionism's inclusivity, rather than a coercive Exodus vision
of collective religious observance in the state. It aims to ensure that
all Jews in the Homeland of the Jewish people can serve in the army
and participate together in state institutions. No one will be excluded
because of their Jewish faith. *A Jew, even if Orthodox, is still a Jew.*

With the education clause, Ben-Gurion conceded to state funding
of religious public schools. It is important to note that the adopted
education policy was to fund parallel educational systems for every
major Jewish and non-Jewish ideological community in Israel. While

public education in the Israeli model is not religion-neutral, no particular Jewish denomination is given control over others. And, parallel to the free exercise clause of the First Amendment, the state does not limit parents' ability to educate their children in the spirit of their own traditions and values—that is, their own Exodus Covenant.[18] This is one of the only instances of Israeli law where the free exercise clause is maintained in the public sphere, and Genesis-inspired religious tolerance is preserved.

The education clause reveals Ben-Gurion's sense of the power balance of his time. The group whose religious freedom was most in need of protection from a hegemonic agenda was, in his view, the Orthodox minority. Orthodox Jews needed to be assured that freedom of religion in Israel would be applied not merely to the state's non-Jewish citizens but to themselves as well. Before offering their implicit support to the Zionist agenda of establishing a Jewish state, the Orthodox needed a guarantee that they would have sole authority over *their* children's education, without any interference from the all-powerful secular state institutions.

This may be the ultimate reason Ben-Gurion was not concerned about the larger consequences of his compromises with Orthodoxy. Based on his reading of his reality, it was inconceivable that they could have any impact on secular Exodus Zionism, either individually or collectively.

How wrong he was.

Marital Law and the State: Orthodoxy's "Deep Need"

Of the concessions listed above, Ben-Gurion's compromise on matters of marital law proved to be the most consequential. In these areas, he argued, it must be accepted that the Orthodox communities have a "*deep need* . . . lest the House of Israel be divided in two."

The "deep need" was code language for Orthodoxy's concern that if marriages, divorce, and conversion were not under their sole control, there would inevitably arise in Israel multiple Jewish communities that did not merely disagree ideologically but whose members under

Orthodox law could not marry each other. To them, non-Orthodox conversions were invalid; such converts could not marry into their community. So, too, any divorce not undertaken under Orthodox auspices was ineffectual: under Orthodox law, the couple was still married, further sexual relationships and marriages prohibited, and any children produced illegitimate (*mamzerim*).

Following Ben-Gurion, the State of Israel granted the Orthodox community sole control over all Jewish marriages and conversions within the state. It did so by preserving the British Mandate law outlined in the Palestine Order-in-Council of 1922:

> Subject to the provisions of Articles 64 to 67 inclusive, jurisdiction in matters of personal status shall be exercised, in accordance with the provisions of this part, by the *courts of the religious communities*. . . . For the purpose of these provisions, matters of personal status mean suits regarding marriage or divorce, alimony, maintenance, guardianship, legitimation and adoption of minors, inhibition from dealing with property of persons who are legally incompetent, successions, wills and legacies, and the administration of the property of absent persons.[19]

As legislated in 1953, the Rabbinic Court Jurisdiction Law stipulated that the "court of the religious communities" representing Israel's Jews would be the Orthodox Rabbinate.[20]

In a telling and perhaps dark irony, Israel proceeded to enact religious jurisdiction provisions for its Muslim, Christian, Druse, and Bahai minorities, but not for its Jewish citizens. In fact, Israel went so far as to establish distinct religious courts wherever there were denominational differences within a religious group, leading to *ten* distinct Christian courts—Greek Orthodox, Latin Catholic, Armenian Orthodox, Armenian Catholic, Syriac Catholic, Chaldean Catholic, Melkite Greek Catholic, Maronite Catholic, Syriac Orthodox, and Evangelical Episcopalian.

Yet for all the Jews, there was only one.

Protecting Minorities, Abusing the Majority

Some background: the 1922 British Mandate Law that had handed religious hegemony to the Orthodox in matters of personal status was a continuation of the Ottoman millet (meaning non-Muslim religious community) system that had governed Palestine prior to World War I.[21] Aiming to safeguard a measure of religious freedom and autonomy for religious minorities, the millet system extended limited self-governance over regulation of internal religious affairs to minority communities within the empire. It functioned under the British Mandate in the same capacity.[22]

Today, the State of Israel recognizes thirteen distinct non-Jewish minorities that together constitute 19 percent of Israeli society and grants each group autonomy over its religious affairs.[23] Each minority has independent religious courts and judges funded by the state. Even Chaldean Catholics, who only number a few families, pursue religious life and govern their personal affairs on their own terms. No non-Jew is forced to abide by a religious authority incommensurate with their beliefs and practices—unless, like their Jewish counterparts, they are secular.[24]

Since the millet system was designed to protect minority rights, the dominant Ottoman Sunni Muslim power was not defined as a protected millet: as the presiding power, its interests were identified with the Ottoman government. Why would it need to define itself as a millet when it could already pass laws that shaped society according to its values?

Thus it makes sense why the millet system of the Jews did not stress secular life at a time when secular Jews constituted the majority of the populace. Yet the courts the Zionist leaders offered to the Jews could have been at least as varied as those given to the diverse Christian community. Instead, treating Judaism as the exclusive concern of one single minority—the Orthodox—Israel's founders withheld the provision of religious courts to any other Jewish religious minority.

In effect, while the nonexistence of Jewish religious freedom in

Israel is often blamed on Orthodox political power today, in fact, it is the direct result of secular Zionists' failure to see themselves as a community of Exodus Jews warranting its own courts. Their abdication of the public sphere to the Orthodox demands has created a reality where only one group lacks religious freedom in the Jewish state: the majority of non-Orthodox Jews.

Why Did Secular Zionists Cede the Public Sphere?

The imperative that Jews in Israel not be further fractured by denominationalism resonated deeply with Zionist leaders' commitment to an inclusive Genesis Zionism. To them, Israel's core objective was to ensure that a functional baseline of cooperation and solidarity would be maintained within the Jewish homeland. Competing versions of Judaism had the potential to undermine the Jews' ability to function as a unified people.

But did the prioritization of inclusiveness really necessitate a unilateral secular withdrawal from the conversation? If the Orthodox were so concerned about Jewish unity, shouldn't secular leaders have placed the onus on *them* to balance their Exodus ideals with the Genesis Covenant's imperative to be as inclusive as possible? The Israeli rabbinate was established as the official religious representative of Zionism without deigning to acknowledge Genesis Zionism at all. Instead the rabbinate embodied the insular sectarian spirit of the nineteenth-century Diaspora that Zionism was ostensibly so intent on leaving behind.

Secular Zionist thinkers were also largely silent in addressing how the many rich formulations of Exodus Zionism they developed should be expressed in the public domain—perhaps because they felt that publicly, the state itself should be a secular liberal entity. If Judaism was to have a role, it was within private homes in accordance with individual conscience and sensibilities.

Furthermore, secular Jews made no effort to secure an alternate rabbinate or religious court that would promulgate a secular Jewish approach to marriage, divorce, conversion, or kashrut. As a result, when their Orthodox counterparts pushed for their version of Judaism to occupy the public sphere, secular Zionists had no "positive" religious agenda to oppose it. They were arguing for an absence, and that vacuum has been filled by an endless rush of negotiated concessions and coalition deals ever since.

From *Hiloni* to Not-Dati

Nowhere is this absence more glaring than in the lack of a serious Exodus-Zionist curriculum in the Secular Israeli school system. This is yet another tragic-but-instructive irony: the one area in which Secular Zionists did *not* cede control to the Orthodox was in the education of their children. The Orthodox could control who and how one married, what food could be sold as kosher, what happened in public sphere on the Sabbath, etc., but not the education of secular Jews.

This decision, however, did not suddenly imbue the secular leadership of the country with new knowledge, ideas, or interest in Exodus Judaism. Just as they were completely at a loss when it came to translating Exodus into a program for public Jewish life in Israel, so too they froze when it came to education. Secular leaders limited, and as the years went on, removed virtually all diaspora-originated subjects, such as Talmud and Jewish Philosophy, which were deemed unworthy of the new secular Israeli Jew, but to fill the gap they did not develop an alternative curriculum presenting a secular vision of Judaism as a framework for moral, ethical, or spiritual growth or engage students in acquiring basic Jewish knowledge.[25]

The ostensible exception was the inclusion of Bible studies as a mandatory subject. The Bible, however, was taught mainly as a book of nationalism, literature, history, and archeology and not as a source for a new Secular-Zionist Exodus Judaism. Through the Bible, students could meet the *last* Jews who spoke Hebrew and lived in, and fought for, the Land of Israel—that was more or less it. By and large the Bible was studied not for its Exodus content but for its ethnic and nationalist symbolism.[26]

These educational choices further reflected—and naturally reinforced—the absence of a secular Exodus-Zionist vision: an absence powerfully witnessed in the contemporary Hebrew vernacular discussed above. In modern Hebrew, the Orthodox are termed *Dati*, which means religious, while "secular" is translated into Hebrew as *Hiloni*. More often than not, though, this descriptor is not used, and secular Jews instead refer to themselves simply in the negative: "not-Dati" (nonreligious).

This negative identification is reflected in the kind of education "not-Dati" children receive: one lacking any formulation of a positive role Exodus Judaism might play in their lives. This absence is ultimately reflected in the allotment of class hours. Whereas state funding enables every student in a Religious Zionist or Haredi school to devote ten to fifteen hours a week to Jewish studies, students in secular schools largely receive no Jewish studies hours, aside from a few weekly hours of Bible—which is taught more as a book of literature than of Jewish values. In 1994 the Shenhar Committee, appointed by the Ministry of Education to explore the status of Jewish studies in public secular schools, exposed the bankruptcy of such courses.[27] In its wake, multiple initiatives were instituted, principally by NGOs supported by North American philanthropists, to reinvigorate Jewish studies. But it took some twenty-five years after the report for the ministry to begin allocating additional hours for Jewish studies in secular schools, and, moreover, these additions proved marginal: currently two weekly hours of Jewish culture, a new subject that combines Talmud and Jewish thought, for grades seven and eight.

Freedom *From*, Not Freedom *Of*

Today, given the growth in number and influence of Traditional Mesorati Jews in Israeli religious, cultural, and political life, a clear majority of Israeli Jews do not want a wall of separation between

Judaism and state. Many secular Israelis too do not advocate for, and do not prioritize in voting, the erection of an impervious wall. As a result, returning to the outline of the Declaration of Independence on this issue will not suffice. In their homeland, the majority of Jews—Orthodox, traditional Mesorati, and secular alike—do not want to be Jewish at home and a person in public.

But what if being Jewish at home could entail Israelis of all stripes bringing their version of Exodus Zionism into their national home, the public domain, and having that home reflect their Jewish commitments?

The problem is, when the different Jewish tribes converge and "talk" about the nature of the public domain, the traditional Mesorati and Orthodox bring their understanding of the Exodus Covenant, while the secular principally arm themselves with their commitment to Genesis Zionism and democracy. They argue for freedom *from* religion instead of demanding freedom *of* religion.

The Question of Religious Sensibilities

In 1997 then–Supreme Court Chief Justice Aharon Barak issued a famous ruling in the case of *Horev v. Ministry of Transportation*. Lior Horev was a secular resident of a majority ultra-Orthodox neighborhood in Jerusalem. At issue was whether the religious demands of Orthodox Jews could force the closure of streets in his neighborhood on the Sabbath to thru-traffic, when those streets served as major traffic arteries and provided access to the homes of the secular Jews. As framed by the petitioners, the conflict was between Orthodox Jews' rights to have their religious sensibilities respected and secular Sabbath-traveling Israelis' rights to free movement.[28]

Chief Justice Barak ruled that in a Jewish and democratic state, Jewish religious sensibilities do have legal standing. In certain instances these must be accommodated, even if they impinge on others' rights. He stipulated, however, a number of conditions.

First, others' human rights could be limited only in cases where the harm to religious sensibilities was definite and extreme. As a result, it was deemed illegitimate to close the main arteries during the hours when Sabbath observers were mostly at home—as distinct from those hours when they were walking to and from synagogue. When in their homes, only the *idea* of vehicular traffic "violating" the Sabbath would be disturbing—and this did not meet the threshold for suspending someone else's basic rights. Alternatively, when walking in the street on their way to synagogue, Sabbath observers had a right to a public sphere that reflected their religious sensibilities—and as a result, the courts could consider closing off the roads to cars at those hours alone.[29]

Barak's second condition stipulated that religious sensibilities could override certain human rights only so long as these did not violate someone else's religious sensibilities.

Tellingly, in presenting their case, the petitioners did not articulate a vision of *their* Sabbath, which might not only have allowed for vehicular travel but perhaps even have been enhanced by it. What if they had argued that access to transportation would enable their families to join them for Shabbat dinners, or allow them to celebrate Shabbat joyfully through access to leisure sites and culture venues? Had such a position been put forth, the issue would not have been framed as religious sensitivities versus human rights; rather, it would have come down to two competing religious sensibilities, which under Barak's own condition would demand equal consideration by the state. Instead, since the secular residents were not offering a competing religious sensibility, Barak determined that Orthodox Sabbath sensibilities would prevail if certain conditions were met: in addition to limiting the time of the closure, identifying an alternative thru-traffic route and finding a solution for the travel needs of the non-Orthodox minority in the neighborhood.[30]

In Israel, when it comes to religion-state issues, the conflict is rarely perceived as being between two distinct religious claims. This may explain why those who assert religious sensibilities most often win. They not only push harder; they are perceived as having more to lose.

The Diasporification of Israeli Jewishness

Redrawing the map of state and religion in Israel will require a deeper synthesis between Genesis and Exodus sensibilities. The societal dysfunction and alienation this long-standing imbalance has produced can only be rectified when public policy is guided by the demands of both. The core framework of Genesis Zionism does not just demand that all Jews be welcome and encouraged to move to the Jewish homeland; it also requires a serious commitment to tolerance for multiple expressions of Judaism. The covenant that embraces all Genesis Jews calls on the Jewish people to rise above their Exodus differences and do the same.

The paradigmatic policy expression of this Genesis-inspired commitment is Israel's Law of Return, which guarantees automatic citizenship to anyone whom Hitler would have persecuted as a Jew:[31]

> Every Jew has the right to come to this country as an oleh. [. . .]
>
> The rights of a Jew under this Law and the rights of an oleh under the Nationality Law, 5712–1952, as well as the rights of an oleh under any other enactment, are also vested in a child and a grandchild of a Jew, the spouse of a Jew, the spouse of a child of a Jew and the spouse of a grandchild of a Jew, except for a person who has been a Jew and has voluntarily changed his religion.
>
> For the purposes of this Law, "Jew" means a person who was born of a Jewish mother or has become converted to Judaism by any Jewish denomination and who is not a member of another religion.[32]

This—emblematic of Zionism's Genesis commitment—is the most expansive definition of Jewish peoplehood in Jewish history. Cognizant that Jews in the twentieth century profoundly disagreed on matters as fundamental as *Who is a Jew?* and how to become one, Israel in this law seemed to acknowledge that the homeland of the Jewish people cannot recognize one kind of Judaism exclusively.

But on its own, opening Israel's doors to the broadest spectrum of Jews is insufficient to achieve the needed recalibration. After all, in as much as Jews of all movements are encouraged to join the Jewish homeland, once those Jews land at Ben-Gurion Airport and attain citizenship, they're routed into a religious millet functioning exclusively under Orthodox law. The essential message is, *You are welcome here, but your Judaism is not.*

Take, for example, an individual who converts to Judaism via non-Orthodox auspices. Israel's Genesis-based law defines this person as Jewish enough to be granted citizenship. Once naturalized, however, the Israeli Rabbinate swoops in with its ultra-Orthodox conversion standards and prohibits this person from marrying any other Jew under its jurisdiction—that is, the entire country. All Jews are free to pursue their individual Judaism in their private homes. But in the national and public domain, only Orthodoxy rules.

Let us return to the Diaspora Jews and their synagogues, the object of so much parody, from which Zionism yearned to redeem the Jewish people. Once upon a time, an essential element of diasporic Jewish collective experience manifested itself through denominational affiliation and synagogue membership. If and when one began to disagree with a particular Exodus articulation of one's synagogue, one left or was asked to leave. In its place, one built or joined a new synagogue or chose to no longer belong at all. In this story, differences on issues pertaining to the Exodus Covenant are grounds for leaving, or being asked to do so.

Conversely, the essence of being at home in a Jewish state is that you can never be asked to leave. Israel is not a synagogue, but the homeland of *all* Jews. To grant Orthodoxy a monopoly and a free hand to alienate other Jews from Judaism on a historic scale is to treat Israel as an oversized diasporic synagogue and not the fulfillment of the Zionist dream.

Additionally, real religious pluralism will only emerge when all Israelis develop their take on Exodus Zionism and demand their rightful place in the public sphere. One only advocates for freedom *of* religion, and not for freedom *from* religion, when one sees oneself as a player in one's own Exodus Covenant and not merely a spectator in someone else's.

An Exodus Zionism for the Twenty-First Century

Instead of treating their respective Exodus Judaisms as bartering chips to be traded for foreign and economic policy support, Israelis must enter into dialogue with each other and begin the difficult process of forging a shared Exodus Zionism. This is what Genesis Zionism demands of us. It demands we stop normalizing insidious dichotomies like Dati vs. not-Dati, which only serve to entrench the disempowerment of non-Orthodox Jews over essential aspects of their lives.

This shared Exodus Zionism will involve compromises. Any liberal, modern synthesis of Genesis and Exodus will advocate for an Israel in which everyone has the right to marry, divorce, convert, and pray in accordance with their own Exodus Covenant. They must have access to their own rabbis, who in turn must have equal status and authority. If the state funds religious institutions, it will fund all of them equally. Israel will sanction multiple rabbinates, multiple Kotels, multiple ways of becoming a Jew. It will create a new status quo for Shabbat in the public sphere, not governed by Orthodox law alone, which will allow Jews to celebrate Shabbat in the public sphere in multiple ways.

Such a Zionist reengagement with the Exodus Covenant must significantly engage the realm of education. Our school systems must be as diverse as our synagogues, with each family having the freedom to send their children to a school that will advocate for, and educate toward, their version of the Exodus Covenant. It is unconscionable and incoherent that in Israel, only the Orthodox have access to a Jewish education.

When everyone has a stake in the public Jewish life of the country as well as the private Jewish identity of their family, Israel will finally fulfill its aspiration to serve at the homeland of the Jewish people.

11

Israel's Relationship with World Jewry

A few years ago I was asked to speak in front of a group of Israeli high school seniors at the opening of their Israel-Diaspora seminar, a recent addition to the curriculum designed to strengthen the bonds between Israelis and world Jewry. Sponsored by Israel's Ministry of Education, with financial support from North American philanthropy, this initiative has been gaining momentum—in direct correlation to spiking anxiety about how strained relations between Israel and much of Diaspora Jewry have become.

As I began to talk about Judaism's Genesis Covenant, the broad-based loyalty to the Jewish people it demands, and its implications for the idea of Israel as the homeland of the Jewish people—and not just Israeli Jews—I felt the lecture hitting its stride. I was even more charming and funny than usual, and my expository remarks were illustrated by colorful personal anecdotes. The students, however—sitting slouched in their chairs, yawning overtly—did not seem to share my enthusiasm. Fair enough. I upped my game, modulated my voice, tapped deeper into my own authentic passion for the subject. Nothing.

Being an experienced lecturer, I stopped the lecture. Turning to the students, I asked directly, "Does this topic interest you?" No answer.

I continued, "Whoever is interested in this topic, please raise your hand." Not one hand went up.

I was taken aback. This was an elite school renowned for academic excellence, intellectual inquiry, social responsibility, and pluralism. A large percentage of the student body had direct familial roots in North America and traveled there often. This wasn't a student body for whom Diaspora Jewry and Judaism was an alien phenomenon.

"Why don't you care?" I asked.

A student raised his hand and answered: "Why should I care? My family chose to make aliyah. My aunts, uncles, and cousins chose not to, even though they could. Beyond my family connection, why should they be important to me as an Israeli? Let them make aliyah, and then I will care."

In front of me was a group of self-confident Israelis raised in a powerful and successful Israel who had never known anything else. They did not need the Diaspora and had no language with which to even think about why they should care about it.

Inadequate Partners: Zionism's Rejection of Diasporic Judaism

Much has been discussed over the last decade regarding the weakening of North American Jewry's commitment to Israel, especially among the younger generation.[1] But very little has been written about Israel's attitude toward Diaspora Jewry, or its responsibility for the deterioration of the relationship.

The historical and intellectual foundations of Zionism are predicated on the notion that Jewish life can never truly thrive outside of Israel.[2] In modern Hebrew, the world is divided into two: *Eretz Yisrael*, the Land of Israel, and *Hutz la-Aretz*, Outside the Land. In rabbinic discourse this division stemmed from the legal distinction between the way one has to treat produce grown in the Land of Israel and produce grown elsewhere.[3] The continued use of this terminology in modern Hebrew is the product of a Zionist-Israeli-centric consciousness in which Israel is the center of the Jewish world.

This attitude, which might best be described as dismissive contempt, is embedded in most Zionist narratives going back to their inception. As Zionists campaigned to chart a new path for the Jewish people, they did so in part by rejecting both the physical and spiritual viability of Jewish life outside of a Jewish sovereign state. From the earliest years of the state, those who moved to Israel were referred to as *Olim*—ascenders, while those who left were referred to as *Yordim*—literally "descenders," a group Yitzchak Rabin once famously compared to the "droppings of insects."[4]

While the original Zionist dream of Israel as the homeland of the Jewish people, and not merely of Israelis or Israeli Jews, was predicated on a familial bond with world Jewry, from the early days of the state it became clear that this core bond entailed a sense of Genesis-based *obligation* toward Diaspora Jewry—but no Genesis-informed tolerance or *respect* for Diaspora Jewry's Exodus commitments. For the average Israeli, Dati and not-Dati alike, only Israeli Exodus Judaism had validity and significance.

Corpse, Vagrant, Beggar, Dog: World Jewry through Israel's Eyes

At the foundation of Zionist ideology lay the belief that the Diaspora was unworthy of respect, as it destroyed the Jew in both body and soul. In the words of some of the movement's most prominent early thinkers:

> Only a dog neither has nor wants a home. A man who chooses to live his whole life as a transient, without a thought for the establishment of a permanent home for his children, will forever be regarded as a dog.[5]
>
> Among the living nations of the earth, the Jews as a nation are long since dead . . . the ghostlike apparition of a living corpse. . . . To the living, the Jew is a corpse; to the native, a foreigner; to the homesteader, a vagrant; to the proprietary, a beggar; to the poor, an exploiter and a millionaire; to the patriot, a man without a country; for all, a hated rival.[6]
>
> The Judaism of the Galut [lit. Exile/Diaspora] is not worthy of survival. . . . The Galut is corrupting our human character and dignity.[7]

Israel was not merely the place where Jews would find a homeland: it was the place where Judaism and the Exodus Covenant would be renewed and restored in the form of a robust Jewish cultural vanguard. Ahad Ha'am had already posited the notion that without a cultural center, Jewish life outside of Israel would become atrophied:

> [Judaism] can no longer tolerate the *Galut* form which it had to take on, in obedience to its will-to-live, when it was exiled from its own country; but, without that form, its life is in danger. So, it seeks to return to its historic center.... Then, from this center, the spirit of Judaism will radiate to the great circumference, to all the communities of the Diaspora, to inspire them with new life and to preserve the over-all unity of our people.[8]

Diasporic existence threatened the Jewish soul and needed a Judaism produced in a Jewish center, a renaissance that would inspire Jews all around the world. That said, Ahad Ha'am viewed the idea of a sovereign Jewish state for all Jews as impractical and assumed Jews would have to continue to live in the Diaspora. But once the idea of Jewish sovereignty captured the imagination of Zionist thinkers, the Diaspora was reclassified as a place of inevitable *spiritual* death:

> Galut [Diaspora] can only drag out the disgrace of our people and sustain the existence of a people disfigured in body and soul.... The *galut* is corrupting our human character and dignity.... For Zionism is an aspiration toward morality and beauty. It has come, as one of its chief purposes, to redeem the man in us....[9]
>
> This is the very curse of the *galut*, that our undertakings do not, indeed *cannot* prosper.... Through cruel and bitter trials and tribulations . . . we have slowly arrived at the realization that without a tangible homeland, without private national premises that are entirely ours, we can have no sort of a life, either material or spiritual.[10]

For the mainstream Zionist, the homeland of the Jews was the only place where Judaism could be safe. With the Jewish people connected to the land, responsible for their own destiny, and free from the assimilationist pull of being a minority in someone else's home, the Exodus Covenant would reinvent itself and be revitalized. All this is unattainable in the Diaspora:

> [As a result of] growing assimilation and the fragmentation of the Jewish soul in the Diaspora, we are increasingly aware that *only* in Israel can a Jew live a full life, both as a Jew and as a human being.[11]
>
> [In Israel] the Jewish Israeli identity has to contend with all the elements of life via the binding and sovereign framework of a territorially defined state. And therefore, the extent of its reach into life is immeasurably fuller and broader and more meaningful than the Jewishness of the American Jew.[12]

From Shoah to Tekumah: Diaspora Darkness and the Light of Israel

While Zionism needed to redeem an unworthy and incomplete diasporic Judaism, it also needed to redeem the Jews who faced continuous and existential threats as long as they continued to live in someone else's home:

> [I]n vain do we make the same sacrifices of life and property as our fellow-citizens; in vain do we strive to increase the fame of our native land in science and art, or her wealth by trade and commerce. In countries where we have lived for centuries we are still cried down as strangers. . . . Everything tends, in fact, to one and the same conclusion, which is clearly enunciated in that classic Berlin phrase: "*Juden Raus!*" [Out with the Jews!].[13]

This sentiment resided deep in the consciousness of leading twentieth-century Zionist thinkers. After the devastation of the Kishinev Pogrom in Russia in 1903, Haim Nahman Bialik, one of Zionism's most significant literary and intellectual figures, wrote a haunting poem,

"The City of Slaughter," offering his assessment of Jewish destiny in the Diaspora:

> It was the flight of mice they fled.
> The scurrying of roaches was their flight.
> They died like dogs, and they were dead! . . .
> Your deaths are without reason.
> Your lives are without cause.[14]

This sentiment was seared into the bedrock of Zionist identity after the Holocaust and the near total destruction of European Jewry. For Israelis, Jewish history and geography were cast within the opposing poles of a stark archetypal dichotomy: Shoah-Holocaust/death on one side, and *Tekumah*-Rebirth/Resurrection/life on the other. Shoah was both the destiny of Jews prior to the rebirth of Israel and the self-evident conclusion of Jewish life outside of Israel. *Tekumah*, on the other hand, is the new Jewish future after the rebirth of the State of Israel and of those Jews who reside within its borders.

An Israel Independence Day Haggadah, written in 1952 for soldiers in the Israeli army, compared the rebirth of Israel to the redemption from Egypt:

> (Avadim Hayinu) We were slaves to the nations in all the lands and countries, from where the sun rises to where it sets. They tortured us, persecuted us, and unleashed upon us pogroms. So we said to one another: "Let us raise our heads and return to our land to work its fields. The house of Jacob, come let us go forth!" So we left from there—our young, elderly, women, our children. And if we had not left, we, our children and the children of our children, would still be enslaved to the nations to this very day.[15]

A few years later, Israel's Ministry of Education produced a collection of readings with a similar message for the family Independence

Day meal. It read, "This day, our day of independence, is a holiday for us, the day in which Israel's independence was restored. This day, it is our duty to sanctify it and celebrate it as Israel from generation to generation sanctified all its holidays. . . . Come let us multiply lights in our homes! These lights will symbolize our *exit from slavery to freedom, from darkness to a great light*."[16]

The redemptive consciousness associated with the rebirth of Israel has also been forged into Israeli sensibilities through what has become the National Israeli High Holiday period, the nine days in the spring between the twenty-seventh of the Hebrew month of Nissan and the fifth of month of Iyar. On the twenty-seventh of Nissan, Israel commemorates Holocaust Memorial Day; on the fourth of Iyar Memorial Day for Israel's fallen soldiers and victims of terror attacks; and on the fifth, Israel's Independence Day. Israelis remember and commemorate the tragedy of the Shoah and directly link it to its antidote, the Tekumah of the Jewish people in Israel.

The Ministry of Education offers the following pedagogical framing for how to teach this holiday period to students:

> "We hereby declare the Establishment of a Jewish State in the land of Israel, to be known as the State of Israel." Thus, 70 years ago, the first prime minister of Israel, David Ben-Gurion, announced the founding of the country. A few years prior, the holocaust occurred wherein six million Jews were killed and destroyed. The founding of the State of Israel in the historical homeland of the Jewish people constitutes the guarantee that never again will any holocaust befall the Jewish people.[17]

Within this zero-sum dichotomy of Jewish life as either destruction or rebirth, existence outside of Israel is, by definition, destruction: an unnatural and unnecessary continuation of the Jewish history of humiliation, powerlessness, and death.

Secular Israelis in Orthodox Clothing

The Zionist narrative has no language for Jews who, like Jacob Blaustein (see chapter 8), see themselves at home outside of Israel. They argue, for example, that "American Jews vigorously repudiate any suggestion or implication that they are in exile. American Jews—young and old alike, Zionist and non-Zionist alike—are profoundly attached to America. . . . *To American Jews, America is home.*"[18]

Israelis, however, can relate all too well to Jewish communities facing immediate and existential threats, such as the Ethiopian and Soviet Jews of the twentieth century, and to some degree French Jews over the last decade or so and Ukrainian Jews today.[19] The precariousness of these communities reaffirms Israeli Jews' sense of self-importance and superiority. Meanwhile, many Israelis, while feeling ideologically reaffirmed by the recent growth of antisemitism in America, have conceptual difficulty with American Jews—Jews who have no yearning to make aliyah and for whom Zionism means supporting the right of *Israelis* to live in Israel.

But Genesis, as argued throughout this book, is not an independent sphere focusing exclusively on the physical viability of Jewish peoplehood. It also exists in a gravitational relationship with its Exodus counterpart, serving to temper the tendencies of overzealous Exodus impulses to sow communal fragmentation. A liberal Genesis Covenant embraced by most Jews entails the understanding that one cannot love Jews and delegitimize their Judaism. *An authentic commitment to this Genesis Covenant demands and fosters tolerance and respect for the multiplicity of Exodus Judaisms so prevalent in Jewish life.*

Israel does not need to devalue world Jewry's contributions to the Exodus Covenant in order to justify its own revolution. In expressing such attitude toward "diasporic" Judaisms, Israeli secular and liberal Jews are, paradoxically, aping Israeli Orthodoxy's claim to hegemony over Jewish life worldwide. They are treating Israeli Judaism as a denomination and claiming it as the only legitimate one. Zionists aspired to redeem the Jewish people from this divisive denominational hubris, only to find themselves turning it on Diaspora Jews who "dared" to believe that Judaism could not merely survive but achieve a thriving renaissance, in its home outside of Israel.

A New Israeli: North American Partnership in the Exodus Covenant

When liberal Jews engage Genesis and Exodus in a healthy self-correcting dialogue, the Exodus Covenant is immunized against denominational monopolization and expands to contain the ideas and values of most Jews who claim it as their birthright. When diverse notions of the Exodus Covenant are open to tolerating, engaging, and learning from each other, advancement in the realm of Exodus itself becomes possible.

Secular and liberal Israeli Jewish approaches to Exodus Judaism can benefit immensely from engaging with their North American counterparts, and vice versa. Secular and liberal Israeli Judaism, mired in a non-Dati identity, have much to learn from North American liberal Jewish denominations, which have spent over a century synthesizing Judaism with modernity. Democracy, human rights, environment, attitudes toward the non-Jew, pluralism, gender sensitivity, racial justice: in Israel, these issues are generally perceived as part of a universal—as distinct from Jewish—discourse. One of North American Judaism's innovative attributes is an interpretive engagement that rereads the Jewish tradition such that "modern universal" values have become an integral part of Judaism and *its* values—a major contribution to Jewish self-understanding.

Free from the hegemony of Orthodoxy, Jewish rituals have also been rewritten and innovated in ways that better speak to a secular and liberal consciousness. For too many secular and liberal Israeli Jews, the synagogue they do not go to is Orthodox. They do not want to be Orthodox and therefore have no synagogue to go to. The challenge that North American Judaism places before Israelis is to build a synagogue they would want to be part of.

Genesis Zionism's challenge to Israel is to free itself from a zero-sum Shoah-Tekumah dichotomy. When Israel becomes Jewish pluralism's greatest advocate—and no longer its most zealous antagonist—it will not only strengthen the World Jewry-Israel relationship but open up possibilities for a new renaissance in Israeli Exodus Judaisms. Then, liberal Israeli Jews, like their counterparts around the world, will no longer tolerate a single rabbinate alien to their Jewish values. They will insist on a marriage and conversion process that reflects their religious sensibilities. They will demand funded hours for their children's Judaic study with a curriculum that reflects *their* vision of the Exodus Covenant. And they will bring their b'nai and b'not mitzvah to the liberal Kotel, now resurrected because they clamored for it, and welcome their children into a Covenant that represents their own deepest commitments and aspirations as Jews.

North American liberal Jewish sensibilities have already influenced Israeli Exodus Judaism—for example, on issues of pluralism, gender, and gay rights—but Israelis rarely acknowledge this indebtedness. When Israelis not only recognize but celebrate the contribution of diasporic Judaism to Israeli life, they will take major steps toward fulfilling their Zionist aspirations to the Tekumah of Israel not merely as a home for the Jews but a Jewish home for all Jews.

12

Unpacking a Not-So-"Basic" Law

In May 2021, in the midst of Hamas's latest rocket campaign against civilian population centers and Israel's military response, some Israeli-Arab-Palestinian youth in the major Jewish/Arab mixed cities of Lod, Haifa, Acre, and Jaffe began to riot and attack Jews, setting fire to Jewish businesses and synagogues. In some neighborhoods, Jewish youth responded in kind. It was the closest we ever have been to a civil war.[1]

Israeli society is one of the most skilled in the world in managing conflict and war on its borders and defending itself against terror attacks, but it is technically and conceptually a novice in managing internal conflict between its fellow citizens. Not only were the police forces overwhelmed, but the public discourse did not know how to classify the riots.

MK and former Mayor of Jerusalem, Nir Barkat, a leading contender for the future leadership in the (right-of-center) Likud party, made an early stab at clarification. He called the Israeli-Arab-Palestinian rioters "Hamas terrorists"—since the riots coincided with the Hamas bombings, Barkat reasoned, those rioters belonged in the same grouping—and classified the Israeli Jewish rioters as "law breakers."[2]

The same acts were performed by fellow citizens—but one was classified as terror, and the other as merely illegal activity.

Similarly, MK Itamar Ben Gvir capitalized on the fear and insecurity that these riots engendered to move his ultranationalist party and ideology to the center of Israeli Zionist political life, ultimately winning over 10 percent of the popular vote in the fall 2022 national elections. He ran a remarkably successful campaign principally on the platform of protecting Jews from Arabs and returning "ownership" over the country to the Jews—ownership they ostensibly lost in the aftermath of the May riots.

Why the riots erupted precisely at that time is not clear. The rioters spoke of the threatened expulsion of Palestinian residents from their homes in Sheikh Jarrah (an East Jerusalem neighborhood) and the police storming the Al Aksa mosque with stun grenades. Whether or not these were the catalysts, Israeli-Arab-Palestinian citizens' loyalty was immediately questioned, whether openly or implicitly—a common occurrence for a group often viewed as on the margins, not fully members of Israeli society and not "really" faithful to the country.[3]

One of my daughters, who lives in Jaffa, a mixed Jewish Arab city, experienced the riots firsthand. When the warning sirens went off as Hamas missiles targeted Tel Aviv, she took cover in her building's stairwell, since the old building did not have a bomb shelter. After the second evening, she noticed that the only people in the stairwell during the attacks were the building's Jewish inhabitants. The next morning she knocked on her Arab neighbors' door, an elderly couple, asking them if they heard the sirens and saying she would be happy to knock on their door and wake them up the next time the sirens went off. They thanked her but declined.

Over the phone, I suggested that maybe she should come home, to Jerusalem, until the current round of attacks subsided. She said she didn't like the idea of someone forcing her out of her home. (This is more the product of her stubborn nature than of some deeper Zionist ideology). Instead, she promised that between the hours of 8 p.m. and midnight, when the missiles were generally launched, she would stay at her friend's house, which had a safety room.

Nonetheless, that evening, at 10:30, after Israel's missile defense system had intercepted an extensive round of missiles launched at the Tel-Aviv area, she decided it was safe to go home. As she walked with her dog, she saw a mob of Arab youths smashing cars and shop windows. One group raced by her, and she quickly crossed the street. The mob saw her and crossed after her, taunting and pursuing. She put her head down, ignored them, and rushed home. She was likely saved because of her gender; some Jewish men who found themselves in similar circumstances that week were severely beaten.

As she opened her apartment door, seriously shaken, her Arab neighbor opened his door and saw her. Immediately realizing her condition, he pulled her into his apartment and proceeded with his wife to feed, comfort, and take care of her.

The next day, she decided to come home.

Five days later she returned to her apartment in Jaffa. For the remainder of the week, until the violence subsided, the Arab residents in the building looked after their Jewish neighbors when Arab mobs passed by. The Jewish neighbors did the same when Jewish mobs were in the vicinity. The bombings ceased, the Gaza campaign wound down, and life returned to its "normal" status quo.

Two weeks later we decided to visit my daughter for Sabbath, staying in an Airbnb nearby. "Coexistence" had returned to the streets, but not until the Military Border Patrol replaced the understaffed police and heavy-handedly patrolled the streets.

Sabbath was restful. Jaffa was beautiful, a tapestry of new and old, Jew and Arab, gentrified and not. The Arab merchants from whom we purchased supplies for the Sabbath welcomed us graciously. Everything seemed normal with the exception of the entrance to the building in which we were staying. A Jewish-owned building on a predominantly Arab street, its doorway alone was charred and black, having been set afire by a Molotov cocktail.

Fellow citizens, enemies, allies, neighbors—who are Jewish and Arab Israelis to each other? One the one hand, we are all citizens of Israel together. At the same time, we do not share in Israel in the same way. For Jews, Israel is our nation and the homeland of the Jewish people, built on the foundations of a two-thousand-year-old dream for Jews to return home. For over 80 percent of Israeli-Arab-Palestinians, as their multihyphenate name suggests, Israel is the land in which they and their ancestors were born, a home they do not want to leave. They are obviously not Zionists and see themselves as part of the Palestinian people but prefer to remain citizens and live in Israel.[4]

Israel is their country, but its establishment was realized through what they experienced as their greatest *Nakba* (catastrophe): many of them losing their homes and lands. In Jaffa, for example, before the war the Palestinian population numbered over fifty thousand, but after the 1948 war, only some four thousand remained.[5] Which brings me to this chapter's central question: how can Israel build a shared society between its Israeli-Jewish and Israeli-Arab-Palestinian citizens? We will focus the discussion on the 2018 Basic Law: Israel as the Nation-State of the Jewish People.

The "Basic Laws" of Israel are thirteen semiconstitutional statutes addressing the formation and role of the principal institutions of the state as well as relations between state authority and basic civil rights that the Supreme Court uses to assess the validity of all other legislation and government policy. The 2018 Basic Law was proposed to reaffirm the Jewish people's connection to Israel. At the same time, the law has emerged as a major source of tension, viewed by some as formalizing discrimination and inequality against citizens who are not members of the Jewish people. The law reaffirms the Jewish people's connection to Israel, but it also institutionalizes Israeli-Arab-Palestinians' marginal status. How would a renewed Genesis-Exodus synthesis reassess—and potentially revise—such a law?

"A Country without a People"?: Israel and Its Palestinian-Arab Citizens

As Zionism endeavored to build a homeland for the Jewish people that would enable them to live in safety, it concentrated its attention on Jewish existential needs. This was its mandate and principal moral responsibility. From a Zionist perspective, it was more convenient to buy into the myth that Palestine was "a country without a people"—an empty desolate land, a perfect match for "a people without a country."[6]

The Palestinians' ensuing animosity toward the Jews, whom they viewed as colonizing usurpers, inevitably generated opposing narratives of mutual delegitimization.[7]

The UN-sponsored Partition Plan adopted by the General Assembly on November 29, 1947, endorsed the proposition that lasting peace between Jews and Arabs would only be achieved through the separation of the two ethnic communities, giving each its exclusive national homeland.[8]

From its inception, Israel as the homeland of the Jewish people did not have a coherent attitude toward its Arab-Palestinian minority. As a result of siding with the Arab states that declared war on Israel in 1948, Israeli-Arab-Palestinians, while granted citizenship, remained under discriminatory martial law until 1966. Like many other nation-states with sizable minorities, Israel failed to bridge the gap between political and legal equality on the one hand, and social equality on the other.[9] The relationship between Israeli-Arab-Palestinians and Palestinians in the West Bank and Gaza, with whom Israel is still not at peace, would further complicate the work of coexistence and mutual accommodation.

Israel as the Nation-State of the Jewish People

Israel does not have a formal constitution. Its so-called Basic Laws function as a quasi-constitution, and as noted, Israel's Supreme Court, since 1992 when the Basic Law of Human Dignity and Freedom and Freedom of Occupation was passed, uses the Basic Laws to assess the validity of all other laws and governmental policy.[10] A classic example is the *Horev v. Ministry of Transportation* case mentioned in a previous chapter, in which Chief Justice Barak used the Basic Law of Human Freedom and Dignity to override the municipal decision to prohibit vehicular traffic in certain neighborhoods on Shabbat.

In 1992 the Knesset instituted this Basic Law of Human Freedom and Dignity, which forbade the violation of life, body, or dignity of any person, regardless of national, religious, or sexual identity.[11] Some constituencies in Israel then argued that this Basic Law needed to be balanced with a parallel Basic Law reinforcing Israel's mission specifically as the homeland of the Jewish people. In effect, they were saying, while the pursuit of human freedom and dignity reflected important universalist Exodus-Zionist aspirations, the lack of statutory expression for Genesis Zionism was too loose a seam in the legal fabric of the state. Viewed strictly through the lens of this Basic Law, for example, could Israel's Law of Return be deemed a discriminatory violation of Israeli-Arab-Palestinian's dignity? What about the primacy of the Jewish calendar as the national calendar of Israel? What about Hebrew?[12]

To clarify and establish the place of Jewishness in the Jewish homeland, in 2018 the Israeli Parliament passed the Basic Law: Israel as the Nation-State of the Jewish People.

Basic Principles

This Basic Law begins with a statement of "Basic Principles":

A. The Land of Israel is the historic homeland of the Jewish people on which the State of Israel was established.
B. The State of Israel is the Nation State of the Jewish people in which it realizes its natural, cultural, religious and its historical right to self-determination.
C. The exercise of the right to national self-determination in the State of Israel is unique to the Jewish people.[13]

Clauses A and B are rearticulations of principles set forth in Israel's Declaration of Independence and represent the core consensual values of all Israeli Zionist Jews, regardless of political and religious affiliation. The problem is not in what these clauses affirm, but in what they omit. Granted, Israel is the nation-state of the Jewish people, but what is Israel's relationship to its two million non-Jewish citizens? Couldn't and shouldn't the law state that Israel is the nation-state of the Jewish people *and* the country of all its citizens?[14] After all, Israel's Declaration of Independence, which served as the inspiration for these clauses, both affirms Israel as the nation-state of the Jewish people and simultaneously asserts that the State of Israel must "foster the development of the country for the benefit of all its inhabitants."

By omitting any mention of Israel's non-Jewish citizens, the law is perhaps not overtly discriminatory, but is implicitly and dangerously so, as it lays the ground to justify discrimination in practice. When a minority of the population is not seen, when their presence and their rights are not explicitly asserted and validated, their status invariably will become more tenuous.

Clause C essentially reaffirms the Israeli side of the UN Partition Plan, which assigned Jews and Palestinians their own nation-states, from which each could pursue its own respective national self-determination. This clause is also the foundation of any future two-state solution to the Israeli-Palestinian conflict.

Note that nowhere does it state that the exercise of the right to national self-determination in the *land* of Israel is unique to the Jewish people. Under this law, Palestinians could form their own nation-state, side by side with the Jewish nation-state, in the same land. The law solely precludes Palestinian national self-determination within the borders of the *State* of Israel.[15]

State Symbols

The second main feature of the law requires that the state's symbols, language, calendar, and holidays give expression to Israel being exclusively the nation-state of the *Jewish* people. Its Jewishness is to be expressed not just in demographic prevalence but in its official public character:

A. The name of the state is "Israel."
B. The state flag is white, with two blue stripes near the edges and a blue Star of David in the center.
C. The state emblem is a seven-branched menorah with olive leaves on both sides and the word "Israel" beneath it.
D. The state anthem is "Hatikvah."[16]

Aside from the national anthem Hatikvah ("The Hope")—which excludes non-Jews who were not a part of the Jewish people's two-thousand-year hope "to be a free people in our homeland"—this section is a standard instance of the international norm of assigning legal standing to national symbols reflecting the majority national group.

The law proceeds to stipulate that Jerusalem is the capital. Later, it legislates that the Jewish and Jewish-Israeli calendar will be the primary national calendar (while allowing the non-Jewish citizens of Israel complete freedom to adopt their religious calendars for their official days of rest):

> Independence Day is the official national holiday of the State.
> Memorial Day for the Fallen in Israel's Wars, and the Holocaust Martyrs' and Heroes' Remembrance Day, are official memorial days of the State.
> The Sabbath and the Jewish holidays are the established days of rest in the State; non-Jews have the right to observe the days of rest on their days of Sabbath and holidays; details regarding this matter shall be determined by law.[17]

A New National State Language

In what became one of its more controversial clauses, the law stipulates that Israel will henceforth have only one state language:

> Hebrew is the State language.
> Arabic in state institutions or vis-à-vis them will be set by law.
> Nothing in this article shall affect the status given to the Arabic language before this law came into force.

What is controversial in this section is not the designation of a singular national language. Adopting the language of the majority is standard and the norm in many states (e.g., France, Italy, and most states in the United States).[18] However—as distinct from the sections quoted above, which merely elaborated on the current state of affairs and folded them into a Basic Law—this section altered the prior legal status quo. Prior to the law, Israel had two official languages: Hebrew and Arabic. This legal status derived from Britain's Palestine Mandate of 1922, which stated that "English, Arabic, and Hebrew shall be the official languages of Palestine."[19] The Palestine Order-in-Council (1922) further required that "all ordinances, official notices, and official forms of the Government . . . shall be published in English, Arabic, and Hebrew."[20]

In 1948, with the establishment of the state, Israel enacted the Law and Administration Ordinance, which adopted the laws prevailing in the country in 1948 as Israeli law, with several amendments and exceptions. Section 15(b) specified that "any provision in the law requiring the use of English language is repealed."[21] This left Israel with the two official languages of Hebrew and Arabic.

In practice, as the language of the majority, Hebrew is dominant. However, as the principal language of 20 percent of Israel society, and the language of educational instruction for most Arabic speaking students, the place of Arabic was de jure and de facto preserved. All food labels, medicine brochures, safety regulations, and messages published or posted by the government had to be translated into Arabic. In Hebrew-speaking schools, Arabic is a common subject of study from grades 7 to 10. In Israel's Knesset, Arabic-speaking members could choose to address the plenary in Arabic. The Israeli Supreme Court ruled to protect the place of Arabic in public signage, alongside Hebrew in mixed Jewish Arab cities, as an essential implication of Israel's bedrock legal commitment to Human Freedom and Dignity.[22]

However, with this new legislation, henceforth, only Hebrew maintains its status as a state language, with Arabic redesignated from state language to one of "special status." That said, the law also stipulates that nothing in this law shall affect its de facto standing prior to the law's passage.

If so, what purpose does the law serve? Its proponents posit that it is merely a symbolic expression of the Jewish national character of the state. Its opponents argue that this section serves to denigrate the Arab-speaking population and to designate Arabs as second-class citizens with a second-class language in the nation-state of the Jews.[23]

Who is right?

In assessing the significance of any legislation, it is important to ask, *what problem is it purporting to solve?* And, *what are the consequences? How will it function de facto?* In Israel, where the status of Hebrew is stronger than ever and proficiency is an essential condition of social and economic advancement, the problem this legislation solves is unclear. Moreover, in functionally maintaining the status quo, the law's primary impact is as a symbolic declaration that is insulting to the Arab-speaking minority, not a buttress to the primacy of Hebrew in Israeli society. Finally, insults of this form never remain declarative alone. Inevitably they influence social and cultural norms and deepen discrimination toward those whose principal language is not the "official" one.[24]

Israel and World Jewry

Reflecting Genesis Zionism's longstanding commitment to preserving Israel's Jewish majority, and again echoing the Declaration of Independence, the law stipulates, "The state will be open for Jewish immigration and the ingathering of exiles." Yet the Basic Law also significantly expands on the position outlined in the declaration.

Understanding twenty-first-century reality—after mass immigrations from the former Soviet Union and Ethiopia, the majority of Diaspora Jews worldwide have no intention to move to Israel—the new law expands on Israel's Genesis responsibilities to World Jewry, asserting its commitment to protect Jews anywhere in the world who are in danger and to ensure their ongoing connection with the State of Israel:

A. The state will strive to ensure the safety of the members of the Jewish people and of its citizens in trouble or in captivity due to the fact of their Jewishness or their citizenship.

B. The state shall act within the Diaspora to strengthen the affinity between the state and members of the Jewish people.

C. The state shall act to preserve the cultural heritage and religious heritage of the Jewish people amongst Jews in the Diaspora.[25]

Here, Israel is viewing World Jewry as being at risk, physically *and* spiritually. As the nation-state of the Jewish *people*—and not Israeli citizens alone—Israel is duty-bound to provide any and all forms of protection and service Diaspora Jewry may require. This is an interesting expansion of the obligations of Genesis Zionism. Admittedly paternalistic, it does acknowledge the permanent status of Jewish life in the Diaspora, a measure of acceptance Israel did not always extend.

What is problematic about this section again lies in what it omits: its expanded sense of responsibility to non-Israeli *Jews* spotlights (and arguably expands) the glaring gap in status between Israel's Jewish and non-Jewish citizens. While embracing additional responsibilities to all Jews, including noncitizens, the Nation State Law nowhere speaks of any obligations to the non-Jews who *are* its citizens. This sin of exclusion gives further credence to the claim that the law does not merely protect the Jewishness of Israel but denigrates its Arab Palestinian citizens, reinforcing their second-class status. While fleshing out its responsibility to Jews who do not live in Israel, the law renders Israeli-Arab-Palestinians legally and culturally invisible.

Jewish Settlement Alone?

The most morally dubious section of the Nation State Law (section 7) is entitled "Jewish Settlement." It states, "The state views the development of Jewish settlement as a national value and will act to encourage and promote its establishment and consolidation."[26]

This section was the subject of extensive debate, criticism, and editing in the Knesset committee. Prior to its final iteration quoted above, the original language stated as follows:

A. Every Israeli resident, regardless of religion or nationality, is entitled to take action to preserve his culture, heritage, and the preservation of his language and identity.
B. The State may allow a community, including members of one religion or of one nationality, to maintain separate communal settlement.[27]

On the surface, subclause A seems to be a broad-based call for equality and tolerance for all Israeli citizens, akin to the equal rights paragraph in Israel's Declaration of Independence. In fact, however, the purpose of sub-clause A was to serve as a preamble and justification for subclause B, which was viewed as legalizing the creation of an apartheid-like state of affairs by sanctioning segregated, ostensibly separate-but-equal, Jewish-only cities.

Israel's Supreme Court had set the precedent that Israeli-Arab-Palestinians must not be impeded from purchasing land or houses in cities with a Jewish majority.[28] Section 7 would effectively nullify this ruling. Under its newfound "enlightened" right to preserve one's distinct culture, heritage, language and identity, Israeli Jews would be able to legally exclude Israeli-Arab-Palestinians from their communities and neighborhoods.

The public protest this language provoked proved effective. Then-prime minister Netanyahu ordered the clause removed and replaced with a more neutral articulation, couching the support for Jewish settlement as a "national value."[29]

While no longer sanctioning segregation among Israeli citizens, this new language remains problematically discriminatory. According to the law, only the development of Jewish settlement is a "national value." But while Israel seeks to define itself as the nation-state of the Jewish people, close to 20 percent of its citizens do not fall into this category. What about land allocation for the economic development of principally Arab-Palestinian cities and towns? According to the law, this does not count as a national value, which amounts to state-sponsored inequality in the distribution of its resources. The law does not merely symbolically strengthen the legitimacy of Genesis Zionism—it does so by making Israeli non-Jewish citizens invisible, "strangers" in their own country.

"For You Were Strangers": An Exodus-Zionist Basic Law

As we've seen, the Basic Law affirming Israel as the nation-state of the Jewish people reaffirms the Jewish people's connection to Israel while institutionalizing Israeli-Arab-Palestinians' marginal status—and, some say, formalizing discrimination and inequality. Defenders of the law argue that its function is to enshrine into the legal fabric of Israeli society principles already articulated in its Declaration of Independence. Opponents argue that the law is morally flawed, a racist manifestation of unbridled Jewish nationalism that views Israel as principally the nation of the Jews, and not of all its citizens.[30]

In my view, some aspects of the Basic Law may hold value as a legal backstop to safeguard core Genesis-Zionist policies, which reflect principles shared widely among most sectors of Israeli Jewish society across the political spectrum—that is, the Jewish Right of Return, Israel's responsibility to World Jewry, the Jewish calendar as the national calendar. It is conceivable that under the existing Basic Law of Dignity and Freedom, these particularistic policies could have been overturned.

However, when public expressions of Genesis Zionism are not balanced by the moral aspirations of Exodus Zionism and its commitment to Israel as not only a Jewish but also a democratic state, a core anchor of our collective Jewishness is uprooted. The nation-state of the Jewish people must be more than a security blanket for insecure Genesis-Zionists to clutch tightly and feel reassured; it must also be a canvas for the collective expression and celebration of our Exodus commitments. Leaving the latter exclusively under the jurisdiction of the Law of Human Freedom and Dignity creates an unnecessary dichotomy between Israel as a democratic state and Israel as a Jewish state; between its liberal Western values and its Jewish ones; between its Genesis and Exodus Zionism.

What would it look like if the Basic Law of Israel as the Nation State of the Jewish People took into account a more liberal Exodus Covenant? What if it sought to enshrine not merely nationalist values, but Jewish moral imperatives?

Israel was never a land without a people. Today, while serving as the homeland of the Jews, it is also home to two million Israeli-Arab-Palestinians. Exodus Judaism has much to say about how we are meant to live with non-Jewish citizens in our midst. The critical principles guiding our attitude are (1) the core belief in the equality of all humankind as created in the image of God, and (2) Jewish history. "They [i.e., the stranger] shall be to you as one of your citizens; you shall love him as yourself, for you were strangers in the Land of Egypt" (Lev. 19:34). Since we know what it means to be a vulnerable minority defined as noncitizens and treated as outsiders, we are commanded to love the minority in our midst and treat them as we yearned to be treated—as equal citizens. Hillel converts this biblical logic into the talmudic "Golden Rule": "What is hateful unto you, do not do to others. That is the whole Torah."[31]

Israel as the homeland of the Jewish people is the antidote to a bitter legacy of persecution and alienation. But as the sovereign *nation-state* of the Jewish people, the injunctions to "remember that you were strangers in the Land of Egypt" and "what is hateful to you do not do unto others" obligate us to recognize not only our own rights but those of the minority. Israel-Arab-Palestinians are not strangers in our midst, but full and equal citizens by law, and Exodus demands that we create a society that embraces and protects them too. No countervailing force should legitimate treating Israel-Arab-Palestinians (or any non-Jew) with anything short of full equality. As the Declaration of Independence declares, Israel's founding commitment is dual in nature: to be the homeland of the Jewish people and to advance the interests of *all* its inhabitants and treat *all* its citizens equally, regardless of national or religious identity. This precise sensibility is absent from the nation-state law.

Heeding the voice of both Genesis and Exodus Zionism requires defining Israel as the nation state of the Jewish people *and* of all its citizens. It might even include, as argued by one of the law's critics, former MK Benjamin Begin, a clause like that found in the Declaration of Independence committing Israel to the equal rights of all its citizens. Such a statement would not undermine the Jewishness of the State of Israel. To the contrary, what better fulfillment of a pillar precept of Exodus Judaism could there be than to raise up the non-Jewish minority and say, *I see you! You are not invisible. I know what it's like to be invisible and therefore I never invisible-ize others.*

In a similar vein, maintaining the status quo and retaining Arabic as an official language is clearly justified by the size of the Palestinian Arab minority and would pose no threat to the Jewishness of Israel. Yet another substantive gesture might be the inclusion of a number of Muslim holidays as days of rest for all citizens.

In this conversation, it is critical to update our context and recognize the advances that have occurred since 1948, when only some 715,000 Jews resided in Israel.[32] In 2021 the Jewish population of Israel is 7.2 million and the Arab minority 2 million, with similar birth rates.[33] The Zionist project succeeded; there is no longer a "demographic challenge" to a sustained Jewish majority. Today, a Basic Law committed to the principles of both Genesis and Exodus Zionism should not only emphasize the right of Jewish immigration but also recognize and affirm rights of family reunification to the spouses and children for all of Israel's citizens. Moreover, it would designate not merely the development of Jewish settlements but the development of settlements for all its citizens as a national value.

The Declaration of Independence's commitment to "foster the development of the country for the benefit of all its inhabitants" is what a liberal Exodus Zionism demands. Anything less devalues the nation-state of the Jewish people.

Defenders of the nation-state law have argued that there is no need for it to protect Israel's non-Jewish minority, as sufficient protection is already provided in the Basic Law of Human Freedom and Dignity. But this argument obscures how, through its Genesis-only focus, the nation-state law itself legitimizes legal and cultural discrimination—and renders these impervious to being overridden by the Basic Law of Human Freedom and Dignity. Furthermore, proponents of the law are enshrining a core tension within Israel between Genesis and Exodus Zionism, between democratic and Jewish values, between Jews and non-Jews. Such a dichotomy is not only unnecessary but detrimental to, and unworthy of, the Jewishness of Israel.

The challenge of Jewishness is to build our collective identity through an ongoing synthesis. As Israel was struggling to birth itself and survive in a hostile environment, Exodus aspirations at times seemed, to paraphrase Jabotinsky, somewhat of a luxury. That may or may not have been true. It is certainly not the case in the twenty-first century. Israel is a remarkable success story: its Jewish identity is secure, its safety is protected by one of the most powerful armies in the world, its economy is thriving, and the outlook is bright. But, as this flawed Basic Law illustrates, Zionism's success has not been fully integrated into the story we are telling ourselves about ourselves.

13

Yearning Again for Peace

I went to war for my country. My tank was blown up. I should not be alive.

The truth is that I should not have been a tank commander in the first place. I have an amblyopic right eye out of which I barely see. Because of a cornea disease, I can only see out of my left eye with the assistance of special contact lenses that I cannot wear under battle conditions. Moreover, both corneas are extensively scratched, and I am significantly visually impaired at night. The army picked up on my condition during my medical examinations and assigned me a noncombat classification. It did not consider the possibility that I would request to be retested and subsequently cheat on the eye exam. I became a combat soldier in the tank corps and eventually a tank commander—the eyes of the tank.

Six years later, as a newly married reservist, I was called up to serve in the 1982 Lebanon War. Since moving to Israel as a thirteen-year-old boy, I had been waiting for this moment: the moment I would join the ranks of my people who fought to defend our country, to defend our right to *be*.

As a Jew I was taught to pray for peace. As an Israeli I was taught to yearn for it but to be ready to go to war when it is forced upon us. As was explained to me many times in many contexts, Israel only fights wars of self-defense. We do not engage in what in Israeli parlance is termed "other-option wars"—*milkhemet yesh breirah*, wars where all nonmilitary options are yet to be exhausted. I was taught how all our wars since 1948 were wars of self-defense. (The 1956 Sinai campaign was notably absent from this conversation.) I was certain that the future would be the same, and if I were called upon by my country, it would only be for a "*no*-other-option war."

As we convened at our staging area to set out for battle, the battalion commander gathered all his officers and tank commanders and said, "We all know why we are here." He did not offer any further explanation; this concluded his motivational remarks. He ordered us to load the tanks onto transporters: we were heading north, tasked with engaging and destroying the Syrian forces in the eastern sector of Lebanon. Our ultimate objective was the Beirut-Damascus highway on the Lebanese-Syrian border, where we were to block any and all Syrian forces from entering Lebanon.

Truth be told, we did not all know why we were "here." We had no idea why we were about to go to war. Israel had not been invaded. We had a general idea that PLO terror against Israel required a response. After being exiled from Jordan in 1971, the PLO had reestablished itself in Lebanon, which became the launching pad for a global and anti-Israeli terror campaign. In 1982 Palestinian terrorists attempted to assassinate Israel's ambassador in London, Shlomo Argov, triggering this Israeli incursion into Lebanon aimed at wiping out the PLO.

Was it a "no other option" war? I didn't really know, but I trusted my country, my government, full of faith that they would be loyal to the implicit covenant between us. I was willing to give my life, but on the condition that my country would ask me to do so only when it was necessary for Israel's survival.

As we headed north to the border with Lebanon, it wasn't clear why we were being tasked to fight the Syrian Army, which, while allied with the PLO, nevertheless had not attacked Israel and was not directly involved in the current terror campaign. While most of the IDF went to fight in the coastal and central regions, charged with eliminating the PLO throughout Lebanon, my brigade eventually came to discover that there were no PLO terrorists in our area, only the Syrian army, and it didn't feel like a war of self-defense. The entrenched Syrian forces we attacked adopted exclusively defensive positions designed to hinder and delay our progress. We engaged the Syrian army when we attempted to advance. For their part, they never attacked us.

As my brigade suffered horrific casualties—25 percent of all the fatalities up to that moment in the war—we were withdrawn from Lebanon and the eastern campaign was suspended. Later we came to learn that we were part of a separate insidious campaign, the brainchild of then–defense minister Ariel Sharon, to change the balance of power and establish a new order in Lebanon led by the Lebanese Christian minority. Achieving this required the neutralization of Syrian influence over Lebanon.

This was not a war of self-defense. We were not acting as the Israel *Defense* Forces. We were the vehicle through which a strategic war of aggression could be used to advance Israeli political and long-term security interests This doctrine was classical Carl von Clausewitz, who declared that war was politics by other means.[1] This was not, and should not have been, an accepted Israeli doctrine.

Israel broke its covenant with me. That was why I then found myself working as a rabbi in New Jersey. It would take me eleven years to return home.

Our Covenant with Our Children

The 1982 Lebanon War ultimately gave birth to massive protests and to the rise of a powerful Israeli peace movement. Over time, their pressure helped force Israel to withdraw from Lebanon. The Israeli military never reordered the Lebanese political landscape. Their only "victory" was deeply pyrrhic: removing the Sunni PLO from Lebanon, which facilitated the rise of the more powerful and capable Shiite Hezbollah, Israel's most dangerous enemy to this very day.

Opting to embark on the War in Lebanon was expressive, even if unconsciously, of an Israeli belief that Zionism had already achieved victory on its Genesis front. Pre-1967, Israel had perceived itself as David facing Goliath, but after the 1967 Six-Day War, Israel emerged as Goliath and saw itself as such. In fact, it became the new regional superpower. Since the 1973 Yom Kippur War, the IDF has only engaged in asymmetrical combat (two wars in Lebanon, two Intifadas, and four operations in Gaza), where, by definition, the enemy we faced was vastly inferior and, while capable of inflicting harm, did not pose an existential threat.

Post-Lebanon, the peace movement turned its critique of the war into a challenge to Israel to internalize its newfound reality: to aim past its Genesis goals and challenge a status quo that assumed Israel's destiny was to live by the sword in a neighborhood bent on our destruction. We would begin to believe in peace not merely as a value but as a real, possible achievement. We would not only believe but work to transform enemies into friends and to alter our shared destiny.

This newfound commitment to actualizing peace led to an openness to see Palestinian national claims in a new light. Going beyond the 1978 Camp David Accords, which were willing to grant the Palestinians autonomy under a sovereign Israel but not their own sovereign state, Israel embarked on negotiations with the PLO and launched the Oslo peace process with the aim of forming a Palestinian State side by side with Israel.

Two stages of the Oslo Accords were signed, in 1993 and 1995. But, as most Israelis understand it, instead of embracing and cultivating peace, in 2000 the Palestinians launched the Second Intifada, which not only caused the death of over one thousand Israelis and three thousand Palestinians but also killed the peace process itself. Since then, the thinking is, we have reverted to being a nation that lives by the sword. We have returned to functioning principally within the modality of Genesis Zionism.

But in truth, we have not returned to the Genesis sensibilities of old. While peace continues to evade us, power has not. Israel has immense and disproportionate power. Our Palestinian enemies are real, but they do not threaten our existence. Our military force provides us with the option to maintain the current status quo, but the lesson of Lebanon challenges us to ask, *If we continue to rely on the military alone to manage our current challenges, are we still engaging in a "no other option war"?*

Peace now, today, tomorrow, even next year, may be beyond our grasp. But what about peace in five years? Is there anything we can do now, besides protecting ourselves, to change our destiny?

We can't return to a "Lebanon consciousness"—where the use of military force is simply Middle Eastern politics by other means. Our covenant with our children demands that we never stop exploring new and other options before we ask our children to endanger their lives. Accepting that the volatile, precarious status quo of Israel's military control of all of Judea and Samaria can go on for another generation, sustained by our children, is a violation of that covenant. We owe them to work harder.

How might a different synthesis of Genesis and Exodus Judaism help us to chart a new future?

"All Her Paths Are Peace" (Prov. 3:17): Israel, Palestinians, and Peace

A major theme in the story Jews tell ourselves about ourselves is that we are a people whose ultimate aspiration is peace. "Seek peace and pursue it" (Ps. 34:14) is a foundational commandment of Exodus Judaism across denominations. It permeates all of Jewish prayer. The tradition elevates it, along with truth and justice, to the rarified status of "one of the pillars upholding the world."[2] We are taught that God is the God of peace and that all of Torah was given only for its sake.[3] The story of Exodus Zionism fully embraces this conception of peace as a core value and aspiration. So does Israel's Declaration of Independence: "freedom, justice and peace as envisaged by the prophets of Israel" are meant to form the country's moral bedrock.[4]

Post-1967, after the remarkable military victory, Israel did not valorize its power as an end unto itself. It still yearned for peace, and what was to become Israel's peace anthem, Yaakov Rotbit's 1999 song "Shir LaShalom" (lit. "Song for Peace,"), galvanizing Israelis to

"Don't say that the day [of peace] will come, bring on that day," became instantly iconic.

The signing of the Oslo Accords led to, among other things, a new wave of peace songs, among them Dag Nahash's "Shalom Salaam Peace," exhorting that peace is "possible here too, not just in Paris or Nice or Boston."

Israel Planned, Neighbors Laughed

Today, however, the broad sentiment among Israelis is that *we offered everything, and the Palestinians said no.* They rejected the UN Partition Plan in 1947 and repeatedly rejected Israel's right to exist, as exemplified in the famous "Three No's Resolution" adopted by the Arab League in Khartoum after the 1967 Six-Day War:

> The Arab Heads of State have agreed to unite their political efforts at the international and diplomatic level to eliminate the effects of the aggression and to ensure the withdrawal of the aggressive Israeli forces from the Arab lands which have been occupied since the aggression of June 5th. This will be done within the framework of the main principles by which the Arab States abide, namely, **no** *peace with Israel,* **no** *recognition of Israel,* **no** *negotiations with it,* and insistence on the rights of the Palestinian people in their own country.[5]

The Palestinians then rejected Oslo in 2000, and all of Israel's peace proposals since, including a proposed withdrawal from over 95 percent of Judea and Samaria and sharing Jerusalem.[6] Moreover, when Israel unilaterally withdrew from Gaza in 2005, the PA-and then Hamas controlled territory quickly turned into a launching pad for violence against Israeli civilians.

In the words of then–prime minister Barak, immediately after the Palestinians launched the Second Intifada:

Citizens of Israel, good evening. . . .

A new situation is indeed taking shape. This is one of the most important struggles in the history of the State of Israel—a struggle for our very right to live here in this difficult and tormented region as free people. . . . Since Madrid and Oslo, throughout a decade, three or four consecutive governments in Israel have strived to achieve a peace agreement with our Palestinian neighbors, on the premise that we have a partner for peace. *Today, the picture that is emerging is that there is apparently no partner for peace.* This truth is a painful one, but it is the truth, and we must confront it with open eyes and draw the necessary conclusions. . . . We will be united. We have no cause to blame ourselves. Our hands are clean. We have turned every stone and were prepared to discuss almost every possible idea in order to explore whether the other side is prepared to pursue the road of peace. . . . An agreement can be reached, but the other side, for whom the choice between agreement and violence is not an easy one either, has apparently chosen violence, and will bear the responsibility for the consequences of this choice.[7]

From "Peace Now" to "Separation Now"

With the Palestinian rejection of Oslo and the emergent belief that there was no peace partner on the Palestinian side, the era of peace as a central preoccupation of Israeli political and cultural life effectively ended.[8] Israel stopped all peace negotiations with the Palestinians. Israelis stopped composing new songs about peace.

"Separation Now" replaced "Peace Now." In 2005 Israel unilaterally withdrew from Gaza. If peace was unattainable, Israel had its own interests in separating from the Palestinians: protecting its citizens, fostering economic growth, and maintaining its Jewish majority. As then–acting prime minister Ehud Olmert argued:

The State of Israel is still a young nation. There are many more steps we must take in order to build an ethical society with strong values. . . . However, there is no doubt that the most important and dramatic step we face is the determination of permanent borders of the State of Israel, to ensure the Jewish majority in the country. Ze'ev Jabotinsky defined the importance of a Jewish majority in his insightful and keen way: "The term 'Jewish nation' is absolutely clear: it means a Jewish majority. With this, Zionism began, and it is the basis of its existence. It will continue to work towards its fulfillment, or it will be lost."

The existence of a Jewish majority in the State of Israel cannot be maintained with the continued control over the Palestinian population in Judea, Samaria, and the Gaza Strip. We firmly stand by the historic right of the people of Israel to the entire Land of Israel. . . . However, the choice between the desire to allow every Jew to live anywhere in the Land of Israel, and the existence of the State of Israel as a Jewish country, obligates relinquishing parts of the Land of Israel. This is not a relinquishing of the Zionist idea, rather the essential realization of the Zionist goal—ensuring the existence of a Jewish and democratic state in the Land of Israel. In order to ensure the existence of a Jewish national homeland, we will not be able to continue ruling over the territories in which the majority of the Palestinian population lives. We must create a clear boundary as soon as possible, one which will reflect the demographic reality on the ground.[9]

Instead of a peace project, the discourse around the two-state solution essentially became a divorce agreement. Pursuing peace shifted from an Exodus to a Genesis project.

But separation *now* has become as unattainable as peace now. In its stead, a cold status quo has ensued, with both sides growing ever distanced not merely from the possibility of peace but from its necessity and even from its value.

Genesis Cannot Subsume Exodus

In the world of realpolitik, Genesis duties and sensibilities may at times take priority. They cannot, however, subsume our responsibilities to the Exodus Covenant.

Israel's place in the millennia-long story of Jewishness is contingent upon an ongoing engagement with Exodus, which demands that our national rebirth be founded on the Jewish principles of human equality, freedom, justice, and peace. While Genesis Zionism grounded our right to a Jewish home in the Jewish homeland, Exodus Zionism teaches that it will not be a Jewish home as long as the Palestinians do not have their own home as well. The challenge of Hillel—"What is hateful unto you do not do to others, *this is the whole Torah*"—demands that Israel treat everyone in accordance with how we would want to be treated. Israel cannot permanently disregard Palestinian inalienable rights as human beings created in the image of God and simultaneously fulfill its Exodus mission to be a "kingdom of priests and a holy nation," much less a "light" unto the other nations of the world.

Israel may be forced to embrace the current status quo in the short term, but if it silences its Exodus aspirations—if peace ceases to be an active pursuit, and if justice and freedom are not viewed as the inalienable rights of all, including the Palestinian people—it will jeopardize its core identity. While Israel must be a nation like other nations, if it is *only* a nation like other nations, it will forfeit its Jewish soul and raison d'être.

The critical question is, how do we fulfill this challenge in the midst of an environment where ending Israel's military control of Judea and Samaria unilaterally is perceived to be suicidal? Without the ability to limit Hamas and Islamic Jihad's terror activities, Judea and Samaria would become like Gaza, terrorist enclaves armed with missiles capable of undermining Israeli life and threatening its very viability. How can we realistically integrate our Genesis and Exodus responsibilities and aspirations?

The Exodus Doctrine of Peace: In Pursuit of a Value

Peace is a complicated value to implement, precisely because we must make peace with our enemies—and the effort is dependent as much on their willingness to change as our own. As a result, the Jewish tradition does not command that we *make* peace, but rather that we *pursue* it—and equates its pursuit with basic virtue: "Turn from evil and do good: seek peace and pursue it" (Ps. 34:14).

The Rabbis explained that the pursuit of peace requires us to embrace policies that create the conditions for it to flourish:

> "When you encounter your enemy's ox or ass wandering, you must take it back to him." (Exodus 23:4). . . . The Torah did not obligate one to pursue the fulfillment of the commandments. Rather, when you encounter [the moment or opportunity to fulfill a commandment, such as an animal wandering astray], your obligation becomes activated. You do not have to pursue after it. *Regarding peace, on the other hand, seek it where you are and pursue it in other places as well.*[10]

The Exodus Covenant obliges us to construe peace as a concrete objective that we are obligated to further through our own policies and actions, even—especially—when it does not seem to be possible.

What does this mean in our current reality?

If Israel believes it made a sincere offer to end the conflict with the Palestinians, and the offer was rejected, it does not mean that we should embrace the current status quo as a permanent reality. It does not mean that we allow Genesis to silence Exodus. If we offered and they said no, the challenge of Exodus is to regroup and try again. And again. And again.

Ultimately, whether our potential peace partner will reciprocate is up to the Palestinians. But their actions do not determine our values or our commitment to create a world in which Exodus values can be actualized.

Genesis requires that we do not embark on a peace initiative that endangers our right to live and be—yet this never translates into permission to forsake its calling. The obligation to pursue peace never lapses, no matter how many times the other side spurns the offer.

"Shrinking the Conflict" and Reducing Moral Failure

Furthermore, the Exodus Covenant demands not merely that we continuously initiate final status negotiations, but work to expand the conditions that may enable such status negotiations to begin.

It is not enough to formally pursue peace through political discourse if we are concurrently pursuing policies that undermine our very aim. We cannot pursue peace with "dirty" hands. We must studiously desist from actions that could impede ending Israeli military control of Judea and Samaria on the day that a serious Palestinian peace partner finally emerges.

Specifically and most importantly, I believe Israel should cease all settlement building and expansion outside the main settlement blocks contiguous with Israel's pre-1967 borders—East Jerusalem, Gush Etzion, Ma'ale Adumim, and Ariel. The international community has long recognized that these will remain under Israeli sovereignty in any future peace agreement, as given the size of their populations their dismantlement is not feasible, and in any event, they do not hinder the creation of a contiguous Palestinian state.[11] Building outside of these blocks, however, further entrenches Israel's hold on all of Judea and Samaria and precludes the possibility of the Palestinians' forming their own sovereign state alongside Israel in the future. This is a critical step toward empowering the peace partner we desire. While the Israeli narrative speaks of a Palestinian people and leadership that have never accepted Israel's right to exist, the Palestinian narrative speaks of an Israeli people and leadership motivated solely by the desire to own all of the land.[12] Palestinians claim that Israel's peace overtures have never been sincere: Israel aimed to procrastinate, gain time, and distract the international community so that enough settlements could be built, and enough Israelis moved into the territories, to make the two-state solution impossible to implement. Perhaps by freezing settlement-building until a peace treaty is signed, we can help change this Palestinian narrative. Perhaps, instead of building settlements, we can begin to build trust. While Israel may not be able to unilaterally establish peace, it can unilaterally establish foundations for peace.

That in itself is not sufficient. Anywhere and any way Israel's military control over the Palestinian people creates injustice and discrimination must be shut down—what my colleague Dr. Micah Goodman calls "shrinking the conflict."[13] One cannot speak of future coexistence without working to diminish military rule to its minimum possible footprint *now*, and without committing to build significant economic infrastructure to benefit Palestinians, *now*.

For example, the number of roadblocks within Judea and Samaria must be kept to a minimum, and transportation infrastructure must be created to enable Palestinians to travel uninhibited by the IDF throughout most of the West Bank. Work permits and security checkpoints at crossings into Israel must be upgraded to allow routine passage that is safe, efficient, and dignified. Palestinians must be granted greater zoning leeway that allows for more robust expansion of both private homes and industrial areas. Military administrative detention without trial must be significantly curtailed, with more impartial courts installed where Palestinians can pursue equitable justice. Violence by "hilltop youth" against Palestinian farmers must be met with greater opposition from the state, and injustices against Palestinians must be addressed with the same severity as Palestinian offences against Jews. As Exodus Jews we must translate our values into policies, *now*.

To facilitate a peaceful resolution to the conflict, we should also begin to reverse the current status-quo of the settlements in Judea and Samaria. Today, roughly six hundred thousand Jews live in the territories captured by Israel in 1967. Half a million of them are concentrated in the major settlement regions—East Jerusalem, Gush Etzion, Ma'ale Adumim, and Ariel.[14] Changing the current status quo requires facilitating the voluntary relocation of the approximately one hundred thousand Jews dispersed in the other settlements throughout Judea and Samaria. Instead of offering tax incentives for Israeli Jews to live in these settlements, Israel needs to create tax *liabilities* for anyone who chooses to remain there. Meanwhile, a massive building initiative needs to be launched to expand the major settlement areas, so that these can accommodate the approximately hundred thousand Jews who need to be relocated. Doing so will ensure that every family that needs to move can relocate to a home no more than thirty minutes from where they currently reside, enabling them to continue to commute to their workplaces and live in the social and cultural environments to which they have become accustomed.

We need to remember that during Israel's unilateral withdrawal from Gaza in 2005, it took Israel mere days to remove the eight thousand settlers from Gaza—but because of Israel's lack of advance planning, coupled with its cumbersome bureaucratic zoning process, it took *a decade* to develop adequate housing for them. In the interim, eight thousand people were forced to live in temporary trailer houses or to fare otherwise on their own. The lesson of Gaza is that you cannot remove people from their homes without a long-term plan and extensive preparation. A failure to do so itself constitutes a travesty of justice. Exodus requires protecting the rights of settlers and Palestinians alike.

The process of relocating one hundred thousand people will take years, but without a viable place for the residents of Judea and Samaria to move, the current stalemate in the peace process will not change, irrespective of Palestinian readiness. Let the buildings be built now, even if some of them remain uninhabited, awaiting a time when peace will be actualized. In the meantime they will be a powerful monument bearing witness to an Exodus-centered Israel which will never accept the occupation of another people as a permanent reality. They will bear witness to what a nation committed to the idea of pursuing peace looks like.

The fact that we cannot unilaterally end the conflict does not mean that we cannot—and must not—reduce its moral failures, now.

The Moral Cost of the Status Quo

Efforts to overcome the conflict will have greater currency when we as a society recognize and openly talk about the moral costs of its perpetuation. The obligation to pursue peace takes on added urgency when one realizes that while there may be a political status quo, there is no moral status quo. The reality of a military occupation of another people—no matter how ethically or politically justified—has an inevitably morally corrosive effect. No matter how ostensibly defensive in nature, it will entail discriminatory practices. And these practices will inevitably lead to discriminatory sensibilities.

As Jews, we are not obligated to love those who want to destroy us. We are not permitted, however, to view any human being, each created in the image of God, as anything less than equal, endowed with the same rights and aspirations as our own. As the Rabbis teach us, God chose to have all of humanity emanate from a single human being so that no one would ever be able to say that their ancestry is superior—and to teach us that since our world emanated from a singular human being, henceforth anyone who takes a life, it is as if they have destroyed a whole world.[15] The only time taking another life is morally justified (indeed required) is in the context of self-defense.

Over time, the military occupation of another people corrodes the moral fiber of both the occupier and the occupied. It inevitably leads to mutual demonization and denigration. On this point alone, *we offered and they said no* cannot serve as a blanket exemption giving moral license to perpetuate the current reality. If it is near-impossible to be an occupier and preserve a sensibility of the equal humanity of the occupied, then the current status quo is nothing short of a cancer eating away at our Exodus covenantal commitments.

This covenant that demands that we treat others the way we yearn, and yearned throughout our history, to be treated, obligates us to embrace Palestinian national aspirations as an integral part of our Zionism. Zionism was an expression of the Jewish people's right to be free and sovereign in our homeland. We cannot be loyal to our Exodus roots if we allow our Zionist dream to be founded on the destruction of another people's dream. "What is hateful unto you do not do to others." As Jews and Zionists, we must pursue the two-state solution not merely as a byproduct of peace but as an imperative of justice: the same justice we demanded for our own people.

We do not need a Palestinian state living side by side with Israel in peace and security merely to ensure Israel's Jewish majority; we need it for our Jewish character. The "Jewishness" of Israel refers not merely to the numerical predominance of Jews within Israel's borders but to the centrality of Jewish values in our national homeland.

Next Year in Jerusalem

It is critical to remember that unfulfilled yearning is not a new condition for the Jews. Starting in 70 CE, when the Temple was destroyed and the Jewish people exiled, we began to pray, *Next year in Jerusalem.* For 2000 years we maintained the deepest aspiration of our Genesis Covenant. Year after year, century after century, millennium after millennium, we never allowed reality to define—much less limit—our aspirations. We never stopped hoping for that new day when we would again be a free people in our homeland.

Now that the Genesis Covenant has become a reality, our challenge is to maintain the same aspiration for our Exodus Covenant. Herzl challenged the Jewish people, "If you will it, it is not a dream"—if you will it, it will become a reality.[16] The story Jews tell ourselves about ourselves is that our will and our dreams have the power to shape reality. Now we need to develop the same determination in pursuit of peace.

2036: Toward a New Story

In 1971 I moved to Israel with my family. I was then thirteen, five years before the age of conscription into the IDF. As their oldest son,

I remember the nervousness my parents expressed: *will Donniel have to go to war?* It is one thing to make a commitment to move to Israel, another to expose one's child to the possibility of death.

In 1971, five years before my age of conscription, the future seemed open with possibility. But peace did not come, and soon after my 1982 Lebanon War experience ended, I moved my family to New Jersey. When we returned to Israel in 1995, my wife and I had three children: daughters Michal (twelve) and Talya (five), and a son, Yitzchak (nine). Israel was in the midst of the Oslo Peace negotiations, and the possibility of peace—the hope that maybe our children would not have to experience what we experienced—was exhilarating. In any event, I reasoned, it would be nine years before Yitzchak was conscripted into the IDF; certainly, peace would be achieved by then. (While my daughters were also to be drafted into the army, at the time, women were not exposed to the dangers of combat.) My son would be safe and not suffer the consequences of our decision to return.

Little did I know that five years later (2000), the second Intifada would erupt and bury hope for at least another generation. Michal lost her best friend to a terrorist bombing at age fourteen. Talya lost her fifth-grade teacher to a vicious terror attack while on maternity leave in her ninth month of pregnancy. Michal and Talya, while shopping for Talya's bat mitzvah dress together, were just fifteen feet away from a suicide bomber whose vest failed to detonate. Ten years after our return, in 2005, peace was still not at hand—and my son, like his father before him, was conscripted into the tank corps. In 2012 it was his turn to put his life on the line—this time, to fight in Gaza.

As of the writing, I now have, thank God, three granddaughters: Mia, Sophia, Libby Or; and two grandsons, Elori, who is now five, and Lavie, who is a newborn. In 2036 Elori will be drafted into the army. To me, that is the year by which our pursuit of peace must be actualized. But every Israeli family—and every Palestinian family—has a year: a year in which our children, or grandchildren, are officially drawn into the cycle of tragedy, pain, and death.

As Israelis, we are living in what may be the most remarkable time in Jewish history. We are a free and powerful people, sovereign in our own homeland, with achievements beyond our wildest expectations. But we have no choice but to pursue peace, for the sake of our moral fiber as a people and for the lives of our children and grandchildren.

PART THREE   A Diaspora Future

14

At Home

The rebirth of Israel and the success of North American Jewish life have transformed Jewish life in the twentieth and twenty-first centuries. From a people who, for much of our history, were seen as "scattered and dispersed . . . whose laws are different from those of any people" (Esther 3:8–9), in Israel and North America, Jews have found a home.

Even so, like many Israelis who left Israel to spend a few years in America, I thought I was coming to live in the Diaspora—a wealthy and comfortable Diaspora, but a Diaspora, nonetheless. It was impossible for me to imagine that anywhere other than Israel could feel like home for a Jew. Yet, as I traveled across North America lecturing, I marveled at how comfortable I was, as a Jew. During one scholar-in-residence weekend, in Corpus Christi, my hotel was a half-hour walk from the various synagogue lecture venues. As I walked alone at 11 p.m. on a Friday night through the suburbs of a city named for the Feast of the Body of Christ, I reflected on how safe and unafraid I felt. How unique this experience was in Jewish history.

But it was on an American Airlines flight that I experienced the fullness of Jewish at-homeness in America. At the time, American Airlines had its own in-flight Sharper Image catalog offering hundreds of novelty items. As an Israeli experiencing the vast scope and quantity of American products, I happily passed many a flight perusing pages offering solar-powered flashlights with built in screwdrivers and pool floats bigger than the average Israeli bedroom. On one flight in early December, the featured catalog item was a Jewish Star Christmas tree ornament designed for the "blended family." It took me a minute to understand what I was seeing, and a few more to comprehend the enormous significance of the product.

For most of history, Jews—routinely accused of being Christ-killers and refusers of divine salvation—were on the receiving end of Christian antisemitism. Christianity saw itself as superseding Judaism and constituting a new, universal Children of Israel. Jews gave the world the *Old* Testament, Christianity the *New* one. In 1965 this began to change as the Second Vatican Council issued *Nostra Aetate* (Latin for "In our time"), a declaration redefining the church's relationship to non-Christian religions in general and to Judaism in particular. Judaism, the church declared, was the root of the tree that sprouted Christianity, and by the witness of the Apostle, "God holds the Jews most dear for the sake of their Fathers; He does not repent of the gifts He makes or of the calls He issues."[1]

Of course, like the unfolding of European Emancipation, there was a chasm between official policy declarations and the reality on the ground, which inevitably adapted more slowly.

Yet by the close of the twentieth century, as evidenced in a Sharper Image catalog, Jews and Judaism were not being superseded in the public consciousness; they were being given a place on the Christmas tree. Christmas was seen as a holiday that Christians and Jews could share. In a very deep sense, Jews were no longer outsiders. They were integrated with Christianity within the umbrella of a shared Judeo-Christian faith. Their experience had contributed to Chrismukkah (the merging of Christmas and Hanukkah)—a term I misspelled when writing this chapter, but, notably, Word's dictionary knew and swiftly corrected.

In the Beginning There Was Otherness

By contrast, the Jewish historical narrative starts with the experience of a singular original Jew whose identity lies precisely in his opposition to the rest of the world. In Genesis chapter 12, in a marked departure from the universal stories that precede it, the Jewish journey begins with a divine commandment. *"Lekh-lekha,"* God charges Abraham. *"Go forth. Leave your homeland, your birthplace, your father's home—and go to the land that I will show you"* (Gen. 12:1).

Our covenantal relationship begins when we are willing to walk alone. "Go forth," God commands: *Leave everything behind and go to a land where you will be a stranger.* The message is clear: the core of your identity cannot be built in the midst of familiarity and comfort with your surroundings.

For this reason, the Rabbis posit, Abraham is called "Abraham the *Ivri*"—"Abraham the Hebrew." Hebrew did not refer to the language Abraham spoke but came from the root *ever*, meaning the other side of the riverbank—the whole world was metaphorically on one side of the river, and Abraham was on the other.[2]

Only when Abraham embarks on a journey of otherness does the Jewish story begin.

Egypt: Nationalizing Otherness

Throughout the book of Genesis, this otherness is maintained. As the nation grows, the Israelites remain separate from the various nations residing in Canaan. Indeed, it is precisely when Abraham's descendants start to assimilate into Canaanite culture via intermarriage (Jacob's sons, unlike both their father and grandfathers, took local wives) that they are sent into exile from that land and into a new crucible of othering, Egypt—where, as segregated strangers and ultimately slaves, the Children of Israel's distinctiveness is maintained.[3] Even if the Israelites want to assimilate, their inferior status ensures that they and the Egyptians will never become one.

Our experience in Egypt becomes a paradigm for much of Jewish history—the "iron furnace" through which our national identity is forged as our otherness is externally enforced. Upon the Exodus from Egypt, the Jewish people begin their own *Go forth* moment, leaving civilization to journey in the desert—an undomesticated place owned by no one, where no one is at home. The Moabite prophet Bil'am will later observe, "They are a people that dwells apart, not reckoned among the nations" (Num. 32:9).

Opposing Idolatry: Legislating Otherness

Jewish law picked up on this theme and worked to fortify it. We had to refrain from intermarriage with the local Canaanites and to avoid following their practices (Lev. 18:3; 20:23). Emulating their mode of worship—idolatry (Heb. "Avodah Zarah")—becomes the quintessential biblical prohibition. A core meaning of the term is "foreign" or "alien" worship. It is not that idolatry is false; rather, it is worship that must remain foreign to Israel. Jews, who are not a part of the world, do not worship the way the world worships:[4] "And when you look up to the sky, and behold, the sun and the moon, and the stars, the whole heavenly hosts, you must not be lured into bowing down to them or serving them. These the Lord your God allotted to other peoples everywhere under heaven. But you the Lord took and brought out of Egypt that iron blast furnace, to be God's very own people, as is now the case" (Deut. 4:19–20).

Jewish law does not merely obligate a distinct mode of worship but forbids any emulation of our surrounding practices:

> We should not follow in the customs of the Gentiles, nor imitate them in dress or in their way of trimming the hair, as it is said, "*and you shall not walk in the customs of the nation which I have cast out before you.*" (Leviticus 20:23) . . . These texts all refer to one theme and warn against imitating them. The Israelites shall, on the contrary, be distinguished from them and be recognizable by the way they dress and, in their activities, just as they are distinguished from them by their knowledge and their principles. As it is said: "*and I have set you apart from all the nations.*" (Leviticus 20:26)[5]

Complex Identities and the Decline of the Singular Other

Our story of "otherness" began to change in the eighteenth and nineteenth centuries. In many ways, the burden of otherness over the two preceding millennia had been too hard for us to bear. We couldn't continue to live in the ghetto. We wanted to be free; to possess what other newfound citizens in modern nation states already did: citizenship, equal rights, equality under the law. With Emancipation we hoped to bring Jewish otherness to an end, while still retaining just the appropriate measure of distinctness. We wanted to be, per the French Sanhedrin, Frenchmen of Jewish persuasion.[6]

Up until now, our Jewishness had been principally singular—we were Jews as distinct from "the goyim," Gentiles, which, from the rabbinic period on, categorized everyone else.[7] Being Jewish defined everything about us. It was who we were as distinct from others; it was what we believed in as distinct from others; it was our practices as distinct from that of others. And as a result of this totalizing singularity, we saw ourselves almost exclusively through the lens of our Jewishness.

Antisemitism, too, played a key role in reinforcing this singularity: You think you're a Frenchman, but your society finds countless ways to tell you every day that you are simply a Jew. You think you're a German, a sophisticated Berliner, but are continually reminded that you are simply a Jew. Antisemitism does not only affect Jewish survival or limit our social interactions, it flattens and homogenizes Jewish experience and self-perception to be always and overwhelmingly a singular Other: a nation that dwells apart.

In North America, Jews hoped to further the aspiration of Emancipation: to be part of a society where they would not be othered. Multicultural America, with its tapestry of identities, would allow Jews to be at home, living as both American citizens and Exodus Jews simultaneously.

Jews did experience antisemitism in America, particularly through the first part of the twentieth century.[8] It is still a growing concern as we enter the third decade of the twenty-first.[9] Until the middle of the twentieth century, many universities, jobs, neighborhoods, and social clubs were closed to Jews, but by the final quarter of the century, and continuing into our current twenty-first-century moment, this institutional antisemitism has been basically eradicated.[10] Unlike in nineteenth-century Europe, the transformation has been both legal and cultural. True, antisemitism in America has been and continues to be a feature of Jewish experience and is recently increasing in both scope and acceptability; but it no longer carries an existential threat to Jews or Jewish identity.[11] Antisemitism in America is no longer a condition that creates a person who is *singularly* a Jew.

Thus, American Jews discovered they could be both Americans *and* Genesis and Exodus Jews. Not only could Americanness and Exodus Judaism coexist, because American values could live in synthesis with Exodus Judaism, but Americanness also allowed for a Genesis Jewish identity, for Americanness did not require an exclusive national identity, either. Precisely as both American, Genesis and Exodus Jews, Jews left behind their status as the "other" and found themselves very much "at home" in America.[12]

This unprecedented environment and the new possibilities it offered allowed for the flourishing of Jewish complex identities.[13] Jews joined their fellow Americans in being fellow Democrats/Republicans, in living principally as middle/upper class Americans, in belonging to common cultural institutions, in sharing philanthropic causes, in largely supporting the feminist revolution and the unfolding of diverse gender identities, and more. They were not merely Jews, but Jews *and* . . . In fact, these additional identities helped them to transcend their otherness and more fully experience "at homeness."

American "At-Homeness" and Jewish Collective Identity

This reality of "at-homeness" in America would alter the experience of Jewish collective identity. In the twentieth century, by and large, North American Jews mostly married other Jews, saw a relationship with Israel as foundational to their Genesis and Exodus Covenants, and viewed their Jewishness as part of collective peoplehood.[14] By the twenty-first century, however, all three of these realities have ceased to be self-evident. Today the majority of Jews outside of Orthodoxy marry non-Jews (over 70 percent); alienation from Israel, while still affecting a minority, has become an integral feature of mainstream

Jewish communal discourse; and increasing numbers of Jews are asking, why should I belong to the Jewish people?[15]

The next few chapters delve into how a dramatic transformation in collective identity catalyzed the shift in the story twenty-first-century North American Jews tell themselves about themselves. Answers to today's dilemmas are not to be found in Americans somehow stripping themselves of the core sensibility of American-Jewish at-homeness, as if such a thing were possible. Our responsibility as twenty-first-century Jews is to be honest with ourselves about the reality we find ourselves in and continually generate authentic, creative responses to both the challenges it raises and the opportunities it affords.

15

Intermarriage and the Meaning of Jewishness

In the mid-1980s, while on "hiatus" from Israel, I embarked on my rabbinic career as the scholar-in-residence at a Jewish community center (JCC) in suburban New Jersey. JCC policy was that an intermarried Jew could not serve on the board of directors. At that time in my life, this rule made sense to me. In Jerusalem, where I grew up, intermarriage was nothing short of unthinkable—a self-evident act of assimilation.

A few years into the JCC position, I had my first rabbinic experience of counseling a Jew about intermarriage. An Orthodox woman in her late thirties had approached me, tortured by a dark secret she was keeping from her parents: after years of being single, she had fallen in love with a non-Jew. This was the first serious and committed relationship she had experienced in her life. She had no intention of relinquishing her Orthodox observances but was struggling with how to tell her parents she planned to intermarry.

"Rabbi," she asked me one afternoon, "what is more important: to maintain Jewish law and be alone for the rest of my life, or to violate one part of the law, even a central one, and to be free of the loneliness and sadness that overwhelm me?"

I granted her that a life of loneliness should not be an option. Yet, I asked her, would marrying a non-Jew foster loneliness of a different kind: a loneliness from her Jewish self, which was obviously critical to her? Moved greatly in those moments by what I felt was the depth of my own words, I only vaguely registered her distance as she sat in polite silence, waiting for me to finish.

In the end, she married the individual in question and never came to me again for advice.

In retrospect, I came to understand that it was obvious to her that while her family and community did not recognize her choices, she was not choosing between having a Jewish identity and leaving it. She was choosing between a life of loneliness and the crossing of what was previously a red line.

Over the years, as I reflected on this event, it became obvious to me that my understanding and categorization of exogamy—the act of marrying outside of one's community—needed to change. Both my personal experience working in Jewish communities and the broader trend of intermarriage evolving from a marginal phenomenon to virtually the norm of Jewish life, with more than 50 percent of American Jews intermarrying, challenged inherited traditional Jewish thinking around this issue.[1]

An understanding of Jewishness and its boundaries, shaped by a synthesis of Genesis and Exodus, is critical for understanding and relating to this new reality in the unfolding story of twenty-first-century Jewish life.

Legal Exogamy: The Biblical Model

Is exogamy the beginning of the end of North American Jewishness—or simply the beginning of yet another new chapter?

In the context of Jewish history, intermarriage between Jews and non-Jews is not an unknown phenomenon. While prohibited by Jewish law for most of the last two thousand years, prior to that, in the biblical period, exogamy was, under certain conditions, normative.[2]

In the biblical period, Jewishness was determined by the father (patrilineal descent). With the exception of only a single case, in Lev. 24:10-11, until the Book of Esther—set in Persia at the conclusion of the Babylonian Exile, marking the beginning of the end of the biblical period—the Bible does not record cases of intermarriage between a Jewish woman and a non-Jewish man. At that time, there was simply no possibility for Jewishness being transmitted matrilineally.

This is the case with Abraham, Isaac, Jacob, and Jacob's sons: in this early patriarchal era, all our forefathers and their children marry non-Jews. Indeed, as the story is told, there were no Jews (other than their sisters) that they could marry. Nevertheless, both the fact that they married non-Jews and the lack of comment or discourse around this are initial indicators of the idea of exogamy as a legitimate element of our patrilineal system.

The first true intermarriage accounted for in the Bible—where a non-Jewish spouse was chosen even though there were Jewish options—occurs with Moses. As he travels to Midian to escape the Egyptian authorities, he meets and marries Zipporah, the daughter of Jethro, a Midianite priest. Interestingly, as with our forefathers, the act itself is recorded in the most matter-of-fact manner, without any pejorative or even reflective commentary: "Moses consented to stay with [Jethro, the priest of Midian], and he gave Moses his daughter Zipporah as wife. She bore a son, whom he named Gershom" (Exod. 2:21–22).

This biblical validation of exogamy has a single, telling qualification. When the time comes for Abraham to seek a wife for his son, his lone instruction is that she may not be from Canaan, the land and culture in which Abraham currently resides and sojourns: "Swear by the Lord, the God of heaven, and the God of the earth, that you will not take a wife for my son from the daughters of the Canaanites among whom I dwell, but will go to the land of my birth and get a wife for my son Isaac" (Gen. 24:2–4).

Jacob is similarly instructed: "So, Isaac sent for Jacob and blessed him. He instructed him saying: 'You shall not take a wife from among the Canaanite women. Up, go to Paddan-aram, the house of Bethuel, your mother's father, and take a wife there from among the daughters of Laban, your mother's brother'" (Gen. 28:1–2).

While the Bible does not couch this preference in any explicit rationale, a likely explanation connects it to the desire to mitigate the danger of competing familial identities and cultures. In essence, the patrilineal system is designed to ensure that patriarchal control over the family's faith is not undermined by the faith of the spouse. Unmoored, much like Abraham, from their own geographical, cultural, and familial roots, these ancestral women embark on their own Lekh-lekha ("Go forth") moment, shedding all they have inherited and known to embrace the Genesis/Exodus identities of their husbands. As a result, when they arrive in their newly adopted homes, there are no competing bonds to draw them away from the religious identity of their husbands.

This idea that exogamy is permitted *as long as the intermarriage does not threaten the patrilineal system and undermine the family's Genesis-Exodus commitments* shapes biblical law. The Bible explicitly prohibits intermarriage *almost exclusively* between Israelites and the Seven Canaanite nations that inhabit the land promised to Israel, on the grounds that their proximity will inevitably draw the Jews away from God:

> When the Lord your God brings you to the land that you are about to enter and possess and God dislodges many nations before you . . . And the Lord your God delivers them to you and you defeat them, you must doom them to destruction: grant them no terms and give them no quarter. You shall not intermarry with them: do not give your daughters to their sons or take their daughters for your sons. For they will turn your children away from Me to worship other gods. . . . For you are a people consecrated to the Lord your God. (Deut. 7:1–6)

By contrast, when a male Israelite encounters an idolatrous woman in a military campaign against nations outside of the Promised Land, he is legally permitted to take her as his wife, intermarriage notwithstanding (Deut. 21:10–14). The biblical assumption is that when she accompanies her husband to the Land of Israel, his God and family will supersede her gods and family ties.

"Your God Is My God": Ruth and the Biblical Legitimization of Exogamy

This acceptability of intermarriage is a central motif in the book of Ruth, which tells the story of a Jewish family that moves to Moab: Elimelekh and Naomi, and their two sons Mahlon and Kilyon. The sons marry Moabite women: Orpah and Ruth. Elimelekh, Mahlon, and Kilyon die prematurely, leaving Naomi, Orpah, and Ruth without any means to protect, feed, and support themselves. As a result, Naomi decides to move back to her family in Israel and encourages her daughters-in-law, in turn, to return to theirs. Orpah listens and returns, but Ruth refuses to abandon Naomi, despite Naomi's plea: "'See, your sister-in-law has returned to her people and *her Gods*. Go follow your sister-in-law.' But Ruth replied: 'Do not urge me to leave you to turn back and not follow you. For wherever you go I will go; wherever you lodge, I will lodge; your people shall be my people. And your God, my God'" (Ruth 1:15–16; emphasis added).

The story implies that Orpah, while married to a Jewish man, adopted both the people and the God of the Jewish family. When she leaves the Jewish family she un-adopts them, returning to her people *and* her family's gods. This is precisely the type of intermarriage the Bible permits: intermarriage devoid of assimilation. The wife assimilates her husband's Judaism as her own Genesis-Exodus paradigm for as long as she is married to him.

Conversely, Ruth, who chooses to stay, recognizes that in doing so she is committing to Naomi, her people, and their God. She subsequently remarries Naomi's late husband's cousin Boaz. The ultimate sign of the Bible's sanctioning of nonassimilationist exogamy finds expression in the fact that the progeny of their marriage is David, who becomes not only the biblical king of Israel but also the forefather of the Messiah. There can be no greater validation of the acceptability of intermarriage than this.

Undermining Intermarriage: The Biblical Shift

The attitude towards exogamy begins to change at the end of the biblical period—precisely because it is no longer viewed as compatible with the Genesis and Exodus Covenants.

The book of Ezra gives voice to this shift. Some sixty years after the destruction of the Temple (586 BCE) and the subsequent exile of the Jewish people to Babylon, a small remnant of Jews returns to Israel and begins to intermarry with the indigenous population, including with the Samaritans, who themselves had been exiled *to* Israel. While formally the Samaritans are not included in the Seven Canaanite Nations and thus not subject to the intermarriage ban, Ezra nevertheless extends the intermarriage ban to include them as well:

> The land that you are about to possess is a land unclean through the uncleanness of the peoples of the land, through their abhorrent practices with which they, in their impurity, have filled it from one end to the other. Now then, do not give your daughters in marriage to their sons or let their daughters marry your sons; do nothing for their well-being or advantage, then you will be strong and enjoy the bounty of the land and bequeath it to your children forever. (Ezra 9:11–12)[3]

Since the Samaritans permanently occupy the same geography as the Jews, the book of Ezra establishes that their status should be considered as identical to that of the Seven Canaanites nations, because their behavior is "*like* those of the Canaanites, the Hittites, Perizzites, Jebusites, Ammonites and Moabites, the Egyptians and the Amorites" (Ezra 9:1–2).

Ultimately, Ezra's expanded prohibition against exogamy becomes codified as Jewish law after the destruction of the Second Temple. Similar to intermarriage with neighbors, given the dominance of Hellenistic culture at the time, intermarriage regardless of the geographic location of one's spouse was virtually guaranteed to lead to assimilation into the larger Hellenistic Roman Empire. To marry outside the Jewish community was to leave it. As a result, for the first time, the Rabbis prohibited *all* intermarriages, designating them as legally null and void.[4] This position was subsequently codified into Jewish law:

An Israelite man who had marital relations with a non-Jew from amongst the nations, or an Israelite women who had marital relations—are subject to biblically mandated corporal punishment, as it states: "and you shall not intermarry with them: do not give your daughters to their sons or take their daughters for your sons." (Deut. 7:3) This prohibition includes those from the Seven Nations as well as those from all the other Nations.[5]

For two thousand years, throughout the diasporic exile, exogamy remained prohibited, as it continued to imply an exit from both the Genesis and Exodus dimensions of Jewishness. Meanwhile, for centuries, pervasive, virulent antisemitism made it nearly incomprehensible that a non-Jew who married a Jew would even consider joining the Jewish community. What would be the incentive to do so: to check out life in the ghetto, to experience a pogrom? Only Jews could conceivably benefit from intermarriage, if they shed their Jewish otherness and became "normal."

This assumption—that exogamy can only imply the exit of the Jewish partner to the religion of his or her spouse—is precisely what has changed in contemporary North America. Today, as in biblical times, marrying a Jew is not seen as strange or dangerous. Generally speaking, Judaism and Jews are largely respected, and marrying a Jew who wants to stay Jewish or embracing the religious identity of one's Jewish spouse are viewed as legitimate life choices.[6]

When intermarriage does not inherently entail an act of exit, and it can be assumed that the Genesis and Exodus identity of the family can be Jewish as well, exogamy ceases to be synonymous with assimilation.

Complex Identities and the Disintegration of "Intermarriage" as a Category

The Genesis-Exodus boundary discourse (chapter 4) can help to conceptualize this critical reclassification of exogamy. As shown, intolerable deviance is limited to the Whole-Torah Meshumad, that is, one who rejects any and all association with either the Genesis or Exodus Covenants. In the past, it was perhaps logical to infer such a wholesale rejection from a Jew's decision to intermarry, which generally meant marrying into the faith, and faith community, of the dominant culture. But in contemporary North America, not only does exogamy not inherently imply such a sweeping rejection—it rarely does so.

Moreover, as we've also seen, a defining feature of American Jewish life in the postmodern era is the phenomenon of complex identities, in which we are no longer simply Jews, but many things—liberals/conservatives, white/brown/black, different genders, etc.[7] In the context of these multiple nonhierarchical identities, it is not just that intermarriage does not necessarily imply assimilation—it's that *it is no longer really intermarriage.*

Exogamy implies a union between two individuals with clear, distinct, different, and competing identities: for example, a biblical monotheist and a Canaanite or Mesopotamian idolater; or a shtetl Jew and a Catholic peasant in Medieval Christendom. But in the America of multiple and complex identities, Jews and non-Jews who enter into a romantic relationship may just see themselves as two people who are falling in love. They can embrace their shared identities without contemplating or rejecting any of their other identities. A Jewish or Christian identity is usually not the principal identity at play in the act of exogamy. In lived reality—and amounting to one of the most significant transformations in twenty-first-century Jewish identity—most North American Jews who marry non-Jews do not primarily see themselves as rejecting their Jewishness or marrying someone who is meaningfully different from them. In fact, as argued by the American Jewish Population Project, a majority of intermarried couples give their children some form of a Jewish education.[8]

If we now consider the rabbinic boundary principle, dictated by a nuanced Genesis-Exodus synthesis (chapter 4), that as long as a Jew continues to embrace the Genesis Covenant as well as some aspect of the Exodus Covenant, Judaism sees the violation as "tolerable deviance" at the very worst, with the individual in question remaining a community member in good standing, then *the "sin" of exogamy is consequently no longer a core boundary violation* but one of many issues of observance Jews may disagree about.

The reality of complex identities changes the self-perception of the Jew, and this self-perception must in turn influence the Jewish tradition and community's attitude toward intermarriage. If most of the Jews who intermarry are not assimilating, exogamy can no longer be deemed as inevitable assimilation. We might view nonassimilationist exogamy as no different than not keeping the Sabbath, holidays, or Jewish dietary laws. The Jew who intermarries may not be a perfect Jew, but there are no perfect Jews.

The New Normal

In like vein, Genesis Judaism requires that Jewishness take into account the social realities created by Genesis Jews. Because the majority of North American Jews who marry are marrying non-Jews, the act of exogamy can no longer be a boundary that defines Jewishness—it is now the norm of Jewish life.

Recognizing exogamy as the new normal does not mean that one must personally embrace it as part of one's Exodus Covenant, or agree to officiate, or disregard the challenges intermarriage poses to a future vibrant and committed Jewish life and community. Two Jewishly committed parents are almost always more able to communicate their love and dedication to Judaism than one, especially if the other parent is inclined toward a different faith community.

The question, however, is not whether we can imagine a better scenario for the Jewish future. That is easy. It is best if both parents are committed. It is best if both parents belong to a synagogue and send their children to Jewish day schools and Jewish camps and travel often to Israel. It is best if the family engages in ongoing study and observes the Jewish calendar in a regular, consistent, and joyful manner.[9]

The issue is not whether we can imagine ideal scenarios, but how we relate to the current one. Internalizing the Genesis teaching whereby

Jewishness is also simply who we are, and not merely what we do or believe, expands the parameters of Jewish identity and the notion of "good Jews" and requires the inclusion of intermarried Jews and their spouses who choose to join us, independent of any assessment of their Exodus bona fides. The Genesis limitation on Exodus-inspired boundaries—only one who chooses to leave the Jewish people is intolerable—requires that we look differently at exogamy in our era. We can no longer exclude intermarried couples who may be actively choosing to be part of the Jewish story.

We can debate whether exogamy is good for Jewishness: whether it makes assimilation more likely or, on the contrary, creates opportunities to assimilate non-Jews into the Jewish people and the Jewish covenants.[10] But this debate is in many ways secondary. In the story Jews will tell themselves about themselves in North America in the years to come, most Jews will have only one Jew-by-birth parent. Synthesizing Genesis and Exodus demands that, rather than digging our heels into a self-defeating discourse of denial, we marshal our collective creativity to ensure a vital next chapter in the Jewish people's story.

16

The Eroding North American-Israel Relationship

Jewishness for me is first and foremost a sense of belonging to a people with whom I have shared a history and story for three thousand years. My Judaism starts with Genesis—where my core identity as a Jew lies.

I have two national identities, Israeli and American. While Israel is my home, where I live and work, I work throughout North America too. I love North America, and feel deeply connected to the Jewish community both in the United States and Canada. A large part of my job, and in fact my life's mission, is to ensure that the respective Jewish communities do not walk away from each other.

If Israeli and North American Jewry were to disengage from each other, my principal concern would not be about Israel's political well-being but whether my Jewish story is in danger of coming to an end—a Genesis emergency. I have no Judaism without my people.

Yet today, we are on the precipice of precisely such a disengagement.

Since the establishment of Israel, inherent disparities between Israelis and North Americans have been a constant source of friction. Besides living in dramatically different environments, separated by thousands of miles, we have very different social and political sensibilities. To give but one example: every Israeli family has, at most, one degree of separation from someone who was killed or injured in the conflict with the Palestinians. Because of these losses, and because of the drafting of our children into the military, we all suffer to some degree from post-traumatic stress. Despite the recent spike in antisemitic incidents across the United States, almost no North American Jews live with this reality.

While over the years our two communities have remained connected to each other overall, more recently there have been calls in the United

States for separation from Israel, along with an increase in anti-Zionist sentiment.[1] As an Israeli American, I experienced this growing gap very painfully during Israel's Gaza military operation against Hamas in May 2021.

To most Israelis, this was one of the most just wars Israel has fought. As the Palestinian Authority and Hamas fought for Palestinian hegemony, Hamas attempted to position itself as the de facto leader of the Palestinian People.

On an annual basis, Ramadan commemorations are a source of extensive friction between Palestinians in Jerusalem and Israeli authority. The focus is around the Old City in Jerusalem, in particular the Al Aqsa Mosque on the Temple Mount, where violent demonstrations break out and rocks are thrown on the Western Wall below. Each year these demonstrations lead to violent clashes, which have included Israeli forces storming the Al Aqsa Mosque with stun grenades.

Manipulating this annual event, Hamas began to fire missiles into Israel under the justification that they were the protectors of Al Aqsa.

Over four thousand missiles rained on Israel's population centers. Thanks to Israel's Iron Dome missile defense system, the casualties were not extreme—twelve fatalities and two hundred injured.[2] But all of Israel was being terrorized, with the majority of its citizens running in and out of shelters throughout the day and into the night. Life was brought to a standstill. No country would endure such an intolerable act of aggression.

With the support of almost every Israeli Jew, and the backing of many Western democracies,[3] Israel launched a defensive air-bombing campaign against Hamas's and Islamic Jihad's command centers, as well as the tunnels in Gaza from which the perpetrators maintained their ability to move about undetected.

Israel explicitly outlined the rationale behind the bombing campaign at the outset.[4] As distinct from previous campaigns, there was no discussion of either defeating Hamas or downgrading its military and missile capabilities, both of which would necessitate a ground incursion and the bombing of sites in close proximity to civilians. All prior Gaza operations had resulted in Gazan casualties in the thousands, a result of moving ground troops and tanks into the densely populated areas of Gaza and Hamas locating their soldiers and missile launchers near schools and civilian buildings.

To most Israeli Jews, the Hamas agenda was to terrorize Israel, murder as many Israelis as possible, *and* cause Israel to kill enough Palestinian innocents so that the Palestinians could win the battle for international support and sympathy.[5] Israel's aim, in turn, was to generate enough infrastructure damage (as distinct from military casualties) to convince Hamas that frequent missile attacks were not in *their* interests. If preventing Gazan civilian casualties were not a sufficient deterrence, maybe hampering Hamas's own ability to function would be. And instead of Hamas launching missiles every other week or month and initiating a large missile campaign every other year, maybe Israeli civilians would be afforded five years of quiet. In its strategy, Israel shifted its aspiration to deterrence—a far more reasonable and achievable objective.[6]

From the dominant Israeli perspective, the war was morally obligatory, morally fought, and operationally well-managed.[7] In a rare anomaly, there was almost no political debate or second guessing. While not free of mistakes—some two hundred civilians were killed, including a large number of children—the overall Gazan deaths were limited to the low hundreds. After twelve days, Hamas agreed to a unilateral ceasefire, seemingly giving credence to Israel's having successfully achieved some measure of its objectives.

Life quickly returned to the Israeli definition of normal.

"When You Have This Much Power, What Is Your Responsibility?": The Other War

Such was reality as most Israelis, including myself, experienced it. Then I watched Trevor Noah and John Oliver, popular TV political commentators and satirists, and heard a completely different narrative of the events. Noah:

But I just want to ask an honest question here: If you are in a fight where the other person cannot beat you, how hard should you retaliate when they try to hurt you? Honest question. And I ask this question because I think of it like this. When I was a teenager, I would always get into fights with my little brothers. And little kids can be vicious right? They're trying to punch you in the legs, trying to punch you in the nuts. They're kids. They do that. But my mom would say to me, whenever I would get angry, "Trevor, don't hit the kid back, because they can't hurt you, you're a teenager and the kid is four." And I was, like "Yeah, but the kid is hitting me. He could hurt me." But my mom was like "Yeah, but you're also so much bigger than the kid. You can crush him in an instant." ...

What my mom made me understand is that as a person who has immensely more power, I had to ask myself whether my response to this child was just or necessary. Could I find different ways to deal with this? Whether I felt aggrieved or not or whether they were fighting fair was almost irrelevant. Was I even able to ask myself the question about why they were doing what they were doing? Was I willing to admit guilt? This was all part of the question that I had to ask myself.

But the main question I ask in this situation is about power. And please, again, I know, it's not a great analogy because I'm not saying the Palestinians are children. I'm not just saying they're all children, right? I'm not saying that they are harmless, or irrational or acting out. I'm not saying any of that. I'm not. I'm just talking about the difference in power, which is something we do all the time. . . . Because, at the end of the day, they brought a knife to a gun fight. . . . All I'm asking is, when you have this much power, what is your responsibility?[8]

John Oliver had a similar take:

But this week has actually been a pretty good reminder that while some things are incredibly complex and require a great deal of context, other are just wrong. . . . And look it is true the militants from Palestinian groups like Hamas fired over a thousand rockets towards Israel this week and that is reprehensible. But, and I realize this is the most load-bearing conjunction in history, but the majority of those rockets thankfully didn't reach their targets. . . . This isn't tit for tat. There is a massive imbalance when it comes to the two sides' weaponry and capabilities. While most of the rockets aimed towards Israeli civilians this week were intercepted, Israel's airstrikes were not. They hit their targets, including a house in a refugee camp, a building housing the Associated Press and al Jazeera, and this 13-story office and apartment building. And while Israel insisted that they were military targets in that building and they destroyed it as humanely as possible, even warning people to evacuate beforehand, for the record, destroying a civilian residence sure seems like a war crime.[9]

I could not believe what I was hearing. Were the Hamas missile attacks raining on our citizens, injuring and killing dozens, and terrorizing millions, really being compared to a younger brother who can't really hurt you? Was our war of self-defense morally problematic simply because of an imbalance in our military capabilities, and because Israel's Iron Dome was effective and the casualties disproportionate? Did more Israelis need to die so that we could have the right to defend ourselves? Is Israel's new moral sin its success, and so long as Hamas remains a relative failure, it is assigned permanent victim status, exempt from judgment, and granted carte blanche to attack and terrorize Israel?

I was confused. I was angry. I was certain that everyone would condemn Noah and Oliver. I was wrong.

While condemned by the traditional pro-Israel institutions and leaders, Noah's and Oliver's voices echoed the sentiment of an ever-growing number of Jews, in particular young Jews.[10] At the same time that they were offering their moral condemnation, in the midst of the missile attacks, ninety future American rabbis and cantors from the major liberal rabbinic and cantorial seminaries penned a letter of deep concern and condemnation of Israel not only for the war but for its ongoing occupation of the Palestinian people:

> Blood is flowing in the streets of the Holy Land. Fires are burning on the hills of Jerusalem and buildings are smoldering in Gaza. Violence is spilling onto the streets of Lod and Haifa. With each refresh of the news and each rocket that falls, new images of terror sear themselves into our minds. We find ourselves in tears . . . .
>
> This year, American Jews have been part of a racial reckoning in our community. Our institutions have been reflecting and asking, "How are we complicit with racial violence?" Jewish communities, large and small, have had teach-ins and workshops, held vigils, and commissioned studies.
>
> And yet, so many of those same institutions are silent when abuse of power and racist violence erupts in Israel and Palestine. So many of us ignore the day-to-day indignity that the Israeli military and police forces enact on Palestinians, and sit idly by as Israel upholds two separate legal systems for the same region. And, in the same breath, we are shocked by escalations of violence, as though these things are not a part of the same dehumanizing status quo.
>
> As American Jews, our institutions tell stories of Israel rooted in hope for what could be, but oblivious to what is. Our tzedakah money funds a story we wish were true, but perpetuates a reality that is untenable and dangerous. Our political advocacy too often puts forth a narrative of victimization, but supports violent suppression of human rights and enables apartheid in the Palestinian territories, and the threat of annexation.
>
> It's far past time that we confront this head on. We can no longer shy away or claim ignorance.
>
> What will it take for us to see that our Israel has the military and controls the borders? How many Palestinians must lose their homes, their schools, their lives, for us to understand that today, in 2021, Israel's choices come from a place of power and that Israel's actions constitute an intentional removal of Palestinians?[11]

Two months after the war, the Jewish Electorate Institute reported statistics from its 2021 National Survey of Jewish Voters in the United States echoing and amplifying these sentiments: 25 percent of voting Jews believe that Israel is an apartheid state, 21 percent believe that Israel is carrying out the genocide of Palestinians, and 34 percent believe that Israel's treatment of Palestinians is similar to racism in the United States. When focusing on Jews aged forty and below, the numbers rise to an astonishing 38, 33, and 43 percent respectively.[12]

As I talked with my North American friends and colleagues, a completely different war unfolded before me. From their perspective, which I came to understand and respect, Israel's bombing of Gaza was not merely a response to Hamas's bombing but part of a larger pattern of abuses made possible by Israel's disproportionate power.

While an asymmetry of power is not morally problematic per se, it becomes problematic when it intoxicates the powerful. Israel's power is so readily available, and the results so guaranteed, that more difficult yet potentially constructive long-term strategies go unexplored. The question my North American friends were asking was not whether Hamas was justified in bombing Israel, but whether Israel had done all that it could to end the occupation and its subsequent abuses, and, what is more, to prevent—not only deter—the next round of Hamas missile attacks.

To many in North America, the Gaza conflict was widely understood to be sparked by two events. First, Israel planned to evict several Arab families living in Jerusalem's Sheikh Jarrah neighborhood, in homes which their Jewish owners had been forced to abandon when Jordan took control in the aftermath of the 1948 war and subsequently granted the Arab families the right to live there. Israel was now claiming the homes on behalf of Jewish citizens who bought the rights to the homes from their original Jewish owner. The second event was the perception of an overly aggressive Israeli police response to growing unrest at the Al-Aqsa Mosque.

Consequently, the story quickly became about Israel's ongoing actions as an occupier, relying on its disproportionate power to "solve" its problems. Ostensibly, then, the ensuing Gaza campaign was not primarily a response to Hamas's missile attacks but an "Occupation War," that is, part of a continued unjust occupation. If Israel wanted to claim the moral high ground and define its response as an act of self-defense, it needed to show through words and deeds that it used power as an instrument of last resort. After decades of occupation and associated power abuses, many Diaspora Jews now believed that Israel had not made that case.

As an Israeli, I was upset at how Israel had handled both the Palestinian claims in Sheikh Jarrah and the Al Aqsa Mosque situation. First, Israel should not give credence to pre-1948 Jewish property claims unless it is willing to do so for equivalent Palestinian refugee property claims as well. Since Israel does not do the latter, it should not do the former. Second, security forces with a proven ability to implement strategic long-term plans should certainly be able to foresee the annual Ramadan demonstrations and develop preventative and deescalating protocols when it comes to the Al Aqsa Mosque. Wrong in themselves, these missteps handed Hamas the opportunity to manipulate the restive Palestinian response to its advantage.

I didn't connect my anger at these unforced errors, however, with my overarching assessment of the war. Almost no Israeli did. As outrageous as these mistakes were, they had nothing to do with our right to self-defense. Hamas was to blame, and our actions were both just and morally required.

For decades, we in Israel could trust that our narrative of reality, especially of our wars, would be embraced by world Jewry. In Gaza in 2021 that clearly was no longer the case.

Partisanship

There is no doubt that American partisan politics is fueling some of this gap in narratives. The mutual embrace of Israel and former president Donald Trump has painted Israel as a partisan Republican issue, on the wrong side of most North American Jews who are liberal Democrats.

Meanwhile, the campaign to uproot systemic discrimination and injustice in America, correctly supported by the liberal Jewish community, has generated greater awareness of, and intolerance toward, systemic oppression. Finally, the radical progressive embrace of universalism and rejection of nationalism, and the attack against white power and privilege, has drawn a direct line between Black Lives Matter and Palestinian Lives Matter and mainstreamed the criminalization of Israel.[13] Put together, these circumstances have strengthened an American milieu that at times challenges Israel's legitimacy, not to speak of questioning its use of power in the Gaza conflict and elsewhere.

All things considered, however, I believe that the principal cause of the deteriorating connection between Israeli and American Jews today is that the central categories through which North American Jews engaged with and related to Israel in the twentieth century are no longer relevant. While there are centrifugal political forces beyond our control, there are also realities we can control, and through a new infusion of Genesis and Exodus sensibilities, a deeper relationship is possible.

Family, Shared Believers, Consumers, and Partners

Throughout the twentieth century, the Jewish commitment to Zionism and Israel was expressed through four principal frameworks that served to carry, sustain, explain, and even justify Diaspora Jewry's relationship with Israel:

1. A relationship to Israel as family;
2. A relationship to Israel as fellow believers;
3. A relationship with Israel as consumers; and
4. A relationship with Israel as partners.

By understanding the way these categories claimed twentieth-century Jews—and the way they have ceased to claim twenty-first-century

Jew—we can better navigate our way out of the tricky landscape we find ourselves in.

Relationship as Family

The Genesis Covenant is the historical and ideological source for the first model: family. As family, I am bound to you by virtue of who you are, and not by what you do. Family speaks to our inherited relationship—one not chosen or earned, but one grounded in a narrative of shared origins and passed down from generation to generation.

For North American Jews, the family model of relationship casts Israelis as brothers and sisters. By virtue of this family tie, Diaspora Jews are obligated to stand with Israelis in good times and bad. As family our loyalty is not contingent on whether we agree.

For much of the twentieth century, this family consciousness was a defining framework for the North American-Israeli relationship, fueling support for Israel and Israel-related causes.

Relationship as Fellow Believers

The Exodus Covenant, on the other hand, has been the framework for an Israeli-North American Jewry relationship based on shared beliefs and values. The shared belief in our roots in the land, and for many its holiness, the shared value of preserving historical memory—both are nurtured by the stories of God's connection to the Land of Israel, its distinction as the birthplace of the Jewish people, and its capacity as a sovereign state to shape a Jewish public space. In this context, Israel becomes a destination for all manner of identity-building pilgrimages: bar and bat mitzvah celebrations, family visits, holiday trips, missions, individual quests of a more personal, seeking nature.

Shared beliefs and values also transcend the broader elements of Jewish history and identity to encompass our liberal Jewish aspirations:

Israel as a beacon of democracy and decency
Israel as a representation of the best the Jewish people can be

Israel as a model of our ultimate mission to be a light unto the nations

Relationship as Consumers

This third category, another outgrowth of an Exodus sensibility with a particular North American hue, denotes a person who "buys" or consumes a product because they believe there is some gain or benefit they will accrue from it. While "consumerism" can carry negative connotations of superficiality and self-centeredness, it has become at the same time a catalyzing feature of North American Jewish life.

North American Jews have emerged as Jews by Choice in every aspect of their Jewish identity, and their relationship to Israel is no different. An integral part of the experience of being a Jew by Choice is a consumerist sensibility whereby one continually asks, *What value am I deriving from the relationship?* This is not necessarily because of a heightened sense of self-centeredness, but can also be because one's multiple identities are constantly competing. A relationship to Israel as consumers does not merely search for shared beliefs but for beliefs that are a source of inspiration, excitement, and meaning. As a consumer I want to know what I'm receiving. Does this "product" enrich my life?

Unlike the familial distinction, the consumer framework does not assume loyalty as a given. The relationship is contingent. For much of the twentieth century, especially after the Six-Day War, Israel was a constant source of pride, a product Jewish consumers were honored to partake in. Israel was victorious, powerful, and righteous. It provided Jews worldwide with a similar sense of power and pride. We were no longer the victims to be pitied and protected. Through a relationship with Israel, Jews were strong and capable of protecting themselves. Israel's ability to serve as the refuge for Soviet and Ethiopian Jewry, its growing military prowess as modeled in the raid on Entebbe, its courageous embrace of peace as exhibited in the Oslo Accords, and its transformation into Start Up Nation, all served as vehicles for consumerist interest.

Relationship as Partnership

This last model for the North America-Israel relationship involves partners who join with each other in a common undertaking with shared risks and benefits. North American Jews who see themselves as partners view the building of Israel as a mission that they share with Israelis. Unlike consumers, partners are committed to building Israel even when the current Israel does not reflect their highest aspirations. For partners, this discrepancy is a call for greater action—the responsibility to build Israel as they envision it should be.

The Collapse of the Family Model

For over a century, the story North American Jews told themselves about their deep and often unconditional commitment to Israel was a story about family. But in the twenty-first century, this model, like the others, is being challenged.

The intensity of loyalty contained within the family model assumes a family living in close proximity to each other. But what happens to brothers and sisters who live six to ten thousand miles away and allow years to pass between visits—who, as time passes, have increasingly less direct family ties? The assumption of loyalty is built on the nuclear family model, but over time, family ties generally have become attenuated and abstracted, the relationships more akin to those of cousins.

Today, as years pass since the dramatic and emotional founding of the state, among those North American Jews who see Israelis as family, only a small minority see them as siblings (11 percent). More see them as first cousins (15 percent), or at best as mere extended family (47 percent).[14] As the family becomes ever more extended, it is only natural that the loyalty claim becomes more tenuous.

This attenuation is further exacerbated by the phenomenon of complex identities. When one's Jewish identity is no longer singular, but one of many parallel and competing identities, a Genesis-like bond with an extended family will not necessarily outweigh a competing bond with, for example, a fellow liberal Democrat. In a Jewish community with complex identities, the experience of a distant family does not offer a compelling framework for maintaining an engagement with, let alone prioritizing, Israel over that of their other identities.

Jews' core experience of at-homeness in both Israel and North America challenge their respective loyalty bonds as well. Even assuming that the model of siblings still applies, Israel and North American Jews are certainly not young brothers and sisters living in the same household; they are more akin to siblings who have grown up, moved away, and entered into new relationships in distinct homes which now claim their principal loyalty.

Adults who have married or who are in long-term relationships are supposed to prioritize the needs of their spouse or significant other over those of a sibling. This is doubly the case when needs are in conflict, or when a sibling or parent is disrespectful of one's partner. To fail to do so is to fail to "grow up" and mature into an adult.

The reality of "at-homeness" in North America has created a unique circumstance in Jewish history whereby Jews are "married" to America and Canada. Most Jews in North America are not merely or even primarily Jews but have a Jewish identity completely intertwined with their American and Canadian ones. Similarly, in Israel, Jewish citizens are "married" to Israel and Israeliness; the claim of the Jewish People is often secondary to that of the State of Israel and its interests.

A powerful example of the complexity of the "extended family" model was dramatized on the international stage in the conflict between Israelis and North American Jews around the Iranian nuclear agreement ultimately adopted in 2015. Then–prime minister Netanyahu, along with much of his considerable constituency, saw a nuclear Iran as a fundamental threat to the existence of the State of Israel and believed that the agreement failed to offer Israel adequate protection. Their expectation was that North American Jews would therefore naturally fall into line and support Israel's position against the agreement; after all, we are family.

But when Prime Minister Netanyahu delivered a presentation before

Congress that critiqued President Obama, hoping to rally the Jewish community around him and marshal their political clout to Israel's cause, he was deeply surprised and disappointed—not just at the rejection of support, but at the strong condemnation he received from the vast majority of North American Jewry.[15]

Why aren't you with me? he seemed to be asking, baffled.[16] What Netanyahu and many Israelis did not understand is that even when North American Jews are connected to Israel, they are married to America. America is their home, and Netanyahu's visit was akin to an adult brother or sister visiting their sibling's family home and insulting their spouse. Demanding that American Jews choose Israel over their president, Netanyahu failed to recognize the extent to which the family model had changed.

Conversely, when American Jews expressed bewilderment and outrage with the Netanyahu government's affiliation with the Trump administration, which many saw as dangerous to Jews and their sense of at-homeness in America—the clear subtext of their complaint was: *Aren't we brothers and sisters? Aren't you supposed to stand with me and combat what I believe to be an existential threat?* They failed to recognize that for Israelis, the first consideration is not the well-being of Jewish life in America but Israel's interests. For most Israelis, Donald Trump was experienced as an ally who made the world more hospitable and safe for Israel. Whether he was a good president for America and its Jews simply did not rank as a consideration. If Jews felt threatened, they could always make aliyah to their home in Israel. American Jewry's demand that Israelis take their side on this issue was to ask—outrageously in their eyes—that Israelis divorce themselves from Israel and *its* needs.

North American and Israeli Jews, embracing the Genesis Covenant, may see each other as a part of the same family. But family is complicated. The notion that a sense of family connection, broadly construed, will be sufficient to create an assumed sense of commitment immune from questions and impervious to outside forces is no longer credible. In the twenty-first century, we have emerged as an extended, multigenerational family juggling numerous constituencies, identities, interests, loyalties, and homes. This new reality, shaped by both distance and a newfound sense of at-homeness, renders the Genesis Covenant and its family model *alone* inadequate to sustain the North American Jewry-Israel relationship.

That said, the family model, in its classic sense, could conceivably undergo a renaissance if Israel faces a clear and present existential threat, or if there is a massive resurgence of existentially dangerous antisemitism in North America. As with all families, loyalty is reprioritized in times of crisis. We are a people who are always ready to sit together at a shivah house. Which table we are designated at a wedding is another matter altogether.

Not-Shared Beliefs

In the twenty-first century, the assumptive model of shared beliefs is increasingly questioned as well. For the majority of North America's liberal Jews, whether they are Reform, Reconstructionist, Conservative, Modern Orthodox, Humanistic, secular, or unaffiliated, Israel's Orthodox monopoly over much of public Jewish life—in which North American rabbis and their denominational affiliations claim no respect—creates a deep gulf and a sharp challenge to the notion of a shared belief system uniting us. As they see it, the retrograde ultra-Orthodox rabbinate has enshrined a Judaism in Israel whose values and practices could not be farther removed from their own. Many liberal Jews feel that the possibilities for expressing their Jewish life are harshly restricted in Israel and that the fullness of their Exodus commitments can be expressed only in North America.

The Kotel or Western Wall fiasco of 2017 was a powerful and, for many North American Jews, galvanizing example of this phenomenon.[17] As the holiest site in the Jewish world—the last remaining remnant of the Second Temple (destroyed in 70 CE)—the Kotel ought to be a place where all Jews feel welcome and respected. However, since its return to Jewish hands in 1967, the Kotel has been transformed into what is de facto an Orthodox synagogue governed by the Orthodox

Rabbinate, with separate sections for men and women. Egalitarian services and women's prayer groups, spurned by the Kotel Rabbi, are banned from the Kotel area and relegated to an outside plaza.

The status of these services, in particular the monthly Women of the Wall prayer services, which generated constant Orthodox harassment and suppression, became the focus of numerous petitions to Israel's High Court. Recognizing the explosive nature of the issue, the courts encouraged the politicians to forge a compromise that all sides could live with. After over a decade of procrastination, Netanyahu appointed the then-head of the Jewish Agency Nathan Sharansky to convene and lead a committee tasked with forging just such a compromise.

The compromise ironed out after decades of contention was to leave the current Kotel under Orthodox jurisdiction but to expand "the Kotel" to include a newfound southern section that would be under the jurisdiction of liberal Jews. A common entranceway would lead all Jews to one shared plaza, from which each group could then proceed to "their" Kotel.

This compromise, however, assumed an equality between Orthodox and liberal Jews within Israel, which ultimately proved a dealbreaker for the former. What easily could and should have been a win-win was squandered because it would have required Israel to officially accept the legitimacy of liberal Judaism. According to many polls, most Israelis were willing to do so—but living up to their principally not-Dati identities, they did not muster sufficient pressure on Netanyahu by standing up against a deeply invested and organized ultra-Orthodox block for whom "liberal Judaism" is itself an affront to their deepest values.[18]

In the end, under pressure from his ultra-Orthodox coalition partners, Netanyahu reneged. There is now a small wooden prayer deck with a convoluted side-entrance available for liberal Jews, devoid of any of the majesty, openness, and grandeur of the Kotel.

The failure of the "Kotel Compromise" left North American Zionists more alienated than before. If the great majority of North American Jewry cannot have a true place at the Kotel, even when it is not infringing on any Orthodox practices, then what *is* shared?

This sense of alienation from Israel has dramatically increased following the 2022 national elections and the forming of the most religiously right-wing government in Israel's history. With unprecedented power, the Haredi parties (Shas and Agudat Yisrael), supported by the National Religious Party—now controlled by its ultra-Orthodox nationalist wing—are committed to uprooting all vestiges of liberal Jewish legislation and policies. The extensive targeted list includes, among others, changes to the Law of Return, delegitimizing liberal conversions performed in Israel, enforcing the current illiberal status quo at the Kotel into law, legitimizing gender segregation in state-sponsored events for the religious community, allowing providers of services (including doctors) to refuse services to individuals who they find religiously abhorrent, greater enforcement of Orthodox Shabbat observance laws in the public sector, and removal of liberal Jewish curriculum from the educational system. Most significantly, the coalition aims to limit the ability of the Supreme Court—the body that almost singlehandedly protected Israel's liberal Jewish values on the basis of the Basic Law of Human Dignity and Freedom—to override any legislation that the latter deems discriminatory. Under these conditions, to claim that the relationship with Israel is based on shared values seems naïve.

Moreover, there is the reality of Israel's continued occupation of the West Bank. The term "occupation" denotes military control over Judea and Samaria and the approximately three million Palestinians who reside there, leaving them devoid of either Israeli citizenship or citizenship in their own state. The majority of North American Jews are committed to a two-state solution, out of both a recognition of Palestinian human rights and a commitment to an Israel that embodies Jewish humanist principles.[19] The continued occupation, with its inevitably discriminatory policies, violates their core Exodus beliefs and their hopes and vision for Israel. When Israel controls the lives of three million Palestinians in Judea and Samaria, it cannot fulfill its mission to be a Jewish and democratic state. If the three million Palestinians are not given equal rights, then Israel is no longer a democracy. Yet if they are incorporated as citizens in the State of Israel, Israel's Jewish majority is threatened and Israel is no longer a Jewish state.

Over the years, North American Jewry's criticism of the occupation was mitigated, and at times suspended, by the assertion that the occupation was temporary.[20] Israel's supporters also contended that Israelis did not want to occupy another people (see Oslo and the unilateral withdrawal from Gaza); the Palestinian rejection of any peaceful resolution to the conflict had forced this reality upon them. In any event, supporters argued, Israel was constantly pursuing peace (again see Oslo and the unilateral withdrawal from Gaza), and if the Palestinians would simply recognize Israel's right to exist, the horrific reality of occupation would immediately come to an end.

Now, however, over half a century later, more American Jews are questioning Israel's intentions vis-à-vis the occupation and whether it makes sense to still call it temporary. Bolstering this concern is the fact that since 2005 Israel has not initiated any significant peace proposal. Meanwhile, it is continuing its decades-long massive state-sponsored settlement campaign, which has facilitated the movement of hundreds of thousands of Israelis into Judea and Samaria, making a two-state solution increasingly impossible to envision.

Here too, the makeup of the 2022 Netanyahu government is exacerbating the divisions. At the heart and leadership of the government are individuals for whom the pursuit of peace with Palestinians and a two-state solution are not a value. They firmly believe in the holiness of all the Land of Israel and advocate for policies that will ensure that Israel's current control over Judea and Samaria continues. They want to undermine the Palestinian Authority, legalize all currently illegal settlements, remove any barriers from Jews expanding and building new ones, and place administrative control over Jewish settlements in the hands of the Israeli civil government, effectively annexing them to Israel. In addition, their support for calls to change the status quo on the Temple Mount will guarantee the perpetuation of the conflict and Israel's reliance on its military power to enforce order. What in the past could be claimed as temporary is now feeling permanent. Israel as a permanent occupier of another people is an Israel that is losing its Jewish and democratic roots.

Consumer Fatigue

This challenge of ideological dissonance grows even more significant when viewed from the vantage point of a consumer relationship. A consumer is committed to a product because it adds tangible value to their lives. As ever-growing numbers of North American Jews become increasingly uncomfortable with Israel's policies in Judea and Samaria, and on issues of state and religion, it becomes harder for Israel to sustain its "market share" in a consumerist culture. Granted, for many North American Jews, Israel is still Start Up Nation, and a major center of innovation and tikkun olam—but for many others, this is no longer sufficiently compelling to override the ideological and moral dissonances. This is particularly the case when it comes to Jewish power, a primary catalyst for pride and consumerist identification with Israel. The same power which in the past was ennobled by its perceived significance in protecting Israel's safety is now tainted by its facilitation of the occupation and oppression of Palestinian human rights. Thus power, once a source of pride, is today a principal source of the problem. In general, consumer interest cannot sustain itself on past successes; for the consumer, present experiences are more significant than historical motivations, no matter how compelling or authentic they once were. The saving of Soviet and Ethiopian Jewry in the '80s and '90s is simply not sufficiently compelling for Jews several decades hence.

Consumers do not have to articulate a position on why Israel is violating their shared beliefs. The same Jews who choose to terminate their synagogue membership when they experience it as no longer vital can do the same with Israel. Even if these growing ideological conflicts do not lead to full-scale rejection of Israel's policies, in a consumerist universe a "product" can be simply dropped, or used less frequently, if it no longer provides a compelling case.

One-Sided Partnership

Finally, the partnership model—the framework embraced by the most Zionist of North American Jews—is being undermined too, both by ideological chasms, and paradoxically, by Israel itself.

When Israel's policies are challenged, the partner might agree with the criticism but nevertheless point out that the meaning of partnership is commitment. A partner may say, for example, *I disagree with the Occupation. I disagree with Israel's position on state and religion. But it is precisely at this moment that my partnership must express itself, as I redouble my efforts to fight for the Israel that I want.*

Today, however, as partners take responsibility to work toward the Israel they believe in, supporting religious pluralism and liberal Jewish educational centers, and vocally critiquing any moves that further inflame or entrench the Occupation, or alienate Palestinians, they increasingly find themself in opposition to the current Israeli government. The growing tension between Israel and its partners expresses itself in escalating cycles of mutual condemnation and delegitimization: North Americans critique Israeli policies; Israelis reject their right to critique altogether.

Further undermining the viability of the partnership model is the fact that Israel has never acknowledged World Jewry as partners. As we saw, the dominant Israeli perspective on World Jewry has ranged from disrespect to outright disdain. If, as the thinking goes, Israel alone is where the Jewish people are redeemed and have a possibility for a vibrant future, then World Jewry's task is not to partner with Israel, but to move to Israel.

Over the first five decades of the State of Israel, this attitude toward World Jewry was tempered by Israel's political and financial weakness. In its diminished capacity as a young nation facing existential dangers, Israel was in no position to correct, much less reject, North American Zionists who had anointed themselves as Israel's partners. In fact, in order to (begrudgingly) seek, and accept, financial and political aid, Israel engaged in a form of kabuki theater, where despite the ideological

rejection of Diaspora Jewry and Judaism, Israel nevertheless granted every supposed "North American Leadership Mission" access to
the prime minister and other top national figures. While both North
American and Israeli leaders spoke openly of their deep partnership,
in fact Israel saw Diaspora Jews as mere supporters and philanthropic
donors—individuals whose money and clout at home were welcome,
but not their voice or opinion about Israel itself. For most Israelis, the
partnership model is actually an option *only* for those who make aliyah.

As Israel achieves greater prosperity, it has even less tolerance toward
self-anointed partners and is less willing to humor their criticisms. In
fact, many on Israel's political right speak openly of their yearning to
disassociate from liberal Jewish "partners" and their Exodus sensibilities and replace them with Evangelical Christians.[21] Many on the
right believe that the latter can provide Israel with far more significant
political support, and without the same Exodus expectations.

Crisis of Relationship, Deficit of Discourse

Family, shared believers, consumers, partners: as the twenty-first century takes shape, we are challenged by the sobering extent to which
each of the primary models of North American Jewry's commitment
to Israel has been compromised.

For too long, the pro-Israel community counted on the Genesis
"family model" as a safety net mitigating the gap between the Israel
that liberal American Jews envision and Israel as it is. But that safety
net has become threadbare, no longer able to support the weight of
North American Jewry's estrangement. Genesis-inspired whitewashing
of Israel's failures will no longer be tolerated.

Devoid of meaningful categories on which to base a relationship,
Jews who are at home in North America will no longer experience Israel
as a meaningful or critical part of their Jewishness. North American
Jews by Choice will simply choose something else.

In the story they will tell themselves about themselves, Israel will
play a significant role in their past, but an increasingly marginal one in

their future. The Genesis and Exodus Covenants will shape the story they tell, but it will be exclusively a story of North American Jewish peoplehood, with minor references to Jews at risk around the world.

How may we alter this devastating trajectory?

It is my belief that Zionism in North America can still be salvaged—but only if Zionist discourse, and indeed Israel itself, can reclaim liberal Exodus principles. The future will require a far more honest, liberal, Exodus-centric conversation about what Israel has become—and what it must become.

It is to that future that we now turn.

17

The Future of Liberal Zionism in North America

The Untroubled-Committed

Not all North American Jews are experiencing an eroding relationship with Israel. A not-insignificant percentage, roughly 20 percent, many of whom are older, politically aligned with the Republican Party, and/or affiliated with Orthodoxy, reject any and all criticism of Israel.[1] I refer to this segment of North American Jewry as the *untroubled-committed*.

Members of this group believe that one cannot be critical of Israeli government policies and still be "pro-Israel." For them, Jewish life and Jewish identity are intertwined with Israel, which lays claim to their undivided loyalty. There are two main types of untroubled-committed Jews: those who are committed and untroubled because of their loyalty to the Genesis Covenant, and those who are committed and untroubled because of their allegiance to the Exodus Covenant.

Genesis Loyalists

For Genesis loyalists, the family model anchors their core relationship and loyalty to Israel. They may not agree with all of Israel's policies, whether on issues of state and religion or vis-à-vis Palestinians, but they see these policies as irrelevant to the vitality of the relationship. A Jew is a Jew is a Jew, and one's primary responsibility is to stand together with one's family, regardless of what its members do or believe, especially what one's family is under attack.[2]

A second manifestation of this Genesis-motivated untroubled committed-ness locates untroubled-ness in the categorical rejection of any Exodus covenantal expectations that might conflict with Israel's security and foreign policy. As a sovereign nation-state, Israel's core responsibility is to pursue its own interests and its citizens' well-being. Politics is about self-interest, not values. Israel does not have to be a light unto the nations, but simply a nation like any other.[3]

This Genesis-based untroubled-ness is paradoxically prevalent within some segments of the Orthodox community. While Judaism demands their fidelity to the principles of Exodus, their relationship with Israel touches little outside of their Genesis consciousness. For these untroubled-committed, while there is an Exodus Judaism, there is no Exodus Zionism, only a Genesis one.

Exodus Loyalists

A different manifestation of untroubled-committed-ness is founded on an Exodus sensibility. Far from being bothered by the occupation, such Jews tend to support Israel's annexation of Judea and Samaria.[4] When it comes to issues of state and religion, those untroubled-committed whose Exodus Covenant is an illiberal one are not bothered by the lack of support for liberal values.

In addition, the untroubled-committed tend to focus on the part of the cup that is half full and believe that Israel is simply the embodiment of Judaism's highest Exodus-based aspirations: a near-utopia. Israel *is* a light unto the nations, having already fulfilled the objective of: *You shall be unto me a kingdom of priests and a Holy Nation.* Israel is *the* paradigm of democracy and human rights, the most moral country—with the most moral army—in the world. As the "Start-Up Nation," Israel is the embodiment of *tikkun olam*, innovation, and excellence.[5] Evidence to the contrary is glossed over.

Even if embracing a liberal reading of Exodus, when it comes to the occupation, they remain untroubled, for they believe there is nothing to be troubled about.[6] They offer two blanket responses to criticisms pertaining to the occupation and the treatment of Palestinians: the factual and the antisemitism defenses.

The factual defense argues that critics of Israel's policies are either uninformed, ignorant of the facts, or simply biased and/or antisemitic. They fail to consider the century-old pattern of Arab and Palestinian aggression and rejection of all peace proposals. The continued occupation results not from Israel's abuse of its overwhelming military power but from the Palestinians' refusal to accept Israel's legitimacy. Israel's unilateral withdrawal from Gaza only catalyzed further Palestinian aggression. Numerous facts prove that Israel is the morally upright victim of aggression, and the tragic suffering of the Palestinian people is a self-inflicted result of the Palestinians' rejection of peace and embrace of terror.[7]

The antisemitism defense of the untroubled-committed claims that critics of Israel are motivated by antisemitic sentiments.[8] These critics are not really troubled by what Israel *does*, but the fact that Israel *exists*—not by particular exercises of Israel's power, but by Jewish power per se. The nation of Israel has become a stand-in for the Jew—demonized, more than any other country on earth, as the personification of evil and embodiment of corruption, such as white supremacy, colonialism, privilege, nationalism. Anti-Zionism is essentially a new manifestation of millennia-old antisemitic tropes and blood libels. Furthermore, these critics exercise double standards when applying the so-called "moral critique" upon the Jewish state.[9] They single out Israel for criticism, overlooking and excusing far worse abuses of power elsewhere, including by the Palestinians.

In short, the untroubled-committed dismiss any criticism of Israel as an unfair distortion bolstered by Israel's flawed public relations and/or a biased press. In the media or institutions in which they play a significant lay leadership role—Hillels, synagogues, Federations, etc.—they are quick to squelch any critical discourse around Israel under the argument that there's enough criticism out "there"; in our institutions, our responsibility is to advocate for our story.[10]

The Untroubled-Uncommitted, Troubled-Committed, and Troubled-Uncommitted

The majority of North American, Jews however, are not members of the untroubled-committed camp. Beyond the untroubled-committed, we can identify three additional archetypes: the *untroubled-uncommitted*; the *troubled-committed*; and the *troubled-uncommitted*.

The majority of North American Jews (70 to 80 percent) are currently either uninvolved or troubled, with the latter ranging from moderate to hypertroubled.[11] They are troubled because ultranationalist and ultra-Orthodox forces are growing in prominence and increasingly shaping Israel's policies and identity on issues of state and religion, minority rights, and democratic institutions and values. They are troubled by the fact that human rights and the Jewish commitment to treating all people as created in the image of God are inconsistently applied in Judea, Samaria, and Gaza and toward Israeli Arab Palestinians. Troubled because Israel, however committed to peace, is no longer resolute in pursuing it. Troubled by the perception that Israel's power has afforded it the ability to maintain the current political status quo while desensitizing it to the moral abuses it conceals and legitimizes. Troubled because Israel can—and must—do better, but Israel no longer seems to be trying. Troubled because the majority of Israelis no longer seem to be troubled.

Like the typological children of the Passover seder, all three groups relate to Israel in distinct ways—from those with no relationship at all to those for whom a relationship with Israel is a core responsibility and necessary part of their Jewishness.

The untroubled-uncommitted and the troubled-uncommitted are on a spectrum of disassociating their Jewishness from Israel and building a North American Jewish identity in which Israel plays little part. Meanwhile, the approximately 60 percent of the total Jewish community that is troubled-committed, still the majority among liberal Jews, remains committed to Israel but nevertheless is deeply troubled by its policies.[12]

The categories of Genesis and Exodus can help to elucidate each of these groups.

The Untroubled-Uncommitted

For the untroubled-uncommitted—typically American Jews with complex identities including a strong American Genesis-like one—Israel is not, or is no longer, a significant aspect of their Jewish life. From a consumerist perspective, Israel neither interests them nor claims their loyalty. The Jewish Genesis sensibilities expressed in the family model are not enough to maintain the relationship—and so, given the Exodus-based discrepancies estranging them from Israel, they have simply walked away. Other untroubled-uncommitted Jews have marginal if any Jewish identities and affiliations—neither the Genesis nor Exodus Covenants play a meaningful role in their lives—and their lack of relationship with Israel parallels their lack of relationship with Judaism in general.

The Troubled-Uncommitted

The second group, the troubled-uncommitted, is currently the smallest in the American Jewish community, but growing every day.[13] Many in this group began as troubled-committed Jews or were raised in vibrant troubled-committed families, but by now the State of Israel and Zionism have ceased to claim their loyalty and self-identity as Jews. They believe they can no longer allow the Genesis family model to obligate loyalty to the State of Israel in its current manifestation as a Jewish ethnocentric nation state. Genesis cannot demand their loyalty to a state that is engaging in intolerably deviant policies, even if that state defines itself as the homeland of the Jewish people.[14]

While uncommitted to Zionism and Israel, these Jews often do remain committed to Israeli Jews as an integral part of their Genesis-inspired commitment to Jewish peoplehood. Doing so, as distinct from supporting the State of Israel, does not conflict with their Exodus values or violate their Exodus red lines.

The third group, the troubled-committed, are troubled as a result of their Exodus commitment—principally because of the abiding sense of discomfort between their more liberal understandings of the Exodus Covenant and some of the behavior they see exhibited within the State of Israel. Nonetheless, these Jews have remained committed to Israel either because they believe that Israel still embraces some of their Exodus values, are still engaged in working to enhance Israel's Exodus commitments and haven't yet despaired, or because their Genesis commitment does not let them walk away.

The Challenge of Sustaining the Troubled-Committed

The future relationship between North American Jewry and Israel will be determined by whether we are able to empower and sustain the troubled-committed community and prevent them from shifting into either the troubled-uncommitted or untroubled-uncommitted camps. To do so, the pro-Israel discourse essentially has to be a troubled-committed one—instead of one working to convert troubled-committed into untroubled-committed Jews by claiming that a true commitment to Israel demands that one embrace its successes and not focus on its supposed failures. The troubled-committed cannot be rewired to believe that despite all they see, Israel is an embodiment of their liberal Jewish values. For the troubled-committed, issues of human rights, state and religion and the occupation and its moral abuses are real, and the fact that Palestinians bear a significant amount of responsibility for its perpetuation does not explain it away.

Untroubled-committed Jews continue to declare that Israel does not have to change its behavior; rather, troubled-committed Jews have to reinforce their level of commitment and become stronger Genesis Jews. This condescending argument is often buttressed with an assertion of the weakness of the liberal and progressive camps' Jewish identity. These so-called globalists and universalists are not strongly identifying Jews. Their rejection of their Jewish identity, not any of Israel's policies, is the source of the problem.

While this type of argument plays well among untroubled-committed circles, it alienates troubled-committed Jews. They cannot be rewired to believe that Israel embodies their liberal Jewish values.

On the Palestinian front, the troubled-committed do not minimize Palestinian responsibility but unlike the untroubled-committed, believe that the Palestinians' failures to take responsibility do not erase Israel's failures to live up to *its* responsibilities. The history of Palestinian rejection of peace does not exculpate occupation power abuses that are unrelated to Israel's legitimate security concerns. The fact that the Palestinians said "no" to Israel's earlier offers of peace and a two-state solution does not alleviate the fact that Israel has continued to expand settlements without advancing any peace proposals for over a decade. Nothing should prevent Israel from actively working toward peace again.

Clearly, then, making troubled-committed Jewry's relationship with Israel contingent on their becoming exclusively Genesis Conservatives will not work. From their perspective, the issue is not their lack of commitment to Genesis but their search to engage both their Genesis and Exodus commitments, and not turn a blind eye when one is violated.

Proposing a North American Liberal Zionist Agenda

Sustaining the community of troubled-committed Jews will necessitate a reorientation of Zionist discourse in North America. In the long run, North American Jews will not embrace Zionism unless it is a liberal Zionism, or Israel unless it embraces liberal values. Trouble-committed-ness necessitates a new balance between Genesis and Exodus Zionism, with liberal Exodus sensibilities playing a more central role. Without this, there will be no future for Zionism in North America.

It is important to stipulate, though, that a relationship with Israel cannot be contingent on it fully mirroring or embodying American liberal values. Given Israel's distinct geopolitical and cultural realities, there will always be differences in both ideology and policy between the North American and Israeli Jewish communities. That said, liberal North American Jews must believe in a possible affinity between Zionism, Israel, and their basic aspirations for a decent and just society. They must believe that their Jewish sensibilities and values have serious advocates and partners in Israel.

Let's begin outlining possible pillars of a liberal Zionism for the North American troubled-committed:

1. Liberal Zionism is first a Zionist movement. It views the Jewish people as members of a national group endowed with the right to sovereignty within the Land of Israel. It believes that a commitment to Israel's physical, moral, and spiritual well-being (Genesis and Exodus), and the opportunity to partner with Israel in shaping the Zionist project, are central precepts of Judaism, and immeasurably enrich Jewish life around the world.
2. Liberal Zionism views Jewish sovereign power as a gift and a responsibility. Using Israel's newfound power to protect the Jewish people, pursue peace and justice, and engage in *tikkun olam* are Zionism's defining challenges and responsibilities.
3. Liberal Zionism believes that a commitment to Israel must be expressed not merely in defending Israel as it is, but also, when necessary, in criticism of its polices and actions, and most significantly, in advocating for and pursuing visions of Israel as it should be.
4. Liberal Zionism is committed to the principle that all human beings are created equal and endowed with inalienable rights, including the right to justice, equality, freedom, and dignity. It seeks to strengthen Israel's independent judiciary; combats all forms of legal, political, and cultural discrimination, whether against women, the LGBTQ community, liberal Jews, or Israel Arab Palestinians; and strives to build

a state founded on religious pluralism in which all of its citizens', including Jews', religious and denominational sensibilities are respected and protected.

5. Liberal Zionism is committed to ending the current occupation and pursuing a peaceful resolution of the Palestinian conflict in a way that enables the Palestinian and Israeli peoples to fulfill their inalienable individual and national rights and live in freedom, dignity, peace, and security. While there may be disagreement about the steps needed to end the occupation, and what a future peace treaty might look like—two states, one state, confederated states, cantons, etc., the core value *"A permanent Occupation of another people is morally wrong"* lies at the foundation of Liberal Zionism.

From Story to Reality

We are the sum of the stories we tell ourselves about ourselves. Israel, however, is no longer just a story; it is a reality. Its policies will ultimately determine the content of the story we tell about it. In the long run, liberal Zionism cannot persevere with its liberal Jewish story in North America if Israel itself does not engage with its Exodus Covenant and aspire to be a liberal Jewish state.

"Troubled-committed" Liberal Zionists—not only in North America, but in Israel as well—are waging a cultural battle over the future character of Israel. North American Jews need to develop a sophisticated, effective strategy of engagement in shaping the future of Israel. They need to develop multiple platforms on which to express their voice and to ensure that it is heard in both North America and Israel. Minimally, North American Jews need to develop Israeli partners and together persuade "untroubled-committed" Israelis to join (or rejoin) the "troubled-committed" camp.

In the meantime, can a troubled-committed liberal Zionist story sustain itself despite the seemingly illiberal Zionist ideology prevalent in many of Israel's recent governments? First, it is critical to remember that liberal Zionism is not an exclusive North American Jewish project. The 2022 election results point to the fact that, at the very least, 40 percent of Israel's Jewish population—those who voted for the Center, Center-Left, and Left—are committed to liberal Zionist principles on issues of state and religion and human rights. In addition, even while voting for parties with illiberal platforms, a significant percentage—possibly as much as 30 percent—of Likud and Religious Zionist party voters are not illiberal, certainly on issues of state and religion and basic human rights. They vote with the Right out of safety and security concerns and are willing to compromise on their liberal values to form a right-wing coalition. While the outcome of elections may change every number of years, this large block of Israeli citizens, and not just the government du jour, are critical allies and partners for North American liberal Jews to engage with in the project of advocating for and building an Israeli liberal Jewish society. They, just as much as any government, constitute the "real" Israel.

Where there is greater discrepancy between the majority of Israeli and North American Jews is with regards to the occupation. The vast majority of Israeli Jews—on the left, center, and right—share the view that the occupation cannot be brought to an end unilaterally and that Israel's legitimate security concerns demand a maintaining of the current political status quo, at least for the near future.[15] This constitutes a clear distinction from many of their North American counterparts. Does this divergence on such a critical and far-reaching issue imply an inevitable schism between the two communities?

The Boundaries of Exodus Zionism: Tolerable and Intolerable Occupations

While it certainly generates significant strains, this difference need not provoke an unavoidable rupture. While the bifurcation cannot be minimized, a possible path forward is dependent on the willingness of each and every one of us to expand the parameters of the liberal Zionist camp beyond our partisan political affiliations.

As difficult as it may sound, it is possible to distinguish between two types of occupations, one tolerable and one intolerable. The "tolerable" one believes that the *political* status quo with the Palestinians must continue until political conditions on the Palestinian side change. This is distinct from the "intolerable" one, which views the occupation as an acceptable or even desirable permanent reality.

If we are willing to transcend limiting partisan thinking, it is possible to allow for multiple reasons why one who accepts the current political status quo can still be included under an inclusive umbrella of liberal Zionism. One can view the occupation as temporary, a position forced upon Israel as a result of a reticent Palestinian leadership unwilling to embrace the compromises necessary to end the conflict. When viewed as a temporary rather than ideal reality, it does not necessarily conflict with ideal liberal Zionist aspirations.

But even those who see the current status quo as more permanent are not necessarily abandoning liberal Zionist values. One can believe that the geography and size of the land between the Jordan and the sea is too small and complex to ever enable Israel to live safely with another sovereign state sharing the land. One can believe that the land is holy and belongs to the Jewish people, and any compromise is a core violation of Judaism's Exodus Covenant. While these positions are often advocated by those who have no concern for Palestinian rights and seem to be embrace a zero-sum, "us-them" consciousness, neither position need inherently deny Palestinian rights or sanctify the current morally problematic status quo. Both can advocate for changing the status quo and ending the occupation without adopting the two-state model. They can advocate for a one-state solution, in which Palestinians achieve full citizenship in Israel; or pursue a broad autonomy plan, under which the Palestinians would achieve 90 percent of national sovereignty through political, civil, and cultural autonomy and a dramatic lessening of the occupation's footprint.[16]

For many, the above may sound like whitewashing the occupation—a way to "morally" legitimize its perpetuation. Indeed, for some it plays this role. That does not mean, however, that it inherently must function in this manner.

My Genesis commitments obligate me to work tirelessly to include as many Jews as possible within my story of Jewishness and to avoid applying the categorization of intolerability to large segments of Jews. The challenge posed by our current partisan political discourse, with its "cancel culture," is that it undermines this Genesis responsibility.

This partisan reality is further exacerbated when we unconsciously adopt other's definitions of ourselves. When the liberal Left advocates for peace and human rights, all too often the Right abandons these principles as the domain and inheritance of the Left and distinguishes itself with exclusive concerns for the security and rights of Jews. Conversely, once security and Jewish rights discourse are seen by the Right as their domain, the Left acquiesces and dissociates itself from them. Partisanship does not merely create discord and sectarian consciousness; it flattens our political discourse and reinforces each of our beliefs in the insurmountable divide between us.

When looking to expand the parameters of the liberal Zionist camp, Genesis demands that we work to reverse this trend. Instead of entrenching ourselves in the delegitimation of each other, we can explore a different path. We can differentiate between those who clearly reject liberal Jewish values and those who do not need to, and in some instances do not want to. Both the "not now two-statist" and some within the "anti-two-state" political Right can share liberal moral Exodus sensibilities and can be committed to altering the moral status quo between Israel and the Palestinians. All of the above must be included within the troubled-committed camp and can be partners with liberals in a shared Exodus Zionist discourse.

By contrast, we should accept that we will not be able to find common ground with some within Israeli Jewish society—those Jews who from a liberal Jewish Zionist perspective inhabit an intolerable moral universe: Jews for whom the occupation does not constitute a moral challenge; Jews for whom holding on to all the Land of Israel is believed to be the fullest expression of their Exodus Zionism, regardless of the consequences to Palestinians; Jews for whom justice, equality, and human rights do not apply to Palestinians, or for that matter liberal Jews. Their dissonance is not only one of policy but of essential Jewish values. While formally these Jews share in the Exodus Covenant, in fact they embody a different covenant altogether.[17]

The essential question is, do we aspire for the success of our partisan platform, or for the victory of a broader platform that provides a framework for the Jewish people in Israel and North America to continue to walk together?

To enable this expansion, we need to recognize that the moral and political complexity of the current reality does not lend itself to only one possible outcome. Each side of the political map needs to relinquish the hubris of claiming monopoly over either Exodus or Genesis, over morality, and even over liberal values. The lines are not always that clear cut, and we do ourselves a disservice when we fail to listen to or allow the possibility of complexity within another's position.

The key challenge facing North America and Israel is to not allow policy debates to devolve into the divisive sectarian culture that typified nineteenth-century Jewish life. We need to recognize that good, intelligent, moral people can share similar values but legitimately disagree on how to best translate them into political programs. Our Genesis and Exodus sensibilities must work together to avoid "pure" manifestation of our Exodus ideologies dominating our discourse, and instead articulate *shared* boundaries that protect a set of core Zionist values that can be shared by the majority of Jews. A synthesized Genesis and Exodus consciousness can lead us to recognize that, given the disparate worlds within which the Jewish people live, there also needs to be room for liberal Zionist lovers of Israel to share values, while at the same time tolerating disagreement about the best ways to implement them.

North American Liberal Zionists need to clearly distinguish between tolerable and intolerable advocates of occupation and to enhance their partnerships with Israelis who can be troubled-committed while nonetheless tolerating the occupation. They also need to understand that for Israelis, fifty-plus years of occupying another people has come at a profound moral cost. It is difficult to sustain a sense of moral obligation toward a people who you believe has rejected your right to exist and who has eliminated peace and coexistence as an option. Palestinians' daily moral abuses have become transparent even to many Liberal Israelis, who suppress their Exodus Zionist aspirations behind a wall of self-protective indifference.

This sectarian culture must—and can—be overcome. Dismantling it on the political Left, Center, and Right is the sacred task of twenty-first-century liberal Zionism.

18

The Choice to Belong

In the 1980s, when I was a faculty member at the Brandeis Bardin Summer Institute outside Los Angeles (a four-week Jewish identity immersion program for college students), a participant confronted me on the first day.

"Are you one of the teachers?"

"Yes."

"Why should I be Jewish?"

By the tone of his voice, I recognized both his anxiety and his combative intent. If I responded, "You should be Jewish because Judaism teaches you to be a moral human being, or connects you to God," he would have justifiably retorted:

"What, only Jews are ethical? Only Jews have a relationship with God?"

So I cut to the chase and offered him the only truthful answer I knew:

"There is no reason why you *have* to be Jewish. You can live a perfectly meaningful, ethical, and valued life as a secular American, or as a Christian or Muslim for that matter. Why then be Jewish? The only reason to be Jewish and to belong to the Jewish people is if doing so adds meaning and value to *your* life. I will be sharing what I love about Judaism, and how it has added meaning to mine. Whether it does so for you is for you to determine."

As Jews by Choice, we don't have to be Jewish. We have to choose, and that choice often requires finding our own personal answer to the "why be Jewish" question. Some prototypical Jewish answers, of an essentialist nature, stress Judaism's unique features and contributions to the world. "You have to be Jewish because *only* Judaism. . . ."[1] While these answers are compelling for some, the more one internalizes one's complex identities, and the more pluralism and tolerance become the default lenses through which Jews looks at difference, the more unlikely it will be for Jews to acquiesce to claims of superiority over others' identities.

As I reasoned with my student, for modern liberal Jews by Choice, the most effective direction is to explore to what extent Judaism enhances one's life and provides it with greater meaning.[2] If it does, then the "why be Jewish" question answers itself. If it does not, then all theoretical essentialist claims about Judaism's importance will surely be ignored.

Some Jews may be apprehensive about such an approach. What if the individual doesn't find Judaism meaningful and compelling? Is the continuity of the Jewish story really dependent on its ability to compete and prevail in the open marketplace of ideas and identities?

In short—yes.

That is the reality of Jewish life in twenty-first-century North America, where as a result of experiencing at-homeness, Jews have developed complex identities and do not feel othered and compelled to embrace their Jewishness.

Why the Jewish People?

As we move further into the twenty-first century, the question of "why be Jewish" from an Exodus perspective—why engage with this particular set of beliefs and practices, why privilege them over any other—is being replaced by a deeper, Genesis-inflected challenge: why be part of the Jewish people at all?

For over three millennia, while offering competing Exodus perspectives on "Who are the Jews?," we nevertheless generally agreed that Jewishness *is a collective identity* (and from the end of the nineteenth century, that Jews constituted a national group as well). It was taken for granted that as a Jew, you were part of a people that claimed you and informed your identity.

But the experience of at-homeness in North America has destabilized this assumption. The mere fact of Jews being welcomed into mainstream society as full and equal citizens has created a compelling alternative Genesis-esque sense of belonging. As a result, for many American Jews, a Jewish Genesis Covenant has come to feel super-fluous. While a North American Genesis–like identity can coexist with a Jewish Genesis identity (a statement that could not be made of nineteenth-century Emancipatory Western Europe),[3] this reality is nonetheless a far cry from necessity: why not simply be an American of Jewish persuasion, an identity a small percentage of American Jews have already internalized?

To the claim that Jewishness is *necessarily* a collective identity, that Judaism's covenants with God have always defined Jews as members of a people or a nation, twenty-first-century Jews by Choice can simply respond: "No." That may have been what Jewishness *was* but is not necessarily what it *is* or will be for me. The most bedrock of questions left before us to address is thus:

What does Jewishness as a particular people and national collective identity provide? What value does it add to the lives of Jews by Choice?

Why *Any* People?

Further complicating this issue is a growing sentiment that particular identities per se are morally dubious, if not altogether suspect. Jews by Choice, like many other liberals, do not merely question their relation-ship with Jewish peoplehood and Israel but ask whether embracing *any* particular collective identity creates unnecessary and discriminatory loyalties. Wouldn't it be better to embrace a universal Jewishness (as the Pittsburgh Platform advocated) and invest our energies in aspiring to create an undifferentiated personhood committed to dignity and equality for all?[4]

This wariness with respect to communal/national identities applies especially to those making explicit claims to exceptionalism. History is replete with nationalist zealotries, rabid patriotisms, and manifest destinies degenerating into fascist nightmares of different kinds. As eloquently argued by the philosopher Martha Nussbaum:

Why do we need an emotion [i.e., patriotism] like this? The very particularity and eroticism of patriotic love make it ripe for capture, it would seem, by darker forces in our personalities.... The first and most obvious danger is that of misplaced values. If we are going to whip up strong passions, we want to make sure we don't generate enthusiasm for the wrong thing. And it is easy to see that patriotic love has served a range of unwise causes: foolish and/or unjust wars, racial or ethnic hatred, religious exclusion, distorted norms of masculinity that contribute to the subordination of women, xenophobia and hatred of other nations....[5]

Many Jews rightly share this concern. At various times throughout our history, Jewish particularity has been woven into notions of exclusive election, the unconditional designation of the Jewish people as superior, uniquely beloved, and blessed by God.[6] "You alone have I known of all the nations of the earth," declares the prophet Amos (3:2), with "known" interpreted as "loved" or "chosen."[7]

For some within our tradition, this notion of Jewish chosenness has birthed a notion of Jewishness steeped in discrimination and prejudice. Ezra prohibits intermarriage on the grounds that Jewish "holy seed" has become intermingled with that of the people of the land (Ezra 9:2). Deuteronomy 20 sanctions any and all wars of aggression that the Jewish people deem to fight against non-Jews. Some within the rabbinic tradition argue that Jews alone are termed human (Heb. *Adam*), and therefore only their dead bodies generate impurity within a closed area.[8] The murder of a Jew is a capital crime, punishable by death, whereas the murder of a non-Jew is not punishable in a human court but left in God's hands.[9] Unlike the case for Jews, some argue that one is forbidden to violate the Sabbath in order to save a non-Jewish life.[10] A Jew is exempt from paying for damages done to a non-Jew's property.[11] As distinct from that of a Jew, the lost property of a non-Jew does not have to be returned.[12]

This list embodies everything I abhor about the corruption that can plague particular ethnic, religious, and national identities.[13] If I believed that this reading of Judaism was a necessary aspect of the Jewish people's story, I would reject my Jewish identity and dedicate my life to combating it.

Fortunately—and it is critical to remember this—we do not inherit only one version of the Jewish story. We have received many stories, and many versions of many stories. As Shakespeare famously posited:

> The devil can cite Scripture for his purpose.
> An evil soul producing holy witness
> Is like a villain with a smiling cheek,
> A goodly apple rotten at the heart.
> O, what a goodly outside falsehood hath![14]

Every one of our traditions and ideologies has a dark side—chapters and verses that legitimize evil that the devil and the evil soul are only too happy to quote. Liberal and illiberal forces are engaged in a cultural war, and as modern liberal Jews we cannot allow others to control or monopolize our story. As Jews by Choice, the central choice, even before deciding whether to belong at all, is deciding which of our stories we claim for ourselves and tell our children.

This is the choice that makes all the difference. The devil can cite Scripture for his purpose—but so can we. Liberal Jews have a different Jewish story to tell.

Primordial Partnership: The First Exodus Covenant and the First Chosen People

Genesis and Exodus are not merely the principal polarities in the story Jews have told themselves about themselves. They also hold the keys to an understanding of Jewish collective identity, a notion of peoplehood free from bigotry and moral blindness. Through a fuller synthesis between the two, we can tell a story of Jewish peoplehood and particularity that is intellectually and morally resonant with our most refined sensibilities and aspirations—the only kind of story twenty-first-century liberal Jews in search of meaning and value can consider.

While the Genesis Covenant starts with Abraham, *our* Jewish story begins "In the beginning": Creation (Genesis 1), where the first biblical covenant is introduced. This covenant, as distinct from the one grounded in the Ten Commandments, is not made with the Jewish people but with humankind as a whole.

In the beginning, God chose to create heaven and earth and everything in between. As the object of divine will and the outcome of divine power, the whole world is endowed with intrinsic value: "And God saw all that God had made and found it very good" (Gen. 1:31). Out of concern for sustaining this world, God created human beings in God's image "to fill the earth and master it; and rule the fish of the sea, the birds of the sky, and all the living things that creep on earth" (Gen. 1:28).

In the beginning, before there were Genesis Jews, there was the human race chosen by God for a mission: to be partners in ruling and caring for the world. This is the universal, Exodus-inflected Covenant of Creation, which mandates that all of humankind take responsibility for the world we inherit.

This Creation Covenant, like the later Exodus Covenant with the Jewish people, did not proceed as God hoped. Here, too, God planned and human beings laughed. Humankind's mission was to "rule the fish of the sea, the birds of the sky, the cattle, the whole earth, and all the creeping things that creep on earth"—*not* to rule over each other. That is no way for chosen people to treat other chosen people, and early humankind's failure to internalize these limits on their power precipitated their downfall.

"For in God's Image Did God Make Mankind": The Fall, the Flaw, and the Fix

In truth though, humankind began to underachieve from the beginning. Adam and Eve ate forbidden fruit from the Tree of Knowledge of Good and Evil (Gen. 3:6), their son Cain committed fratricide (Gen. 4:8), and things only deteriorated from there: "The Lord saw how great was human's wickedness on Earth, and how every plan devised by the human mind was evil all the time," and "The earth became corrupt before God and the earth was filled with lawlessness" (Gen. 6:5, 11).

God attempted to reset the world and the Covenant of Creation by destroying the wicked and preserving the righteous—Noah and his descendants. However, immediately after the destruction wrought by the Flood, God realized that the divine "do-over" would be a failure. Despite being created in the image of God, humans were clearly driven to use their newfound powers to rule over other human beings. Endemic to human nature was the propensity to treat other people as means to the fulfillment of one's own personal desires ("The devisings of humankind are evil from their youth" [Gen. 9:21]).

Attempting to correct this flaw, God amended the Covenant of Creation with the following commandment:

> Whoever sheds the blood of *humans* by other humans shall their blood be shed, for in God's image did God make humankind. (Gen. 9:6)

Instead of assuming that humanity would do good and rule justly simply as a result of being created in God's image, God commanded the just behavior God expected from humankind. With this commandment, the Bible elaborates that being created in the image of God is not merely a *description* of human nature and potential but the basis for a *prescription* explicating how we are to treat others. Since all of humanity is created in God's image, all human beings possess a Divine-endowed value and consequently are charged with moral responsibilities toward each other.

In grounding the commandment to use power justly on the inherent value of being a human being created in God's image, the Bible is also taking an additional step: defining the parameters of this community to include all, without any distinction on the basis of race, religion, sex, nationality, etc. As a result, as a Jew, the Covenant of Creation binds me in ways that the Genesis and Exodus Covenants do not. The latter covenants constitute the foundation of my relationship with the Jewish people. The Covenant of Creation is the foundation of all Jews' relationship with the community of humankind.

Picking up on this Creation Covenant sensibility, the rabbinic tradition admonishes that one refrain from ever saying "My parents are of greater [value] than yours," for we all emanate from the same Adam and Eve.[15] To assert any intrinsic distinction between human beings is to sever the root-structure anchoring and nourishing the Jewish story through its universal Covenant of Creation.

Jewish Particularism, Among Others: "Be a Blessing"—Period

At the end of the biblical Beginning, with the universal Covenant of Creation and the transitional Tower of Babel tale (Gen. 11), the world is divided among peoples, communities, and nations, each inhabiting its own territory, speaking its particular language, shaping its collective culture, and pursuing its individual self-interests. It is in the context of this "particularizing" of the human race that the Bible locates the Jewish people's beginning as a particular people among others. "Lekh-lekha," God commands Abraham: "Go forth" into your own *particular* covenant and national identity.

But Jewish particularity, and even election, is neither particular nor unique. To the contrary, it is but one particularistic covenantal story among innumerable others from across human history—a fact the Bible has no problem acknowledging: "To me, O Israelites, you are just like the Ethiopians—declares the Lord. True, I brought Israel up from the land of Egypt, but also the Philistines from Caphtor and the Arameans from Kir" (Amos 9:7).

From Lekh-lekha forward, the Bible unfolds the particular story of the Jews: their relationship with God, each other, and the world. This move into particularism, however, does not negate, supersede, or otherwise subvert God's initial Creation Covenant, which designates all humankind as God's Chosen People. As a result, when God bestows the Genesis covenantal blessing on Abraham—"I will make of you a great nation, and I will bless you, and I will make your name great" (Gen. 12:2)—the Bible immediately continues, "and you shall be a blessing." While the covenant with God promises greatness for Abraham and his descendants, this greatness is not intended to be in the service of Jews alone, but for all humanity. Chosenness is not about receiving a "status-upgrade" with a prestigious-sounding title and exclusive benefits. It is about raising the bar on what is demanded of us Jews, fulfilling a heightened responsibility towards our fellow humans: "And all the families of the earth shall bless themselves by you" (Gen. 12:3).

This very universalist commitment inspires God's consultation with Abraham on how to respond to the inhabitants of Sodom, whose sins were grave (Gen. 18). God is compelled to engage Abraham in the matter precisely because of Abraham's promised capacity to dispense blessing: "Abraham is to become a great and populous nation, and the nations of the earth are to bless themselves by him." (Gen. 18:19)

Abraham instinctively demands justice for the inhabitants of Sodom. He understands that his role is to fight against any and all injustice, even if initiated by God: "Far be it from You [God] to do such a thing [as destroying Sodom], to bring death upon the innocent as well as the guilty. . . . Far be it from You. Shall the Judge of all the earth not deal justly?" (Gen. 18:25).

Through the story of Sodom, the election of the Genesis Covenant expands to encompass a larger responsibility for all of humankind. As God's partners in the Covenant of Creation and the recipients of the Genesis Covenant blessings, Jews are tasked to be the vehicle through which blessing is shared, ensuring justice and righteousness are the inheritance of all:

> For I have singled him [Abraham] out, so that he may instruct his children and his posterity to keep the way of the Lord by doing what is just and right. (Gen. 18:19)

Complex Identities: Embracing and Transcending Jewish Particularism

Prioritizing loyalty to fellow community members is one of the most foundational features of our moral and political universe. To what extent does prioritization make one unaware of and insensitive to the needs of those who may not be members of one's group? The core moral failure of ultranationalism, fascism, racism, and other such "-isms" is grounded on their demand for *exclusive* concern and care for one's own group and the justification of discriminatory actions towards other groups as a moral necessity.

However, one may care for one's family, community, nation, etc., but that does not imply that one ought to do so over and against *all* other competing concerns. Foreign aid, fighting against injustice beyond one's borders or community, or even the simple act of giving charity to non-family members are all manifestations of a nonexclusive ethos of loyalty.

How do we mitigate the propensity for particular loyalties to become exclusive and morally limiting? How do we save particularism from its worst tendencies?

In my view the solution is not to be found in eliminating all particular loyalties, as advocated by utilitarian universalists who posit that the most effective way to improve the world is to disconnect moral responsibility from all external ties (familial, communal, national) and distribute all resources solely on the basis of need.[16] I agree with the political philosopher Michael Sandel that this level of abstract idealism runs counter to our most bedrock human moral intuitions.[17]

There is a powerful—and considerably more easily achieved—antidote to the dangers posed by exclusivity. Rather than attempt the cancelation of particular identities and loyalties, we can embrace complex identities. To "belong" to only one sphere of identity is to risk it becoming "*uber alles,*" above all else, an exclusive sphere of discriminatory loyalty. When we adopt, instead, a multiplication of spheres of identity and its corollary flowing of multiple loyalty claims, of multiple communities claiming each and every one of us, the dangers of toxic particularism naturally dissipate.

In the Jewish story I have found in my tradition, and told myself about myself, I am simultaneously claimed by three traditional spheres of identity: Genesis, Exodus, and Creation. The Jewish people claim me as fellow members in my ethnic story (Genesis). At the same time, those who embrace some aspect of the Exodus Covenant, who share my values—whether as Jews or as members of other faith or moral communities—have an additional claim on my identity. As Maimonides posits within the framework of his particular reading of the Exodus Covenant as being founded on the pursuit of the knowledge of God:

> Every single individual from amongst the world's inhabitants whose spirit moved them and whose intelligence gave them the understanding to withdraw from the world in order to stand before God to serve and to minister to God, to know God, and to walk upright in the manner in which God made them . . .-behold, this person has been totally consecrated, holy of holy, and God will be their portion and inheritance forever.[18]

The Exodus Covenant, while originally given to Genesis Jews, is open to "every individual from amongst the world's inhabitants" who shares in its teaching. Through Exodus I am claimed by a universal community of shared faith and values.

Finally, humankind, my fellow members in my Covenant of Creation, claim me. They claim my loyalty and my moral concern, for all are created in the image of God and together we are God's partners in ruling and shaping the future of our world. As an expression of these diverse identities and consequent manifold spheres of loyalty, our tradition commands us to both love our neighbor (Lev. 19:18) and love the stranger (Lev. 19:34) and to return the lost property of our brother (Deut. 22:1) as well as that of our enemy (Exod. 23:4).[19] "What is hateful unto you do not to others" is thus not understood as applying to Jews alone.[20] As members of multiple covenants, our fellow covenantal members, Jews and non-Jews alike, claim our attention, allegiance, and moral concern. In the words of Maimonides, "The children of our father Abraham, i.e., Israel, to whom God gave the Torah, and commanded righteous laws and ordinances—show mercy *to all*. And similarly, among the attributes of God which we are commanded to emulate one finds: 'And God is merciful to all of God's creation.' (Ps. 148:9)."[21]

We inherit multiple identities. How we balance and navigate among them is perhaps the central moral challenge of our time. But as long as the story we tell ourselves about ourselves embraces and strengthens the complexity of our identities and the multiplicity of stories to which we belong, we provide ourselves with the tools to expand our moral aperture and avoid the potential pitfalls of particularism.

Why Jewish Peoplehood

"Why Jewish peoplehood?"

As a Jew, my story tells me of my responsibilities to my people and requires that I be a blessing to all humankind, period. Is this a good enough answer? Can belonging to this story add meaning and value to your life? Is it a story worth being told?

You tell me.

Notes

Introduction

1. b. Ber. 32a
2. Geertz, *Interpretation of Culture*, 448, 452.
3. Sofer, *Responsa Hatam Sofer*, Likutei She'eilot ve-Teshuvot 89.
4. "A Portrait of Jewish Americans," Pew Research Center, October 1, 2013, https://www.pewresearch.org/religion/2013/10/01/jewish-american -beliefs-attitudes-culture-survey/.
5. Eisen and Cohen, *Jew Within*.
6. For one of the best depictions of the complex, multiethnic, and multidi-mensional nature of American Jewish identity, see Magid, *American Post Judaism*, 16–34. See also "Jewish Americans in 2020," Pew Research Center, May 11, 2021, https://www.pewresearch.org/religion/2021/05/11/jewish -americans-in-2020/.
7. This distinction featured prominently in Zionist thought. See, for example, Klatzkin, "Judaism Is Nationalism," 316–18.

1. The Genesis Covenant

1. Joseph B. Soloveitchik offers a seemingly parallel distinction in *Kol Dodi Dofek*. There, he distinguishes between the Covenant of Fate founded in Egypt and the Covenant of Destiny founded at Sinai. His Covenant of Fate, however, speaks essentially to the imposed presence of God in the life of the Jew, the coercive and inevitableness of Jewish identity, and the essential and inescapable otherness of Jewishness. It is not by chance that the foundation of his Covenant of Fate is the Exodus from Egypt and God's declaration: "I will take you to be my people and I will be your God" (Gen. 6:7). None of these characteristics apply to the Genesis Covenant, in partic-ular, "I will be your God." In addition, while Jewishness is inherited, it still requires the individual choice to belong. If Genesis is coercive, it is in the fact that the community is obligated to accept Jews regardless of what they do or believe. Furthermore, by seeing the Jews' relationship with God as the

core of the Covenant of Fate, Soloveitchik infuses the Covenant of Fate with Exodus dimensions.

2. See Knohl, "Rise, Decline, and Renewal," 167–80.

3. Neh. 9:26–30; emphasis added. For a similar but shorter analysis, see Mal. 3:7.

4. Rejecting this idea and providing an alternative notion of Jewishness constituted the essence of the Paulian message (see Gal. 3).

5. Another possible exception to this notion of an inherited unconditional covenant is found in Gen. 18:19, a verse clearly indicative of behavioral aspirations and conditions: "For I have singled him (Abraham) out, that he may instruct his children and his posterity to keep the way of the Lord by doing what is just and right, in order that the Lord may bring about for Abraham what the Lord has promised him." However, this verse is part of a private conversation God is having with Godself, and never enters into the Genesis Covenantal framework shared with Abraham.

6. The fact that the sign is marked on the sexual reproduction organ further emphasizes the idea of the covenant as familial continuity.

7. Further evidence of the distinction between the Genesis Covenant itself and the notion of a sign to the covenant is the fact that even the non-family members who reside in Abraham's midst are to be circumcised—see Gen. 17:12–13. Genesis 17 does not claim that they become a part of the covenant by doing so.

 A curious point is that while Abraham immediately circumcises Ishmael (Gen. 17:23–35) and subsequently Isaac (Gen. 21:4), there is no account of the other forefathers circumcising their sons. The Bible does infer that they were circumcised—the children of Jacob saw it as their distinguishing characteristic (Gen. 34:14–15)—but neither Isaac nor Jacob are accounted as fulfilling this commandment; nor is it presented as a condition for their and their descendants' status within the covenant.

8. In the act of circumcising their son, parents actively choose both for themselves and their family to enter into the covenant and embrace their Jewishness. In addition, even though a son is to be circumcised at infancy, he is nevertheless personally responsible for being circumcised. If his parents failed to do so, he is obligated at bar mitzvah age (thirteen) to arrange for his own circumcision.

9. See Gen. 25:21; 26:2; 26:23–25; 27:28; 28:16–32; 32:10–13; 35:1–4; 35:13–15; 48:15–16. Joseph references his faith in Elohim as well. See Gen. 41:16, 25; 42:18.

10. Interestingly, the Passover sacrifice is the only commandment that prohibits the uncircumcised from participating (see Exod. 12:48). See also

Mekhilta d'Rabbi Yishmael, Bo Parasha 5 (12:6), which links the commandments of the blood of the Passover sacrifice and the blood of circumcision and argues that redemption is contingent on the fulfillment of both.

11. See also Lev. 26:42.

12. See also Isa. 41:8–10.

13. For further reference to Israel's pattern of sin and rebelliousness see Exod. 15:22–25; 16:1–3; 16:19–20; 16:27–28; 17:1–7; 32:1–4; Num. 11:1–3; 11:4–6, 33–34; 13–14, in particular 14:1–4; 20:1–5; 25:1–9; Deut. 1:22–36; and Deut. 9.

14. See Midrash Tanhuma, Parashat Bereshit, 11; Rashi, Gen. 1:1.

15. See, for example, Gen. Rabbah, Toldot 63:6; 63:8; 63:10; 65:1; 67:4; and Num. Rabbah 3:2.

16. See Lev. Rabbah 32:5.

17. b. Yev. 47b; emphasis added.

18. b. San. 44a; emphasis added.

19. See Katz, "Halakhah and Kabbalah," 148–72.

20. Responsa Tzitz Eliezer, 13:93.

21. The Four Sons portion of the traditional Haggadah is originally found in Mekhilta d'Rabbi Yishmael Bo Parasha 18 (13:14).

22. Maimonides, *Mishneh Torah*, Laws of Repentance 3:11; emphasis added.

23. Maimonides, *Mishneh Torah*, Laws of Repentance 3:11.

24. Heb. *Shemittat Kesafim*.

25. The Fathers according to Rabbi Nathan, chap. 2.

26. See for example: b. Yev. 61a and b. B. Metz. 114b; Yehuda Halevi, Kuzari, Part 1:95, 103, and 115; Zohar, Hayei Sarah 131a, and Vayehi 120a; Maharal of Prague, Derekh Haim 3:17; Shneur Zalman of Liadi, Tanya Part 1; Abraham Isaac Kook, Orot Yisrael 5:10 and Da'at Kohen 199.

2. *The Exodus Covenant*

1. "The Spirit of the IDF," *Israel Defense Forces*, accessed July 7, 2022, https://www.idf.il/en/minisites/israel-defense-forces/.

2. "Spirit of the IDF."

3. See Mishnah Avot 5:3 and Maimonides, *Commentary on the Mishnah*, Avot 5:3. See also *Pirkei D'Rabbi Eliezer* 26.

4. See BT Mak. 23b; Maimonides, *Sefer HaMitzvot*; and *Sefer Hahinukh*.

5. See Maimonides, *Commentary on the Mishnah*, introduction to *Perek Helek*; Maimonides, *Mishneh Torah*, Laws of the Foundations of the Torah 1–2 and Laws of Repentance 3:6–8.

6. Mak. 3:7.

7. Maimonides, Commentary on the Mishnah, Mak. 3:7.

8. BT San. 97b

9. Gen. Rabbah 38:13.

10. Gen. Rabbah 63:6.

11. Gen. Rabbah 63:8.

12. Gen. Rabbah 63:10.

13. Gen. Rabbah 65:1.

14. Gen. Rabbah 67:4.

15. Num. Rabbah 3:2

16. Maimonides, *Commentary on the Mishnah*, introduction to *Perek Helek*.

17. Maimonides, *Commentary on the Mishnah*, introduction to *Perek Helek*.

18. Maimonides, *Commentary on the Mishnah*, introduction to *Perek Helek*.

19. BT Hul. 5a.

20. Tosefta B. Metz. 2:33.

21. Maimonides, *Mishneh Torah*, Laws of Rebels 3:1.

22. A further example of marginalization is found in the talmudic ruling that annuls a fellow Jew's responsibility to redeem certain deviants from captivity, even when the consequence may be loss of life. See BT Git. 46b–47a.

23. BT Pes. 113b.

24. For a parallel phenomenon in contemporary Orthodoxy, see Jay P. Lefkowitz, "The Rise of Social Orthodoxy: A Personal Account," *Commentary*, April 2014, https://www.commentary.org/articles/jay-lefkowitz/the-rise-of-social-orthodoxy-a-personal-account/.

3. The Rabbinic Synthesis

1. E.g., Ruth 2:2, 2:6, 2:21, 4:5, 4:10.

2. Ophir and Rosen-Zvi, *Goy*.

3. See Ezra 9.

4. Cohen, *Beginnings of Jewishness*, 110.

5. Tosefta Men. 13:22; BT B. Metz 30b; BT San 64b. See also Maccabees I.

6. Maccabees I.

7. Sifrei Bemidbar 108.

8. Mishnah Bik. 1:4; emphasis added.

9. JT Bik. 1:4; emphasis added.

10. See Gal. 3:7 and Rom. 4:12, which make a similar argument.

11. BT Yev. 47a.

12. BT Yev. 47a.

13. Tosefta Dem. 2:6.

14. BT Yev. 47b; numbering added.

15. Tosefta Demai 2:6.

16. BT Shab. 31a.

4. Good Jews and Bad Jews

1. Erikson, *Wayward Puritans*, 10.

2. Berlin, "Two Concepts of Liberty," 216.

3. BT Eruv. 13b.

4. See Sagi, *Elu va-Elu*.

5. Williams, "Toleration," 19.

6. Mishnah Eduy. 1:5. For the record, in 1:6 the Rabbis offer the opposite opinion: minority opinions are recorded so that if one adopts such a position in the future, one can point to the past recording and say that it was already rejected back then.

7. Erikson, "Notes on the Sociology of Deviance," 308.

8. Goode, *Deviant Behavior*, 3.

9. BT Yev. 47b.

10. Hartman, *Boundaries of Judaism*, 36–46.

11. BT Yev. 47b; Tosefta Suk. 4:28.

12. See BT Hul. 5a and BT Git. 47a.

13. Sifrei Bemidbar 111.

14. BT Meg. 13a.

15. See Maimonides, *Mishneh Torah*, Laws of Sacrificial Procedure 3:4. As for why the rabbis did not give circumcision this status, see Koren, "'Fore-skinned Jew,'" 397–438. In some instances, one who reverses one's circumcision (*Mashukh*) is classified as a *Meshumad*, but not designated with a unique status. See Tosefta Hor. 1:5.

16. Hoffman, *Melamed Le-Ho-il* 1:29; Feinstein, *Igrot Moshe* 4.58.3.

17. BT Git. 47a.

18. Maimonides, Mishneh Torah, Laws of Repentance 3:9.

19. For example: Torah study (Mishnah Pe'ah 1:1); settling in the land of Israel (Sifri Devarim 86 and Tosefta Avodah Zarah 5:2); keeping the Sabbath, not only in public (JT Ned. 3:9); circumcision (BT Ned. 32a); wearing tzitzit (BT Ned. 25a); acts of loving-kindness (JT Peah 1:1). See also Mishnah Peah 1:1.

20. Hartman, *Boundaries of Judaism*, 44–46.

21. Tosefta Hullin, chap. 1.

22. See Boyarin, *Borderlines*.

23. See Katz, *House Divided*.

24. Tosefta Dem. 2:2–3.

5. Maimonides

1. Maimonides, *Commentary on the Mishnah*, introduction to *Perek Helek*.
2. Maimonides, *Commentary on the Mishnah*, introduction to *Perek Helek*; emphasis added.
3. Maimonides, *Guide of the Perplexed*, 5–6.
4. Maimonides, *Guide of the Perplexed*, 2:25.
5. See Hartman, *Maimonides: Torah and Philosophic Quest*.
6. Maimonides, *Mishneh Torah*, Laws of the Foundations of the Torah, 1:1–3, 6.
7. Maimonides, *Guide of the Perplexed*, 1:1.
8. Maimonides, *Guide of the Perplexed*, 3:51.
9. Maimonides, *Commentary on the Mishnah*, introduction to *Perek Helek*; emphasis added.
10. Maimonides, *Commentary on the Mishnah*, introduction to *Perek Helek*; emphasis added.
11. Maimonides, *Commentary on the Mishnah*, introduction to *Perek Helek*.
12. Maimonides, *Mishneh Torah*, Laws of Foreign Worship, 1:3; emphasis added.
13. Maimonides, *Mishneh Torah*, Laws of Forbidden Intercourse, 14:1.
14. Maimonides, *Mishneh Torah*, Laws of Forbidden Intercourse, 14:2; emphasis added.
15. Maimonides, *Mishneh Torah*, Laws of Forbidden Intercourse, 14:2.
16. Maimonides, *Mishneh Torah*, Laws of Foreign Worship, 2:5.
17. Maimonides, *Mishneh Torah*, Laws of Shabbat, 30:15.
18. Maimonides, *Commentary on the Mishnah*, introduction to *Perek Helek*.
19. Maimonides, *Commentary on the Mishnah*, introduction to *Perek Helek*.
20. Maimonides, *Mishneh Torah*, Laws of Rebels, 3:1–2; emphasis added.
21. Maimonides, *Mishneh Torah*, Laws of Rebels, 3:3.
22. Maimonides, *Mishneh Torah*, Laws of the Foundations of the Torah, 1:1–3, 6
23. Maimonides, *Mishneh Torah*, Laws of Forbidden Intercourse, 14:1.
24. Maimonides, *Commentary on the Mishnah*, introduction to *Perek Helek*
25. Maimonides, *Teshuvot Harambam*, Letter to Obadiah the Convert, 293.

6. Emancipation

1. De Clermont-Tonnerre, "Speech on Religious Minorities and Questionable Professions," 88.
2. Molé, "Napoleon's Instructions to the Assembly," 125.
3. Molé, "Napoleon's Instructions to the Assembly," 125–26.
4. Molé, "Napoleon's Instructions to the Assembly," 125–28; emphasis added.

5. See Batnitzky, *How Judaism Became a Religion*. Batnitzky uses the categories of nationality vs. religion.

6. See Plaut, *Rise of Reform Judaism*, 3–62.

7. *Likutei She-eilot ve-Teshuvot* 89; emphasis added.

8. Katz, *House Divided*.

9. See Hartman, *Boundaries of Judaism*, 104–67.

10. Central Conference of American Rabbis, "The Pittsburgh Platform–1885," https://www.ccarnet.org/rabbinic-voice/platforms/article-declaration-principles/.

11. Nordau, "Speech to the First Zionist Congress," 237. Nordau also saw the failure of Emancipation as a desired conclusion, as it contradicted his notion of national identity. See Litvak, *Haskalah*.

12. See Batnitzky, *How Judaism Became a Religion*, 147.

7. Zionism

1. "Basle Program (1897)," 540.

2. Herzl, *Jewish State*, 8, 19, 26, 99.

3. Herzl, *Jewish State*, 8.

4. Herzl, *Jewish State*, 26.

5. Balfour, *Balfour Declaration*, 582.

6. See "The Palestine Mandate," July 24, 1922, Avalon Project, Yale Law School, https://avalon.law.yale.edu/20th_century/palmanda.asp.

7. Edwin Montagu, "Memorandum of Edwin Montagu on the Anti-Semitism of the Present (British) Government—Submitted to the British Cabinet, August 1917," available at Zionism and Israel Information Center, https://zionism-israel.com/hdoc/Montagu_balfour.htm.

8. Ha'am, "Jewish State and Jewish Problem," 266.

9. Ha'am, "Jewish State and Jewish Problem," 267.

10. Ha'am, "Jewish State and Jewish Problem," 269.

11. Herzl, *Old New Land*, 248–49.

12. Herzl, *Old New Land*, 253–54.

13. Jabotinsky, "Jewish Needs vs. Arab Claims," 609.

14. Benjamin Netanyahu, Speech at the World Holocaust Forum 2020, January 23, 2020, https://www.gov.il/en/departments/news/event_yad_vashem230120.

15. Benjamin Netanyahu, Address to United Nations General Assembly, New York, October 1, 2015, *Times of Israel*, https://www.timesofisrael.com/full-text-of-netanyahu-2015-address-to-the-un-general-assembly/.

16. Ashkenazi, "Here, in the Most Cursed Place on Earth," 137–42.

8. North American Homeland

1. "About Us," AIPAC, accessed May 8, 2022, https://www.aipac.org/about.
2. Sarna, *American Judaism*, 151.
3. John Hope Simpson, *Palestine: Report on Immigration, Land Settlement and Development*, London: UK Government, October 1930, retrieved from United Nations Information Systems on the Question of Palestine (UNISPAL), https://www.un.org/unispal/document/auto-insert-194707/.
4. Israeli Central Bureau of Statistics, "Population, by Religion and Population Group," 2005, https://web.archive.org/web/20060410121622/http://www1.cbs.gov.il/shnaton56/st02_01.pdf.
5. Sarna, *American Judaism*, 153–56.
6. Central Conference of American Rabbis, "Declaration of Principles: 'The Pittsburgh Platform'-1885," https://www.ccarnet.org/rabbinic-voice/platforms/article-declaration-principles/.
7. See, for example, Kaplan, *Judaism as a Civilization*.
8. Ben-Gurion and Blaustein, "Exchange of Views," 564–68; emphasis added.
9. See Hertzberg, *Zionist Idea*, 88–91.
10. Louis Brandeis, "The Jewish Problem: How to Solve It," speech to the Conference of Eastern Council of Reform Rabbis, April 25, 1915, University of Louisville, available at https://louisville.edu/law/library/special-collections/the-louis-d.-brandeis-collection/the-jewish-problem-how-to-solve-it-by-louis-d.-brandeis.
11. Brandeis, "Jewish Problem."
12. See Pianko, *Jewish Peoplehood*.
13. See Arthur Hertzberg, "American Zionism at an Impasse: A Movement in Search of a Program," *Commentary*, January 1, 1949, 340–45.
14. Hertzberg, "American Zionism at an Impasse."
15. See Cohen, *Americanization of Zionism*.
16. Central Conference of American Rabbis, "The Guiding Principles of Reform Judaism: 'The Columbus Platform'-1937," https://www.ccarnet.org/rabbinic-voice/platforms/article-guiding-principles-reform-judaism/.
17. Central Conference of American Rabbis, "Guiding Principles of Reform Judaism." Emphasis added.
18. "Nuremberg Laws," 463–67.
19. See BT Sanhedrin 44a.
20. See Steven M. Cohen and Jack Wertheimer, "Whatever Happened to the Jewish People?," *Commentary*, June 1, 2006, 33–37.
21. Pianko, *Jewish Peoplehood*, 55ff. Pianko also asserts that the subsequent

campaign to save Soviet Jewry strengthened the sense of Jewish peoplehood throughout the Diaspora.

22. See Morgan, *Beyond Auschwitz*, 79–90.

23. See Ravitzky, *Messianism*.

24. Sharansky, "Political Legacy of Theodor Herzl," 87.

25. See Bernstein, *To Dwell in Unity*, 63.

26. Steven M. Cohen, *The 1984 Survey of American Jews: Political and Social Outlooks* American Jewish Committee, 1985, https://www.jewishdatabank .org/api/download/?studyId=866&mediaId=bjdb\The_1984_National _Survey_of_American_Jews.pdf; Steven M. Cohen, *The 1981–1982 National Survey of American Jews*, American Jewish Committee, 1983, https://www .jewishdatabank.org/api/download/?studyId=867&mediaId=bjdb\1981-82 _ajc_National_Survey_of_American_Jews.pdf; American Jewish Committee, *1997 Annual Survey of American Jewish Opinion Conducted for the American Jewish Committee by Market Facts, Inc.*, https://www.jewishdatabank.org/api /download/?studyId=865&mediaId=bjdb\1997_ajc_Survey_of_American _Jewish_Opinion.pdf; *1999 Annual Survey of American Jewish Opinion Conducted for the American Jewish Committee by Market Facts, Inc.*, 2000, https://www.jewishdatabank.org/api/download/?studyId=868&mediaId =bjdb\1999_ajc_Survey_of_American_Jewish_Public_Opinion.pdf. See also Sarna, *American Judaism*, 333.

27. See Elazar, *Community and Polity*, 219ff.

28. See Sarna, *American Judaism*, 333ff.

29. Borowitz, *Twenty Years Later*, 38–43.

30. See Arthur Hertzberg, "Israel and American Jewry," *Commentary*, August 1967, https://www.commentary.org/articles/arthur-hertzberg/israel-and -american-jewry/.

31. Birthright Israel, "About Us," accessed May 9, 2022, https://www .birthrightisrael.com/about-us.

32. See Sarna, *American Judaism*, 275ff; Elazar, *Community and Polity*, 231–33.

33. Fackenheim, "Jewish Values in the Post-Holocaust Future," 295.

34. Fackenheim, "Jewish Values in the Post-Holocaust Future," 294.

35. Hartman, *Living Covenant*, 287.

36. Hartman, *Living Covenant*, 298.

37. Central Conference of American Rabbis, "Reform Judaism: A Centenary Perspective," 1976, https://www.ccarnet.org/rabbinic-voice/platforms /article-reform-judaism-centenary-perspective/.

38. Central Conference of American Rabbis, "Reform Judaism."

9. A Liberal Jewish Story

1. BT Eruvin 13b.
2. BT Shabbat 31a.
3. See Constitution Annotated, "First Amendment," accessed February 14, 2023, https://constitution.congress.gov/constitution/amendment-1/.
4. BT Shab 31a.

10. Religion-State Status Quo

1. See Shimoni, *Zionist Ideology*, 127–65; Troy, *Zionist Ideas*, 85–101.
2. Salmon, "Zionism and Anti-Zionism," 25–43; Ravitzky, "Munkács and Jerusalem," 67–89. More broadly see Brown, "Orthodox Judaism," 311–33.
3. See Shimoni, *Zionist Ideology*, 269–315; Troy, *Zionist Ideas*, 3–85, 103–23. In contemporary Israel, most secular Israelis observe certain Jewish traditions, mostly around the Hebrew calendar and life ceremonies. See Pew Research Center, *Israel's Religiously Divided Society*, March 8, 2016, https://www.pewresearch.org/religion/wp-content/uploads/sites/7/2016/03/Israel-Survey-Full-Report.pdf, 100–118. A leading force of secular Jewishness after Israel's establishment were the members of the *Shdemot* group in the Kibbutz movement, evolving in the 1960s, leading to the educational workshops at 'Ef'al in the late 1970s and culminating with the establishment of the Oranim Midrasha a decade later. See Ofaz, *Second and Third Generation Kibbutz Members*.
4. See Agassi, *Liberal Nationalism for Israel*; Yehoshua, "Neurotic Solution," 21–74; Fromen, *Secular Road*. In their sociological research of contemporary Israel, Shmuel Rosner and Camil Fuchs suggest a distinction between "Fully Secular" (28 percent of Israeli society) and "Somewhat Traditional Secular" (21 percent) (Rosner and Fuchs, *#IsraeliJudaism*, 124–35). Perhaps the most extreme form of "Secular Israeliness," disconnected from Judaism, was the "Canaanite" movement; see for example Shavit, *New Hebrew Nation*; Diamond, *Homeland or Holy Land?*
5. Yadgar, *Traditional Jews in Israel*; Bezalel, *You Were Born Zionists*.
6. Thomas Jefferson to Nehemiah Dodge, Ephraim Robbins, and Stephen S. Nelson, "Letter to the Danbury Baptists," January 1, 1802, Library of Congress, https://www.loc.gov/loc/lcib/9806/danpre.html.
7. Provisional Government of Israel, "Declaration of Independence," emphasis added.
8. Provisional Government of Israel, "Declaration of Independence," emphasis added.

9. Provisional Government of Israel, "Declaration of Independence," emphasis added.

10. See Elbaum, *Declaration of Independence*, 526–38.

11. See, for example, the writings of J. H. Brenner and M. J. Berdichevsky in Troy, *Zionist Ideas*, 42–44, 115–19.

12. Provisional Government of Israel, "Declaration of Independence," emphasis added.

13. See, for example, Deut. 32:4, 15, 18, 30, 37; 2 Sam. 23:3; Isa. 30:29; Ps. 19:15.

14. Ben-Gurion, "Status-Quo Agreement," 58–59.

15. Ben-Gurion, "Status-Quo Agreement," 58–59.

16. Ben-Gurion, "Status-Quo Agreement," 58–59.

17. Provisional Government of Israel, "Declaration of Independence," emphasis added.

18. U.S. Constitution, Amendment I: "or prohibiting the free exercise thereof."

19. "Palestine Order in Council," section 51, August 10, 1922, Israel National Archive, https://www.archives.gov.il/archives/Archive/0b07170680031ec7/File/0b071706810857fa.

20. Rabbinical Courts Jurisdiction (Marriage and Divorce) Law, 5713-1953, SH 134, 165 (Isr.), August 26, 1953, https://main.knesset.gov.il/en/about/history/documents/kns2_rabbiniccourts_eng.pdf.

21. Layish, "Heritage of Ottoman Rule," 128–49.

22. "Palestine Order in Council," section 51.

23. Pew Research Center, *Israel's Religiously Divided Society*.

24. See Karayanni, *Multicultural Entrapment*.

25. See Shenhar, "Nation and the World."

26. Shapira, "Bible and Israeli Identity," 11–41. See also the extended edition with appendices, Shapira, *Bible and Israeli Identity*.

27. See Shenhar, *Jewish People and the World*. For more background on the report and its aftermath, see Penina Schoor, *Between Jewish Studies and Identity Formation: Trends in Jewish Education in the Non-Religious System*, report submitted to the Avi Chai Foundation, June 2011 (Heb.), https://avichai.org.il/sites/default/files/החינוך20%במערכת20%היהודי20%החינוך20%מגמות.pdf.

28. HCJ 5016/96 *Horev v. Minister of Transportation* (1997), PD 51(4), 1.

29. HCJ 5016/96 *Horev v. Minister of Transportation* (1997), PD 51(4), 1.

30. HCJ 5016/96 *Horev v. Minister of Transportation* (1997), PD 51(4), 1.

31. See Rubinstein, "Curious Case of Jewish Democracy," 33–51. For a critical examination of this link see Fischer, "Untold Story," 87–112.

32. Israel: Law no. 5710-1950, The Law of Return, SH 51, 159, Amendment no. 2, 5730-1970, SH 586, 34.

11. Israel's Relationship with World Jewry

1. See Shalom, "Crisis in the Relations," 103–41; Steven Cohen and Sam Abrams, "Israel Off Their Minds: The Diminished Place of Israel in the Political Thinking of Young Jews," the Berman Jewish Policy Archive at NYU Wagner 2008 National Survey of American Jews, October 27, 2008, https://www.jewishdatabank.org/content/upload/bjdb/552/N_2008 _National_Survey_Spirituality_Politics_IsraelYoungJewsReport.pdf; Steven Cohen and Ari Kelman, "Beyond Distancing: Young Adult American Jews and Their Alienation from Israel," 2007, https://www.jewishdatabank .org/content/upload/bjdb/574/N-Survey_American_Jews-2007-Beyond _Distancing.pdf; Cohen and Kelman, "Thinking about Distancing from Israel," 287–96. For critical discussions of "the distancing hypothesis," see Shmuel Rosner and Inbal Hakman, "The Challenge of Peoplehood: Strengthening the Attachment of Young American Jews to Israel in the Time of the Distancing Discourse," Jewish People Policy Institute, 2012, http://jppi.org.il/uploads/The_Challenge_of_Peoplehood-Strengthening _the_Attachment_of_Young_American_Jews_to_Israel_in_the_Time_of_the _Distancing_Discourse.pdf; Sasson, Kadushin, and Saxe, "Trends in American Jewish Attachment to Israel," 297–319.
2. This was labeled "Negation of the Diaspora." See Schweid, "Rejection of the Diaspora in Zionist Thought," 43–70; Shimoni, "Reappraisal of 'Negation of the Diaspora,'" 45–63; Gorni, "'Negation of the Diaspora' and the Return to History," 349–60.
3. See, for example, Mishnah Halla 2:1; JT Shevi'it 8:3; JT Shekalim 4:1.
4. The Mishnah first introduces the language of ascend, *ma-alin*, to Israel or as a verb. See Mishnah Ketubot 13:11. See also BT Megillah 23a regarding the use of the verb *ma-alin* to also depict one who has an aliyah to the Torah. "Droppings of insects": *Nefolet shel nemushot* in the original Hebrew. Then–prime minister Rabin used this term during a TV interview on Israel's twenty-eighth Independence Day, 1976. *Nemushot* can also denote a person of no character.
5. Smolenskin, "The Haskalah of Berlin," 157.
6. Pinsker, "Auto-Emancipation," 10.
7. Klatzkin, "Boundaries," 322–23.
8. Ahad Ha'am, "Jewish State and the Jewish Problem," 267.
9. Klatzkin, "Boundaries," 322–23, 327.
10. Bialik, "Speech at the Inauguration of the Hebrew University in 1925," 281–89.

11. Ben-Gurion, *Memoirs*, 152.

12. Yehoshua and Troy, "Basics of Zionism," 453.

13. Herzl, *Jewish State*, 8.

14. Bialik, "The City of Slaughter," 114.

15. Meged, *Israel Independence Day Haggadah*, 4.

16. Dinur, *Holiday Readings for the Yom Haatzmaut Dinner*, 1; emphasis added.

17. See State of Israel Ministry of Education, "From Holocaust to Revival: Memorial Days in Hebrew Studies," accessed July 26, 2022, https://pop .education.gov.il/tchumey_daat/ivrit_havana_habaa_lashon/chativat -beynayim/magal-shna-ivrit-htb/ben-shoah-litkuma-yemey-hazikaron -beivrit/, (Heb.).

18. Ben-Gurion and Blaustein, "Exchange of Views," 567; emphasis added.

19. Over the last decade or so, French Jewry has served as the symbol for Israelis of European Jews at risk.

12. *Unpacking a Not-So-"Basic" Law*

1. See, for example, Doron Matza, "The May 2021 Riots and Their Implications," Begin-Sadat Center for Strategic Studies, June 8, 2021, https:// besacenter.org/israel-may-2021-riots/.

2. Nir Barkat, interview at Channel 13 News, May 18, 2021.

3. See, for example, Ya'akov Bardugo, "Political Correctness Reinforces Nationalistic Arab Violence," *Israel HaYom*, May 12, 2021 (Heb.), https:// digital-edition.israelhayom.co.il/israel-hayom/20210512; Akko Mayor Shimon Lankri, "We Will Not Take the Pogrom Silently," *Israel HaYom*, May 13, 2021 (Heb.), https://digital-edition.israelhayom.co.il/israel-hayom /20210513.

4. See the annual reports of Haifa University, led by Prof. Sami Smooha, on Israeli Arabs' positions. For example, Sammy Smooha, *Still Playing by the Rules: Index of Arab-Jewish Relations in Israel 2015*, 2017, https://www .iataskforce.org/sites/default/files/resource/resource-1510.pdf .

5. Palestine Mandate Government, *Village Statistics*, April 1945, http://users .cecs.anu.edu.au/~bdm/yabber/census/vspages/vs1945_p27.jpg. See also Morris, *Birth of the Palestinian Refugee Problem*.

6. Zangwill, "Return to Palestine," 627. For earlier formulations of this sentence see Garfinkle, "On the Origin, Meaning, Use and Abuse of a Phrase," 539–50; Muir, "A Land without a People," 55–62.

7. See, for example, Cohen, *Year Zero of the Arab-Israeli Conflict*; Dowty, *Israel/ Palestine*.

8. See William Peel, "Report of the Palestine Royal Commission" (1937),

380–93, UNISPAL, http://unispal.un.org/pdfs/Cmd5479.pdf; General Assembly resolution 181, *Palestine Plan of Partition with Economic Union*, November 29, 1947, A/RES/181(IIj), https://documents-dds-ny.un.org/doc /resolution/gen/nr0/038/88/pdf/nr003888.pdf?OpenElement.

9. See, for example, Smooha, "Hungarian National Minority in Slovakia," 45–49. For numerous other examples see Jacobson and Rubinstein, *Israel and the Family of Nations*.

10. "The Knesset as a Constitutive Authority," Government of Israel, accessed May 22, 2022, https://main.knesset.gov.il/en/activity/pages /BasicLawsAndConstitution.aspx.

11. Basic Law: Human Dignity and Liberty 5752–1992, SH 1391, 150 (Isr.), https://m.knesset.gov.il/en/activity/documents/BasicLawspdf /BasicLawLiberty.pdf (Heb.).

12. For a discussion of such arguments see Jacobson and Rubinstein, *Israel and the Family of Nations*.

13. Basic Law: Israel as the Nation-State of the Jewish People 5778–2018. SH 2743, 898 (Isr.), https://fs.knesset.gov.il//20/law/20_lsr_504220.pdf (Heb.).

14. See, for example, MK Benny Begin's proposed correction to this law, adding that the state "promotes equality of rights for all its citizens," submitted to the Knesset on October 15, 2018, https://www.nevo.co.il/law_html/law04 /5725_20_lst_517849.htm.

15. For a broad discussion see Tal Becker, "The Claim for Recognition of Israel as a Jewish State: A Reassessment," Washington Institute, February 4, 2011, https://www.washingtoninstitute.org/policy-analysis/claim-recognition -israel-jewish-state-reassessment.

16. Basic Law: Israel as the Nation-State of the Jewish People, 5778–2018.

17. Basic Law: Israel as the Nation-State of the Jewish People, 5778–2018.

18. See Jacobson and Rubinstein, *Israel and the Family of Nations*.

19. "Mandate for Palestine," the Council of the League of Nations, July 24, 1922, retrieved from Israel Ministry of Foreign Affairs, https://www.gov.il /en/Departments/General/the-mandate-for-palestine.

20. "Palestine Order in Council," August 10, 1922, Israel National Archive, https://www.archives.gov.il/archives/Archive/0b07170680031ec7/File /0b071706810857fa.

21. Israel Law and Administration Ordinance, 5708–1948, *Official Gazette*, no. 2, retrieved from Israeli Knesset, http://www.knesset.gov.il/review/data/eng /law/kns0_govt-justice_eng.pdf.

22. HCJ 4112/99, Adalah v. The Municipality of Tel Aviv-Jaffa, PD 56(5) 393

(2002) (Isr.), https://supremedecisions.court.gov.il/Home/Download?path
=HebrewVerdicts\99/120/041/a10&fileName=99041120.a10&type=4
(Heb).

23. For a criticism of the law see Ha'aretz Editorial Board, "Israel's Second-
Class-Citizens Law," *Ha'aretz*, May 11, 2017, https://www.haaretz.com
/opinion/editorial/2017-05-11/ty-article/israels-second-class-citizens-law
/0000017f-f5f1-d318-afff-f7f36e540000; "Nation-State Law," Association for Civil Rights in Israel, July 20, 2018, https://law.acri.org.il/en/2018
/07/20/nation-state-law/. For a defense of the law see Moshe Koppel and
Eugene Kontorovich, "Why All the Outrage Over Israel's Nation-State
Law?" *Mosaic*, October 8, 2018, https://mosaicmagazine.com/essay/israel
-zionism/2018/10/why-all-the-outrage-over-israels-nation-state-law/.

24. See Amir Fox, "The Damages from the Nation State Law," Israel
Democracy Institute, December 3, 2020, https://www.idi.org.il/articles
/33021 (Heb.).

25. Basic Law: Israel as the Nation-State of the Jewish People, 5778–2018.

26. Basic Law: Israel as the Nation-State of the Jewish People, 5778–2018.

27. Proposed Bill, Israel Basic Law: Israel as the Nation-State of the Jewish
People, 5778–2018, as submitted to the Knesset for first round vote, March
13, 2018, https://main.knesset.gov.il/Activity/plenum/Pages/SessionItem
.aspx?itemid=2066728.

28. HCJ 6698/95, Aadel Ka'adan v. Israel Lands Administration, 54(1) P.D. 258
(2002) (Isr.), https://supremedecisions.court.gov.il/Home/Download?path
=HebrewVerdicts/95/980/066/p23&fileName=95066980_p23.txt&type=
4 (Heb.).

29. Basic Law: Israel as the Nation-State of the Jewish People, 5778–2018.

30. See Mohammed Darawshe, "Only Jews Can Stop This Disgrace," *Jerusalem
Post*, August 6, 2018, https://www.jpost.com/opinion/only-jews-can-stop
-this-disgrace-564270.

31. BT Shabbat 31a.

32. *Historical Statistical Atlas, 1948–2018*, Israeli Central Bureau of Statistics,
2021, https://www.cbs.gov.il/en/publications/Pages/2021/atlas-2018-e
.aspx, 16.

33. "Israel's Independence Day 2022," Israeli Central Bureau of Statistics,
May 1, 2022, https://www.cbs.gov.il/en/mediarelease/Pages/2022/Israels
-Independence-Day-2022.aspx; "Births and Fertility in Israel 2020," Israeli
Central Bureau of Statistics, February 21, 2022, https://www.cbs.gov.il/he
/mediarelease/DocLib/2022/062/01_22_062b.pdf, 4–5 (Heb.).

13. Yearning Again for Peace

1. See Von Clausewitz, *On War*, vol. 1, 23.
2. Mishnah Avot 1:18.
3. BT Gittin 59b.
4. Provisional Government of Israel, "Declaration of Independence," May 14, 1948, https://m.knesset.gov.il/en/about/pages/declaration.aspx.
5. "Khartoum Resolution," Arab League, September 1, 1967, Avalon Law Library, Yale Law School, https://avalon.law.yale.edu/20th_century /khartoum.asp.
6. Edy Cohen, "A Short History of Palestinian Rejectionism," Begin-Sadat Center for Strategic Studies, February 16, 2020, https://besacenter.org /palestinian-rejectionism/.
7. Ehud Barak, Statement to the Israeli People, Jerusalem, October 7, 2000, Jewish Virtual Library, https://www.jewishvirtuallibrary.org/statement-to -the-israeli-people-by-prime-minister-barak.
8. See, for example, Lustick, *Paradigm Lost*.
9. Ehud Olmert, Address at the 6th Herzliya Conference, January 24, 2006, https://www.haaretz.co.il/misc/2006-02-04/ty-article/0000017f-f69f -d460-afff-ffffc45b0000 (Heb.).
10. Midrash Tanhuma, Hukat 22; emphasis added.
11. See George W. Bush, "Letter to Prime Minister Ariel Sharon," April 14, 2004, White House Archives, https://georgewbush-whitehouse.archives .gov/news/releases/2004/04/20040414-3.html.
12. See, for example, Khaled Abu Tomeh and Tovah Lazaroff, "Abbas Claims Israel Doesn't Want Peace," *Jerusalem Post*, November 9, 2009, https:// www.jpost.com/middle-east/abbas-claims-israel-doesnt-want-peace; "Israel Doesn't Want Peace, Says Abbas," *Sydney Morning Herald*, January 30, 2009, https://www.smh.com.au/world/israel-doesnt-want-peace-says -abbas-20090129-7t29.html; Pappe, *History of Modern Palestine*, 272–86; Gideon Levy, "Israel Does Not Want Peace," *Ha'aretz*, July 4, 2014, https:// www.haaretz.com/2014-07-04/ty-article/israel-does-not-want-peace /0000017f-db80-df62-a9ff-dfd75c210000; "John Kerry: Israel Has No Interest in Peace with the Palestinians," *Palestine Chronicle*, November 21, 2017, https://www.palestinechronicle.com/john-kerry-israel-has -no-interest-in-peace-with-the-palestinians/; Jonathan Thrall, "Israel-Palestine: The Real Reason There's Still No Peace," *Guardian*, May 16, 2017, https://www.theguardian.com/world/2017/may/16/the-real-reason-the -israel-palestine-peace-process-always-fails; Bashir Abu-Manneh, "Israel

Doesn't Want Peace—It Wants to Prevent Palestinian Self-Determination,"
Tribune, October 10, 2020, https://tribunemag.co.uk/2020/10/israel
-doesnt-want-peace-it-wants-to-prevent-palestinian-self-determination;
Hesham Youssef, "The Israeli-Palestinian Conflict: The Danger of 'No Solution' Messaging: The Six 'No's' That Are Cementing a One-State Outcome
and Perpetual Conflict," United States Institute of Peace, February 17, 2022,
https://www.usip.org/publications/2022/02/israeli-palestinian-conflict
-danger-no-solution-messaging.

13. Micah Goodman, "Eight Steps to Shrink the Israeli-Palestinian Conflict,"
Atlantic, April 1, 2019, https://www.theatlantic.com/ideas/archive/2019
/04/eight-steps-shrink-israeli-palestinian-conflict/585964/.

14. See, for example, Mitchell Bard, "The 'Consensus' Settlements," Jewish
Virtual Library, accessed June 6, 2022, jewishvirtuallibrary.org/the-ldquo
-consensus-rdquo-settlements. The data is drawn from the "West Bank
Jewish Population Stats," http://westbankjewishpopulationstats.com/,
based on the Israeli Ministry of the Interior's Population Registry, compiled
by former MK Yaakov "Katzale" Katz.

15. BT San. 37a.

16. Herzl, *Old New Land*, epigraph.

14. At Home

1. Pope Paul VI, "Declaration on the Relation of the Church to Non-Christian
Religions—Nostra Aetate," October 28, 1965, http://vatican.va/archive
/hist_councils/ii_vatican_council/documents/vat-ii_decl_19651028_nostra
-aetate_en.html.

2. Gen. Rabbah 42:8.

3. The travel and marriage narratives come to an end with the forefathers.
Most of the marriages of Jacob's children are not accounted for; those that
are were local. See Gen. 38:2; 38:6, 46:10. For Joseph, see Gen. 41:45.

4. See Halbertal and Margalit, *Idolatry*.

5. Maimonides, Mishneh Torah, Laws of Foreign Worship 11:1. See Sifra, Aha-
rei Mot, 13:8.

6. See Molé, "Napoleon's Instructions to the Assembly of Jewish Notables,"
128.

7. See Ophir and Ishay, *Goy*.

8. Jonathan D. Sarna and Jonathan Golden, "The American Jewish
Experience in the Twentieth Century: Antisemitism and Assimilation," National Humanities Center, last revised October 2000, http://
nationalhumanitiescenter.org/tserve/twenty/tkeyinfo/jewishexp.htm.

9. See "Audit of Anti-Semitic Incidents in 2021," Anti-Defamation League, accessed May 29, 2022, https://adl.org/audit-antisemitic-incidents-202.

10. See Sarna, *American Judaism*, 219.

11. See Magid, *American Post Judaism*.

12. See, for example, American Jewish Committee President Jacob Blaustein's report, *The Voice of Reason*, at the AJC Executive Committee meeting, April 29, 1950, American Jewish Committee, https://ajcarchives.org/ajc_data /Files/507.pdf.

13. See Magid, *American Post Judaism*.

14. See, for example, "Highlights of the CJF 1990 National Jewish Population Survey," Council of Jewish Federations, 1991, https://www.academia.edu /23066875/Highlights_of_the_cjf_National_Jewish_Population_Survey.

15. See "Jewish Americans in 2020," Pew Research Center, May 11, 2021, https://www.pewresearch.org/religion/wp-content/uploads/sites/7/2021 /05/pf_05.11.21_Jewish.Americans.pdf; also "Jewish Americans in 2020."

15. Intermarriage

1. "Jewish Americans in 2020: 4. Marriage, Families and Children," Pew Research Center, May 11, 2021, https://www.pewresearch.org/religion /2021/05/11/marriage-families-and-children/.

2. See Maimonides, Laws of Forbidden Intercourse 12:1. See also Shulchan Aruch Even Ha'Ezer 16:1.

3. For further discussion of Ezra's expansion of the Deuteronomy ban against intermarriage with the Seven Nations of Canaan, see Fishbane, *Biblical Interpretation in Ancient Israel*, 114–16.

4. See Mishnah Kiddushin 3:12.

5. Maimonides, Issurei Biah 12:1. See also Shulhan Arukh Even Ha'Ezer 16:1. An outgrowth of this ruling was a shift from patrilineality to matrilineality. If there is no legally binding relationship between a husband and a wife, and thus between father and child, Jewish law reasoned that the connection between mother and child was more significant.

6. "Americans Express Increasingly Warm Feelings toward Religious Groups," Pew Research Center, February 15, 2017, https://www.pewresearch.org /religion/2017/02/15/americans-express-increasingly-warm-feelings -toward-religious-groups/ and "Feelings toward Religious Groups," Pew Research Center, July 23, 2019, https://www.pewresearch.org/religion /2019/07/23/feelings-toward-religious-groups/.

7. See Kleinberg, *Hybrid Judaism*; Magid, *American Post Judaism*, 16–34.

8. *Ynet*, February 8, 2023, https://www.ynet.co.il/judaism/article/hjb411vx6o.

9. See "The National Jewish Population Survey 2000–1," United Jewish Communities, 2003, 16–19, https://cdn.fedweb.org/fed-34/136/National-Jewish-Population-Study.pdf.

10. See, for example, Jack Wertheimer, "Conservative Judaism Does Not Need a New Narrative about Intermarriage," *eJewishPhilanthropy*, March 15, 2022, https://ejewishphilanthropy.com/conservative-judaism-does-not-need-a-new-narrative-about-intermarriage/. See also Rabbi Charles Arian et al., "As Rabbis, We Believe a New Intermarriage Narrative Can Strengthen Conservative Judaism," *eJewishPhilanthropy*, April 5, 2022, https://ejewishphilanthropy.com/as-rabbis-we-believe-a-new-intermarriage-narrative-can-strengthen-conservative-judaism/.

16. Eroding North American-Israel Relationship

1. See "AJC 2021 Survey of American Jewish Opinion," American Jewish Committee, July 14, 2021, https://www.ajc.org/news/survey2021. See also "July 2021 National Survey of Jewish Voters," Jewish Electorate Institute, July 13, 2021, https://www.jewishelectorateinstitute.org/july-2021-national-survey-of-jewish-voters/, according to which 20 percent of respondents support "establishing one state that is neither Jewish nor Palestinian."

2. Sam Sokol, "11 Days, 4,340 Rockets and 261 Dead: The Israel-Gaza Fighting in Numbers," *Haaretz*, May 23, 2021, https://www.haaretz.com/israel-news/elections/2021-05-23/ty-article/.highlight/11-days-4-340-rockets-and-261-dead-the-israel-gaza-fighting-in-numbers/0000017f-ef54-d8a1-a5ff-ffde438f0000.

3. "Israeli Voice Index May 2021," Israel Democracy Institute, May 30, 2021, https://en.idi.org.il/media/16382/israeli_voice_index_data_2105_eng-first.pdf; Binyamin Netanyahu [@IsraeliPM], "Thank you for resolutely standing with [Israel] and supporting our right to self-defense against terrorist attacks," *Twitter*, May 15, 2021, https://twitter.com/Israelipm/status/1393691747348320256?s=20&t=ds74cedao2pneofljp6y9w.

4. See Judah Ari Gross, "Gantz: Gaza Operation Aims to 'Strike Hamas Hard,' Make It 'Regret' Rockets," *Times of Israel*, May 11, 2021, https://www.timesofisrael.com/gantz-gaza-operation-aims-to-strike-hamas-hard-make-it-regret-rockets/. See also Binyamin Netanyahu, "Statement by PM Netanyahu-11 May," May 11, 2021, https://www.gov.il/en/Departments/news/statement-by-pm-netanyahu-16-may-2021.

5. See, for example, IDF Editorial Team, "Context Is Everything: What You Need to Know about IDF Strikes in Gaza," Israel Defense Forces, accessed May 19, 2022, https://www.idf.il/en/minisites/wars-and-operations

/operation-guardian-of-the-walls/what-you-need-to-know-about-idf
-strikes-in-gaza.

6. Cf. Israeli Ministry of Foreign Affairs, *The 2014 Gaza Conflict: Factual and Legal Aspects*, May 2015, 33, https://mfa.gov.il/ProtectiveEdge/Documents /2014gazaConflictFullReport.pdf.

7. "Press Release: *Operation Guardian of the Walls* Survey-May 2021," Israel Democracy Institute, May 25, 2021, https://en.idi.org.il/media/16349 /operation-guardian-of-the-walls-survey-may-2021.pdf.

8. Trevor Noah, *The Daily Social Distancing Show*, episode 3567, May 11, 2021.

9. John Oliver, *Last Week Tonight*, season 8, episode 12, May 16, 2021.

10. See, for example, David Harris, "An Open Letter to Trevor Noah," *Times of Israel*, May 13, 2021, https://www.ajc.org/news/an-open-letter-to -trevor-noah.

11. "Rabbinical and Cantorial Students Appeal to the Heart of the Jewish Community," accessed May 16, 2022, https://docs.google.com/document/d /17iNzyOuThn6yecqiBx9t_R-wahf7m2kkxxiq8v0ifpa/edit.

12. "July 2021 National Survey of Jewish Voters."

13. See Hannah Black, "From Minneapolis to Jerusalem: On Black-Palestinian Solidarity," *Jewish Currents*, Fall 2021, https://jewishcurrents.org/from -minneapolis-to-jerusalem. See also Marya Hanun, "How Black Lives Matter Changed the American Conversation around Israel and Palestine," *Slate*, May 14, 2021, https://slate.com/news-and-politics/2021/05/black-lives -matter-israel-palestine.html.

14. "AJC 2021 Survey of American Jewish Opinion."

15. See Nathan Guttman, "Abe Foxman Calls on Benjamin Netanyahu to Scrap Speech to GOP Congress," *Forward*, February 6, 2015, https://forward.com /news/214320/abe-foxman-calls-on-benjamin-netanyahu-to-scrap-sp/; Nathan Guttman, "Reform's Rick Jacobs Presses Benjamin Netanyahu to Call Off Speech to Congress," *Forward*, February 7, 2015, https://forward .com/israel/214346/reforms-rick-jacobs-presses-benjamin-netanyahu-to/.

16. Binyamin Netanyahu, "Address to the Jewish Federations of North America," August 4, 2015, https://embassies.gov.il/washington/NewsAndEvents /Pages/pm-Netanyahu-addresses-Jewish-Federations-on-Iran-4-Aug -2015.aspx.

17. See Ruth Eglash, "Scuffle at Jerusalem's Western Wall Pits American Jews against Netanyahu," *Washington Post*, November 17, 2017. See also Ben Sales, "Suspension of Western Wall Deal Leaves Jewish Leaders Feeling Betrayed," *Jewish Telegraphic Agency*, June 25, 2017, https://www.jta.org

/2017/06/25/united-states/suspension-of-western-wall-deal-leaves
-jewish-leaders-feeling-betrayed.

18. Dan Feferman, *Rising Streams: Reform and Conservative Judaism in Israel*, Jewish People Policy Institute, 2018, p. 106, https://jppi.org.il/wp-content /uploads/2018/10/RisingStreams.pdf; "Ruderman Family Foundation Poll: Israeli Attitudes Toward American Jews," Ruderman Family Foundation, February 2016, http://rrfei.org/wp-content/uploads/2016/02 /ruderman-poll-kotel.pdf.

19. "AJC 2019 Survey of American Jewish Opinion," American Jewish Committee, June 2, 2019, https://www.ajc.org/news/survey2019; "July 2021 National Survey of Jewish Voters," Jewish Electorate Institute, July 13, 2021, https://www.jewishelectorateinstitute.org/wp-content/uploads/2021 /07/jei-National-Jewish-Survey-Topline-Results-July-2021.pdf; "Jewish Americans in 2020," Pew Research Center, May 11, 2021, https://www .pewresearch.org/religion/wp-content/uploads/sites/7/2021/05/pf_05.11 .21_Jewish.Americans.pdf.

20. See, for example, Richard J. Goldstone, "Israel and the Apartheid Slander," *New York Times*, October 31, 2011, https://www.nytimes.com/2011/11/01 /opinion/israel-and-the-apartheid-slander.html.

21. See Jacob Magid, "Dermer Suggests Israel Should Prioritize Support of Evangelicals over US Jews," *Times of Israel*, May 10, 2022, https://www .timesofisrael.com/dermer-suggests-israel-should-prioritize-support-of -evangelicals-over-us-jews/.

17. Future of Liberal Zionism

1. "July 2021 National Survey of Jewish Voters."

2. See, for example, Eve Bartlow [@eve_bartlow], "I was born Jewish and a Zionist. I didn't take up a cause. Many of us Jews recognize this because we are Israel. Wherever we are. Israel was a concept and now it's a reality. You attack Israel, you attack us," *Twitter*, May 14, 2022, https://twitter.com/Eve _Barlow/status/1525505041297297410.

3. See, for example, Jonah Goldberg, "The Real 'Realism' on Israel," *Los Angeles Times*, February 8, 2011, https://www.latimes.com/opinion/la-xpm-2011 -feb-08-la-oe-0208-goldberg-israel-20110208-story.html. See also Oz, *In the Land of Israel*, 95–96.

4. "July 2021 National Survey of Jewish Voters." See also "Survey of American Jewish Millennials," American Jewish Committee, April 25, 2022, https://www.ajc.org/Jewish-Millennial-Survey-2022/American-Jewish

-Millennials, according to which 15 percent of participants surveyed support Israeli annexation of the West Bank.

5. See Singer and Senor, *Start-Up Nation*.

6. See, for example, Avi Mayer, "Another Side of Israel: The Impact of Tikkun Olam," Jewish Policy Center, Spring 2013, https://www.jewishpolicycenter .org/2013/02/28/israel-tikkun-olam/.

7. See Bret Stephens, "Palestine Makes You Dumb," *Wall Street Journal*, July 28, 2014, https://www.wsj.com/articles/bret-stephens-palestine-makes-you -dumb-1406590159. See also Morton Klein, "ZOA President Klein Address- es Knesset about the Importance of Language in Fighting BDS," Zionist Organization of America, July 3, 2014 [transcript], https://zoa.org/2014 /07/10249460-video-of-zoa-president-morton-klein-addressing-knesset -about-the-importance-of-language-in-fighting-bds/.

8. See Blake Flayton, "On the Frontlines of Progressive Anti-Semitism," *New York Times*, November 14, 2019, https://www.nytimes.com/2019/11/14 /opinion/college-israel-anti-semitism.html.

9. See "What Is Antisemitism? Non-Legally Binding Working Definition of Antisemitism," International Holocaust Remembrance Alliance, adopted May 26, 2016, https://holocaustremembrance.com/resources/working -definitions-charters/working-definition-antisemitism.

10. See Amy Sara Clark, "Factions Clash Over Hillel Israel Policy," *New York Jewish Week*, March 4, 2014, https://www.jta.org/2014/03/04/ny/factions -clash-over-hillel-israel-policy. See also "Hillel Israel Guidelines," Hillel International, accessed June 3, 2022, https://www.hillel.org/jewish/hillel -israel/hillel-israel-guidelines.

11. See, for example, Ruderman Family Foundation, "Contrary to Common Wisdom Study Finds Vast Majority of American Jews Are Connected to Israel," accessed March 3, 2023, https://rudermanfoundation.org/wp -content/uploads/2021/03/2020.01.30-english-us-Jewry-Survey.pdf, according to which only 23 percent of U.S. Jews are supportive of the Net- anyahu government.

12. See "POLL: American Jews Remain Strongly Supportive of the Demo- cratic Party," Jewish Electorate Institute, October 16, 2018, https://www .jewishelectorateinstitute.org/american-jews-remain-strongly-supportive -of-the-democratic-party/. Fifty-nine percent define themselves as pro- Israel but critical: "Generally pro-Israel but also critical of some of the current Israeli government's policies" (35 percent) and "Generally pro- Israel but also critical of many of the current Israeli government's policies" (24 percent). See also "July 2021 National Survey Of Jewish Voters," which

reports that 59 percent of American Jews are in favor of restricting U.S. aid to settlements and 81 percent prefer either a two-state solution (61 percent) or one democratic state (20%). See also "Jewish Americans in 2020," Pew Research Center, May 11, 2021, https://www.pewresearch.org/religion /wp-content/uploads/sites/7/2021/05/pf_05.11.21_Jewish.Americans .pdf: only 31 percent of the total respondents, and only 20 percent of the Democratic respondents, believe Israel is making a sincere effort towards peace with Palestinians. See also "Survey of American Jewish Millennials": 47 percent support a two-state outcome, 23 percent support one binational state.

13. See "National Survey of Likely Jewish Voters In 2020," Jewish Electorate Institute, February 28, 2020, https://www.jewishelectorateinstitute.org /national-survey-of-likely-jewish-voters-in-2020/, according to which only 9 percent of American Jewish respondents did *not* describe themselves as "generally pro-Israel."

14. See, for example, "About IfNotNow Movement," *IfNotNow*, first published November 3, 2019. Accessed at https://www.ifnotnowmovement.org /about.

15. See Zipi Israel, "National Security Index: Public Opinion Study 2019–2020," Institute for National Security Studies, Tel Aviv University, 2020, https:// www.inss.org.il/wp-content/uploads/2020/01/-מדד-הביטחון-הלאומי-מצגת אנגלית-השאלות-כל-עם-לכנס_compressed.pdf: only 11 percent of Israelis surveyed believe that a two-state solution is achievable in the near future (while 55 percent of Israeli Jews support a two-state solution in theory). Even the Meretz Party does not support the Israeli military's unilateral withdrawal from the West Bank, supporting only evacuation of "isolated settlements" in advance of a peace agreement (see "English Platform," *Meretz*, https:// meretz.org.il/wp-content/uploads/2021/02/English-Platform.pdf).

16. See Marissa Newman, "Rivlin Backs Annexation with Full Rights for Palestinians," *Times of Israel*, February 13, 2017, timesofisrael.com/rivlin -backs-annexation-with-full-rights-for-palestinians/; see also See Naftali Bennett, "For Israel, Two-State Is No Solution," *New York Times*, November 5, 2014, https://www.nytimes.com/2014/11/06/opinion/naftali-bennett -for-israel-two-state-is-no-solution.html. Also Micah Goodman, "Eight Steps to Shrink the Israeli-Palestinian Conflict," *Atlantic*, April 1, 2019, https://www.theatlantic.com/ideas/archive/2019/04/eight-steps-shrink -israeli-palestinian-conflict/585964/ and Jonathan Lis, "Israel's Lapid to EU's Top Diplomats: Two-State Solution Is Unfeasible," *Haaretz*, July 12, 2021, https://www.haaretz.com/israel-news/2021-07-12/ty-article/

.premium/lapid-to-meet-european-foreign-ministers-in-bid-to-rehabilitate
-israel-eu-relations/0000017f-e125-d38f-a57f-e777b09a0000.

17. See, for example, Tomer Persico, "Why Religious Zionism Is Growing Darker," *Haaretz*, May 16, 2017, https://www.haaretz.com/opinion/2017-05-16
/ty-article/.premium/why-religious-zionism-is-growing-darker/0000017f
-e13a-d804-ad7f-f1faf5f90000. See also Ravit Hecht, "The Face of Israel's
Far Right Wants to 'Abort' Palestinian Hope," *Haaretz*, December 3, 2016,
https://www.haaretz.com/israel-news/2016-12-03/ty-article-magazine/
.premium/the-face-of-israels-far-right-wants-to-abort-palestinian-hope
/0000017f-f2f8-d497-a1ff-f2f875960000.

18. The Choice to Belong

1. See, for example, Prager and Telushkin, *Nine Questions People Ask about
Judaism*.
2. See Woocher and Woocher, "Jewish Education in a New Century," 3–57.
3. Kallen, "Democracy versus the Melting Pot," 190–94, 217–20.
4. "Declaration of Principles: 'The Pittsburgh Platform'–1885," Central
Conference of American Rabbis, https://www.ccarnet.org/rabbinic-voice
/platforms/article-declaration-principles/.
5. Nussbaum, *Political Emotions*, 209–12.
6. See Halevi, *Kuzari*.
7. Rashi on Amos 3:2; RaDak on Amos 3:2.
8. BT Yevamot 61a.
9. Mekhilta d'Rabbi Yishmael Mesekhet Nezikin, Parsha 4.
10. Mishnah Yoma 8:5.
11. Mishnah Bava Kama 4:3.
12. BT Bava Kama 113b.
13. See Hartman, *Putting God Second*.
14. Shakespeare, *Merchant of Venice*, 1.3.107–11.
15. Mishnah Sanhedrin 4:5.
16. See, for example, Singer, *One World Now*.
17. See Sandel, *Justice: What's the Right Thing to Do?*
18. Maimonides, Laws of the Sabbatical Year and the Jubilee, 13:13.
19. See Mekhilta d'Rabbi Shimon Bar Yochai 23:4, where "enemy" is interpreted as the idolatrous non-Jew.
20. BT Shabbat 31a.
21. Maimonides, Laws of Slavery, 9:8, emphasis mine.

Bibliography

Agassi, Joseph. *Liberal Nationalism for Israel: Towards an Israeli National Identity*. Jerusalem: Geffen, 1999.

Almog, Shmuel, Jehuda Reinharz, and Anita Shapira, eds. *Zionism and Religion*. Hanover NH: University Press of New England, 1998.

Ashkenazi, Gabi. "Here, in the Most Cursed Place on Earth." Speech originally delivered at Auschwitz, 2008. In *Devar Hamefaked*, 137–42. Tel Aviv: Matkal/Aka-Anaf Hasbarah, 2011 [Hebrew].

Balfour, Arthur. "The Balfour Declaration" [Letter to Lord Rothchild]. In Mendes-Flohr and Reinharz, *Jew in the Modern World*, 582.

Batnitzky, Leora. *How Judaism Became a Religion*. Princeton: Princeton University Press, 1997.

Ben-Gurion, David. *Memoirs*. Cleveland: World Publishing, 1970.

———. "Status-Quo Agreement." In *Israel in the Middle East: Documents and Readings on Society, Politics, and Foreign Relations, Pre-1948 to the Present*, edited by Itamar Rabinovich and Jehuda Reinharz, 58–59. Waltham MA: Brandeis University Press, 2008.

Ben-Gurion, David, and Jacob Blaustein. "An Exchange of Views: American Jews and the State of Israel." *American Jewish Year Book* 53 (1952): 564–68.

Berlin, Isaiah. "Two Concepts of Liberty." In *Liberty: Incorporating Four Essays on Liberty*, edited by Henry Harvey, 166–217. Oxford: Oxford University Press, 1969.

Bernstein, Philip. *To Dwell in Unity: The Jewish Federation Movement in America since 1960*. Philadelphia: Jewish Publication Society of America, 1983.

Bezalel, Itzhak. *You Were Born Zionists: The Sephardim in Eretz Israel in Zionism and the Hebrew Revival during the Ottoman Period*. Israel: Ben-Zvi, 2007 [Hebrew].

Bialik, Haim Nahman. "The City of Slaughter." In *Complete Poetic Works of Hayyim Nahman Bialik Translated from the Hebrew*, vol. 1. New York: Histadruth Ivrith of America, 1948.

———. "Speech at the Inauguration of the Hebrew University in 1925." In Hertzberg, *Zionist Idea*, 281–89.

Borowitz, Eugene. Symposium participant. In *20 Years Later: The Impact of Israel on American Jewry*, 38–43. New York: American Histadrut Cultural Exchange Institute, 1969.

Boyarin, Daniel. *Borderlines: The Partition of Judeo-Christianity*. Philadelphia: University of Pennsylvania Press, 2006.

Brown, Benjamin. "Orthodox Judaism." In *The Blackwell Companion to Judaism*, edited by Jacob Neusner and Alan J. Avery-Peck, 311–33. Malden MA: Blackwell Reference, 2000.

Cohen, Hillel. *Year Zero of the Arab-Israeli Conflict 1929*. Waltham MA: Brandeis University Press, 2015.

Cohen, Naomi W. *The Americanization of Zionism, 1897–1948*. Waltham MA: Brandeis University Press, 2003.

Cohen, Shaye J. D. *The Beginnings of Jewishness: Boundaries, Varieties, Uncertainties*. Berkeley: University of California Press, 1999.

Cohen, Steven, and Ari Kelman. "Thinking about Distancing from Israel." *Contemporary Jewry* 30 (2010): 287–96.

De Clermont-Tonnerre, Count Stanislas-Marie-Adélaïde. "Speech on Religious Minorities and Questionable Professions." In *The French Revolution and Human Rights: A Brief Documentary History*, edited and translated by Lynn Hunt, 86–88. Boston: St. Martin, 1996.

Diamond, James. *Homeland or Holy Land?: The "Canaanite" Critique of Israel*. Bloomington: Indiana University Press, 1986.

Dinur, Ben Zion. *Holiday Readings for the Yom Haatzmaut Dinner*. Jerusalem: Association of Publishers of Hebrew Books, 1954 [Hebrew].

Dowty, Alan. *Israel/Palestine*. Fourth ed. Cambridge, UK: Polity Press, 2017.

Eisen, Arnold, and Steven M. Cohen. *The Jew Within: Self, Family and Community in America*. Bloomington: Indiana University Press, 2000.

Elazar, Daniel J. *Community and Polity: The Organizational Dynamics of American Jewry*. Philadelphia: Varda Books, 2001.

Elbaum, Dov, ed. *Declaration of Independence: With an Israeli Talmudic Commentary*. Israel: Miskal, 2019 [Hebrew].

Erikson, Kai. "Notes on the Sociology of Deviance." *Social Problems* 9, no. 4 (Spring 1962): 307–14.

———. *Wayward Puritans: A Study in the Sociology of Deviance*. New York: Wiley, 1966.

Fackenheim, Emil L. "Jewish Values in the Post-Holocaust Future: A Symposium." *Judaism* 16, no. 3 (Summer 1967): 266–99.

———. *To Mend the World*. Third ed. Bloomington: Indiana University Press, 1994.

Fischer, Netanel. "The Untold Story about the Law of Return." *HaShiloah* 26 (2021): 87–112 [Hebrew].

Fishbane, Michael. *Biblical Interpretation in Ancient Israel*. Oxford: Clarendon Press, 1985.

First Zionist Congress, The. "The Basle Program." In Mendes-Flohr and Reinharz, *Jew in the Modern World*, 540.

Fromen, Ram. *The Secular Road*. Israel: Miskal, 2019 [Hebrew].

Garfinkle, Adam M. "On the Origin, Meaning, Use and Abuse of a Phrase." *Middle Eastern Studies* 27, no. 4 (October 1991): 539–50.

Geertz, Clifford. *The Interpretation of Culture*. London: Hutchinson, 1975.

Goode, Erich. *Deviant Behavior*. Eleventh ed. New York: Routledge, 2016.

Gorni, Yosef. "'Negation of the Diaspora' and the Return to History." In *Zionism and the Return to History: A Reappraisal*, edited by S. N. Eisenstadt and Moshe Lissak, 349–60. Jerusalem: Ben-Zvi, 1999 [Hebrew].

Ha'am, Ahad. "The Jewish State and the Jewish Problem." In Hertzberg, *Zionist Idea*, 262–69.

Halbertal, Moshe, and Avishai Margalit. *Idolatry*. Translated by Naomi Goldblum. Cambridge MA: Harvard University Press, 1992.

ha-Levi, Yehuda. *Kuzari*. Translated by N. Daniel Korobkin as *The Kuzari: In Defense of the Despised Faith*. Northvale NJ: 1998. 2nd ed. (revised) published Jerusalem: 2009.

Hartman, David. *A Living Covenant*. New York: Free Press, 1985.

———. *Maimonides: Torah and Philosophic Quest*. Philadelphia: Jewish Publication Society of America, 1976.

Hartman, Donniel. *The Boundaries of Judaism*. New York: Continuum, 2007.

———. *Putting God Second: How to Save Religion from Itself*. Boston: Beacon Press, 2016.

Hertzberg, Arthur, ed. *The Zionist Idea: A Historical Analysis and Reader*. Philadelphia: Jewish Publication Society, 1997.

Herzl, Theodor. *The Jewish State: An Attempt at a Modern Solution of the Jewish Question*. Translated by Sylvie D'Avigdor. London: Penguin Books 2010.

———. *Old New Land*. Translated by Lotta Levensohn. New York: Markus Wiener, 1987.

Jabotinsky, Vladmir. "Jewish Needs vs. Arab Claims." In Mendes-Flohr and Reinharz, *Jew in the Modern World*, 609–11.

Jacobson, Alexander, and Amnon Rubinstein. *Israel and the Family of Nations: The Jewish Nation-State and Human Rights*. New York: Routledge, 2009.

Kallen, Horace M. "Democracy Versus the Melting Pot I." *Nation* 100, no. 2590 (1915): 190–94.

———. 1915b. "Democracy Versus the Melting Pot II: A Study of American Nationality." *Nation* 100, no. 2591 (1915): 217-20.

Kaplan, Mordecai M. *Judaism as a Civilization: Toward a Reconstruction of American Jewish Life*. Philadelphia: Jewish Publication Society, 2010.

Karayanni, Michael. *A Multicultural Entrapment: Religion and State among the Palestinian-Arabs in Israel*. Cambridge UK: Cambridge University Press, 2020.

Katz, Jacob. "Halakhah and Kabbalah: First Contacts." *Zion* 54 (1979): 148-72 [Hebrew].

———. *A House Divided: Orthodoxy and Schism in Nineteenth-Century Central European Jewry*. Waltham MA: Brandeis University Press, 1998.

Klatzkin, Jacob. "Boundaries." In Hertzberg, *Zionist Idea*, 316-27.

Kleinberg, Darren. *Hybrid Judaism: Irving Greenberg, Encounter, and the Changing Nature of American Jewish Identity*. Boston: Academic Studies Press, 2016.

Knohl, Israel. "The Rise, Decline, and Renewal of the Biblical Revolution." In *Yehezkel Kaufmann and the Reinvention of Jewish Biblical Scholarship*, edited by Job Y. Jindo, Benjamin D. Sommer, and Thomas Staubli, 167-80. Gottingen: Vandenhoeck & Ruprecht, 2017.

Koren, Yedida. "The 'Foreskinned Jew' in Tannaitic Literature: Another Aspect of the Rabbinic (Re)Construction of Judaism." *Zion* 82, no. 4 (2017): 397-437 [Hebrew].

Layish, Aharon. "The Heritage of Ottoman Rule in the Israeli Legal System: The Concept of Umma and Millet." In *The Law Applied: Contextualizing the Islamic Shari'a*, edited by Peri Bearman, Wolfhart Heinrichs, and Bernard G. Weiss, 128-49. London: Bloomsbury Academic, 2008.

Litvak, Olga. *Haskalah: The Romantic Movement in Judaism*. New Brunswick NJ: Rutgers University Press, 2012.

Lustick, Ian M. *Paradigm Lost: From Two-State Solution to One-State Reality*. Philadelphia: University of Pennsylvania Press, 2019.

Magid, Shaul. *American Post Judaism: Identity and Renewal in a Postethnic Society*. Bloomington: Indiana University Press, 2013.

Maimonides, Moses. *Guide of the Perplexed*. Translated by Shlomo Pines. Chicago: University of Chicago Press, 1963.

Margalit, Avishai. *On Compromise and Rotten Compromises*. Princeton: Princeton University Press, 2010.

Meged, Aharon, ed. *Israel Independence Day Haggadah*. Tel Aviv: Matkal/Aka-Anaf Hasbarah, 1952 [Hebrew].

Mendes-Flohr, Paul R., and Jehuda Reinharz, eds. *The Jew in the Modern World*. Second ed. New York: Oxford University Press, 1995.

Molé, Louis-Mathieu. "Napoleon's Letter to Nobles," "Napoleon's Instructions to the Assembly of Jewish Notables," and "Answers to Napoleon." In Mendes-Flohr and Reinharz, *Jew in the Modern World*, 125-33.

Muir, Diana. "A Land without a People for a People without a Land." *Middle East Quarterly* 15, no. 2 (Spring 2008): 55-62.

Morgan, Michael. *Beyond Auschwitz: Post-Holocaust Jewish Thought in America.* Oxford: Oxford University Press, 2001.

Morris, Benny. *The Birth of the Palestinian Refugee Problem, 1947-1949.* Cambridge UK: Cambridge University Press, 1987.

Nordau, Max. "Speech to the First Zionist Congress." In Hertzberg, *Zionist Idea*, 235-41.

"The Nuremberg Laws." In *Documents on Nazism, 1919-1945*, edited by Jeremy Noakes and Geoffrey Pridham, 463-67. New York: Viking Press, 1974.

Nussbaum, Martha. *Political Emotions: Why Love Matters for Justice.* Cambridge MA: Belknap Press, 2013.

Ofaz, Gad. *Second and Third Generation Kibbutz Members in Search of Jewish Identity.* Jerusalem: Melton, 2016. [Hebrew].

Ophir, Adi, and Ishay Rosen-Zvi. *Goy: Israel's Multiple Others and the Birth of the Gentile.* Oxford: Oxford University Press, 2018.

Oz, Amos. *In the Land of Israel: Essays.* Translated by Maurie Goldberg-Bartura. Orlando: Harcourt, 1993.

Pappe, Ilan. *A History of Modern Palestine: One Land, Two Peoples.* 2nd ed. Cambridge MA: Cambridge University Press, 2006.

Pianko, Noam. *Jewish Peoplehood: An American Innovation.* New Brunswick NJ: Rutgers University Press, 2015.

Pinsker, Leon. "Auto-Emancipation: An Appeal to His People by a Russian Jew." In Troy, *Zionist Ideas*, 9-11.

Plaut, W. Gunther. *The Rise of Reform Judaism: A Sourcebook of Its European Origins.* Philadelphia: Jewish Publication Society, 2015.

Prager, Dennis, and Joseph Telushkin. *Nine Questions People Ask about Judaism.* New York: Touchstone, 1986.

Ravitzky, Aviezer. *Messianism, Zionism, and Jewish Religious Radicalism.* Chicago: University of Chicago Press, 1996.

———. "Munkács and Jerusalem: Ultra-Orthodox Opposition to Zionism and Agudaism." In Almog, Reinharz, and Shapira, *Zionism and Religion*, 67-89.

Rosner, Shmuel, and Camil Fuchs. *#IsraeliJudaism: Portrait of a Cultural Revolution.* Jerusalem: Jewish People Policy Institute, 2019.

Rubenstein, Amnon. "The Curious Case of Jewish Democracy." *Azure* 41 (2010): 33-41.

Sagi, Avi. *Elu va-Elu: A Study on the Meaning of Halakhic Discourse*. Tel Aviv: Hakibbutz Hameuchad, 1996 [Hebrew].

Salmon, Yosef. "Zionism and Anti-Zionism in Traditional Judaism in Eastern Europe." In Almog, Reinharz, and Shapira, *Zionism and Religion*, 25–43.

Sandel, Michael. *Justice: What's the Right Thing to Do?* New York: Farrar, Straus and Giroux, 2009.

Sarna, Jonathan. *American Judaism: A History*. New Haven: Yale University Press, 2004.

Sasson, Theodore, Charles Kadushin, and Leonard Saxe. "Trends in American Jewish Attachment to Israel: An Assessment of the 'Distancing' Hypothesis." *Contemporary Jewry* 30 (2010): 297–319.

Schweid, Eliezer. "The Rejection of the Diaspora in Zionist Thought: Two Approaches." *Studies in Zionism* 5, no. 1 (Spring 1984): 43–70.

Shakespeare, William. *The Merchant of Venice*. Edited by Barbara A. Mowat and Paul Werstine. New York: Washington Square Press, 1992.

Shalom, Zaki. "The Crisis in the Relations between Israel and the Jewish Community in the US: Background and Implications." In *US Jewry and Israel's National Security*, edited by Assaf Orion and Shahar Eilam, 103–41. Tel-Aviv: Institute for National Security Studies, 2018 [Hebrew].

Shapira, Anita. "The Bible and Israeli Identity." *AJS Review* 28, no. 1 (April 2004): 11–41.

———. *The Bible and Israeli Identity*. Jerusalem: Magness Press, 2005 [Hebrew].

Sharansky, Natan. "The Political Legacy of Theodor Herzl." *Azure* 21 (2005): 83–98.

Shavit, Ya'akov. *The New Hebrew Nation: A Study in Israeli Heresy and Fantasy*. London: Frank Cass, 1987.

Shenhar, Aliza. *A Nation and the World: Jewish Culture in a Changing World*. [Hebrew] Jerusalem: Ministry of Education, Sport and Culture, 1994.

Shimoni, Gideon. "A Reappraisal of 'Negation of the Diaspora' in Thought and in Action." In *The Age of Zionism*, edited by Anita Shapira, Jehuda Reinharz, and Jay Harris, 45–63. Jerusalem: Shazar, 2000 [Hebrew].

———. *The Zionist Ideology*. Waltham MA: Brandeis University Press, 1995.

Singer, Peter. *One World Now: The Ethics of Globalization*. New Haven: Yale University Press, 2016.

Singer, Saul, and Dan Senor. *Start-Up Nation: The Story of Israel's Economic Miracle*. New York: Grand Central Publishing, 2011.

Smolenskin, Peretz. "The Haskalah of Berlin." In Hertzberg, *Zionist Idea*, 154–57.

Smooha, Sammy. "The Hungarian National Minority in Slovakia." In *The Status of the Arab Minority in the Jewish Nation State*, edited by Elie Rekhess and Sarah Ozacky-Lazar, 45-49. Tel Aviv: Moshe Dayan Center and Konrad Adenauer Stiftung, 2005 [Hebrew].

Sofer, Moses. *Responsa Hatam Sofer, Likutei She'eilot ve-Teshuvot.* Bratislava, Slovakia: n.p., 1855.

Soloveitchik, Joseph B. *Kol Dodi Dofek: Listen My Beloved Knocks.* Translated by David Z. Gordon. New York: Ktav, 2006.

Troy, Gil, ed. *The Zionist Ideas: Visions for the Jewish Homeland—Then, Now, Tomorrow.* Philadelphia: Jewish Publication Society, 2018.

Von Clausewitz, Carl. *On War.* Volume 1. London: Kegan, Paul, Trench, Trubner, 1918.

Williams, Bernard. "Toleration: An Impossible Virtue?" In *Toleration: An Elusive Virtue*, edited by David Heyd, 18-27. Princeton: Princeton University Press, 1996.

Woocher, Jonathan, and Meredith Woocher. "Jewish Education in a New Century: An Ecosystem in Transition." *American Jewish Yearbook* 113 (2013): 3-57.

Yadgar, Yaakov. *Traditional Jews in Israel: Modernity without Secularization.* Tel Aviv: Keter, 2010 [Hebrew].

Yehoshua, A. B. "The Neurotic Solution." In *Between Right and Right*, translated by Arnold Schwartz, 21-74. Garden City NY: Doubleday, 1981.

Yehoshua, A. B., and Gil Troy. "The Basics of Zionism, Homeland, and Being a Total Jew." In Troy, *Zionist Ideas*, 452-55.

Zangwill, Israel. "The Return to Palestine." *New Liberal Review* 2 (1901): 615-34.

Index

Jewish community center (JCC), 62, 218
Jewish Electorate Institute, 234
Jewish emigration, 149
Jewish history, 18, 145, 170–71, 213
Jewish identity, 7, 15, 16, 19, 31, 32, 37, 44, 49, 50, 90
Jewish immigration, 189
Jewish law, 17–19, 33–34, 55–56, 58–59, 60, 63, 75–76, 83, 91, 100, 148, 214, 218, 219, 223–24
Jewish life, 130–31, 166, 168, 170–71, 211, 226, 242, 250, 254
Jewish majority, 184, 197–98
Jewishness, xvii–xviii, xxii–xxiii, xxv–xxvi, 7, 10, 12, 13, 16, 18, 26–27, 32, 34, 37, 40–41, 46, 48, 51–54, 56, 57, 59, 61, 69, 72, 78–79, 97, 102, 106–8, 123–25, 129, 134, 138, 141, 205, 225, 253, 266–67, 278n4, 278n8; and the Basic Law, 180; and belonging, 228; and the biblical model of exogamy, 219; and boundary discourse, 89; and collective identities, 190, 216, 265–66; and exogamy, 224; and Genesis, 103–4; of Israel, 189; and Israel as a democratic state, 187; Israel's place in, 199; and Maimonides, 80, 84–85, 87; and North American Jewry's commitment to Israel, 248; and the Nuremberg Laws, 126; otherness of, 277n1; of the public sphere, 147; and the removal of racial vestiges to, 93; and the Sabbath, 75; and singularity, 215; and social realities created by Genesis Jews, 226–27; and the state, 149; and state symbols, 181;

and World Jewry, 184–85; and Zionism, 121–22
Jewish nod, 4
Jewish particularity, 267–68, 271–75
Jewish peoplehood, xxiii, 20, 63, 79, 123, 127–29, 148, 162, 172, 249, 254, 266, 275, 285n21
Jewish population of Israel, 189
Jewish principles, 199
Jewish Right of Return, 187
Jewish right to sovereignty, 114
Jewish rituals, 173
Jewish settlements, 124, 148, 185–87, 189, 201–3, 245, 256
Jewish state, 110–13, 147–50, 157, 163
The Jewish State (Herzl), 107
Jewish story, xvii–xviii, 5–7, 27, 141, 195, 213, 258–59, 268–69, 271, 274–75
Jewish tradition, xxi–xxii, 20–21, 24, 33, 42, 65, 81, 148, 200, 226
Jewish values, 144
Jews by Choice, 238, 248, 264–65, 266–68
Jews in good standing, 45, 67, 72–73, 77, 78, 86, 128, 227
jokes, xix–xx, xxi–xxii, 68
Jordan, 21–22, 41, 192, 234, 260
Joseph, 11
Joshua, Rabbi, 40
Jubilee Year, 23–24
Judah, 11, 53
Judaism, xvi–xvii, xxi, xxii, xxvi, 6, 7, 17–19, 20, 26–29, 31–32, 40, 42, 44–47, 48, 53, 55–56, 63, 71, 77–78, 80–81, 82–83, 86, 92–94, 96, 99, 103, 110–11, 120, 123–24, 127–29, 131–32, 138, 139–41, 142–44, 147, 150–51, 156, 157–58, 162–64, 165,

public sphere, 66, 140, 147, 153–54, 157–59, 161, 163, 164

Ra'anana, 95
rabbinate, 132–33, 142–43, 157–58, 164
rabbinic authorities, 66
Rabbinic Court Jurisdiction Law, 155
rabbinic discourse, 75, 166
Rabbinic Judaism, 77–78
rabbinic law, 17–18
rabbinic literature, 74
rabbinic period, 69, 74, 215
rabbinic tradition, 16, 25, 72–73, 87–89, 271
Rabbis, xvi, 15–16, 25, 26, 34, 42, 43, 47, 48, 50–51, 53–54, 61, 66, 73, 74, 75, 76, 77, 78, 79, 200, 204, 213, 223–24
Rabin, Yitzchak, 167
race, 27–28
racial justice, 173
racial vestiges to Jewishness, 93
racism, 27, 234
Ramadan, 229, 235
Rebecca, 15, 43–44
rebirth of Israel, 121, 170–71, 199, 211
reciprocal covenant, 32–33, 35–36
Reconstructionist Jews, xx, 139, 242
reconversion, 18–19, 56, 73
redemption, 13–14, 40, 110, 118, 123, 170, 279n10
red lines, 62–63, 66–67, 71, 76–77, 92, 139
Reform Jews, xx, 71, 103, 139, 242
Reform movement, 100–102, 103, 119, 123–24, 125–26, 132–34
reinterpretation, 42–43, 82–83
relationship with God, 16, 17, 33, 35, 52, 108, 271, 277–78n1

relativism, 65, 70
religious consciousness, 28
religious freedom, 154, 156–57
religious identity, 59, 84, 105, 221, 224
religious institutions, 164
religious minorities, 156–57
religious pluralism, 163, 247
religious sensibilities, 160–61, 174
Religious Zionist party, 259
religious Zionists, 127, 145, 147
Religious Zionist school, 159
renaissance, 110–13, 168
Renewal Jews, xx, 139
Republican Party, 250
responsibilities, 22, 23, 45, 47–48, 100, 184–85, 187, 199, 250–51, 253, 255–56, 280n22
return of God's Temple to Jerusalem, 101
Reuven, 11, 21, 30
righteousness, 84, 272
rights, 96, 99, 151–52, 156, 160–61, 180–81, 199, 203
rights, minority, 188–89
right-wing coalition, 259
riots, 175–76
Rock of Israel, 151
Rosner, Shmuel, 286n4
Rotbit, Yaakov, 195–96
Russia, 169–70
Russians, 70
Ruth, 51; book of, 221–22

Sabbath, 52, 74–76, 100, 101, 152–53, 158, 160–61, 177, 226, 267
sacrifice, 13, 26, 47, 278–79n10
salvation, 12–14, 119, 150, 212

troubled-uncommitted camp, 253, 254, 255

Trump, Donald, 235, 241

truth, 83–84

two-state solution, 181, 198, 202, 205, 244–45, 256, 260

tzedakah, 120, 144–45

Ukrainian Jews, 172

ultranationalist forces, 253

ultra-Orthodoxy, 146, 147, 163, 242, 243–44, 253

unaffiliated Jews, 242

unconditional acceptance, 26–27

unconditional communal love, 23, 48

unconditional loyalty, 19, 30–31, 97

United Nations (UN), 115–16, 147–49, 179

unity, xxi, 157

universalism, 103, 236

universal values, 149–50

untroubled-committed camp, 250–52, 253, 255–56

untroubled-uncommitted camp, 253, 254, 255

utilitarian universalists, 273

value(s), 15–16, 24, 28, 64–65, 101, 139–41, 144, 149–50, 173–74, 180–81, 187–88, 190, 200, 202, 205, 216, 237–38, 242–46, 251, 253, 255–62, 269, 270–71, 274. *See also* pluralism

vigilance, 26, 28

violations, 67, 73–75

violence, 177, 196–97, 202

von Clausewitz, Carl, 193

voting Jews, survey of, 234

Waldenberg, Rabbi Eliezer, 18–19

wars of self-defense, 191–93

West Bank, 30, 179, 202, 244

Western Europe, 80, 96–97, 100, 103, 104, 150, 266

Who is a Jew?, xviii, 57, 162

whole Torah, 60, 74, 76, 188

Whole-Torah Meshumad, 224–25

Wicked Child, 19–20

Williams, Bernard, 65

Wise, Stephen S., 123

women, 17–19, 63

Women of the Wall prayer services, 243

women's prayer groups, 243

World Holocaust Forum, 115

World Jewry, xx, 165–74, 184–85, 187, 247–48

worship, 5–7, 82, 214. *See also* idolatry

yearning, 205

Yehuda, Rabbi, 55

Yishuv (Jewish settlement in pre-state Palestine), 147

Yom Hazikaron, 95–96

Yom Kippur War, 194

Yordim, 166–67

Zionism, xxiii, 204–5; Ahad Ha-Am on, 111–12, 168; and American Jews' Exodus Judaism, 120–25; David Hartman on, 131; and Diaspora Jewry, 162–67; in Europe, 109–10; and an Exodus-Zionist Basic Law, 187–90; and Herzl's revival of Genesis-Jewishness, 106–8; Jewish commitment to, 236–39; and the necessity of Genesis, 113–17; in North America,